Blessing
Family
Strength Through Service
with God's Amazing Grace

Darell Hunt

MW00967153

PRAISE FOR
Silent TEARS

"It is a privilege to call Dorothy Newton friend. Her life is an inspiring example of a courageous woman of God who values faith, family, and friends as our ultimate earthly treasures. She shares her past and present experiences with others in the hope that they too can celebrate life in abundance now and forever."

—PAT & CHERI SUMMERALL
Legendary Television Sportscaster & His Wife

"We've been friends with Dorothy Newton for years and have long admired her strength and courage. She's a devoted mother, who after her divorce, brought that family together and held them so tightly nothing could have ever torn them apart. It was incredibly touching and inspiring to watch. She is also one of the most spiritual people we've ever met, something she leaned on for strength during the trials of her marriage. She has a lifetime of wisdom to impart, and the simple, straight-forward way she does so in her autobiography, *Silent Tears*, makes every page an inspiration. It's a book filled with love, perseverance and proof that in America second acts aren't only for men, women have some pretty remarkable ones as well."

—EMMITT & PAT SMITH
Emmitt is an NFL Pro Football Hall of Famer, Pat is the CEO of Treasure You™

Though the title reads *Silent Tears*, this is a story about triumph and grace; the triumph of Dorothy, her sons, Tre' and King, and ultimately that of Nate Newton as well. Both the good and the bad that we read in this story occur beneath the covering of God's grace, which is the bedrock of Dorothy's strength. In fact, this book is more than a story; it is a witness and full evidence of human capability. Every man should read this biography.

—MONTE & INGRID FORD
Monte is a former Senior Vice President for American Airlines
Ingrid owns Peace of Life, Therapeutic and Oncology Massage

PRAISE FOR
Silent TEARS

Powerful. Straightforward. Honest. Brave. These are the words I use to describe Dorothy Newton. When I first met her, I knew immediately there was a spiritual strength about her that was uncommon. However, it wasn't until she dared to share the story of *Silent Tears* with me that I fully understood how her ability to overcome personal pain had been shaped by her passion for Jesus.

Dorothy chose in the midst of isolation and relational deprivation to turn her tears into floods of victory. In the pages of this book she shares the truth of her personal story in a way that reveals hope for anyone who is facing difficult circumstances, unhealthy relationships, or even devastating loss. It is rare to find such honesty and hope in the same place.

If you have ever wondered how you are going to make it, this book is for you.

—JAN GREENWOOD
Associate Pastor of Women | *Gateway Church*

Truth brings liberty to the captive, gives beauty for ashes, great joy in place of grieving, and high praise to God instead of despair. Dorothy is a living testimony of this. She shares this story courageously so that the reader too can experience God in their own set of circumstances. She found her tears and her freedom. Come, dear reader, and find yours too.

—REBECCA WILSON, LCSW, LMFT

A NOTE FROM THE COLLABORATOR

I met Dorothy for coffee at Grounded Cafe' inside Gateway Church's Southlake Campus. Jan Greenwood had introduced us at her writing club and Dorothy called me after reading my book, *Marketing Your Mind*. She had been inspired and encouraged by it to take this project across the finish line and wanted my help to get the job done. We decided to meet to determine if we were the right fit to work together.

"Ghost writing," I told her, "from my experience is actually *spirit* writing—someone has to be able to bear witness with your spirit, feel your passion, and communicate in your voice. If they don't understand what drives you to get up in the morning and make a difference in the world, then they shouldn't write for you."

In no time we were sharing stories and laughing and feeling completely at ease. I sensed there was something special about this woman and I was drawn to help her. I liked her. In the months that followed, we spent many hours together as she opened her heart and shared the details of her remarkable story with me.

As I worked, sometimes my heart would break, sometimes I would become angry and agitated as the injustice and needless suffering became real to me through her testimony. I was captured by her words, amazed by her strength and desire for God's best for every person, no matter how they treated her. I could see in Dorothy a depth of character that could only have been forged in fiery adversity. She is a remarkable woman with a remarkable mission to see others set free. It is my very great privilege to have been chosen to help put her words on paper and bring her story to life.

Ghost writers are anonymous. Dorothy would not have this. Even though every word of this story is hers, she was not content that my work with her remain completely behind the scenes. Collaborators work together in an intellectual endeavor—they co-labor. This is truly my relationship with Dorothy. We have co-labored in love, hoping that by sharing her story of betrayal, abuse, recovery, and victory, others will find the joy of freedom that she has come to know. I pray you are touched as you read.

—WENDY K. WALTERS

Author of *Marketing Your Mind* and soon to be released *Intentionality—Live on Purpose!*

WWW.WENDYKWALTERS.COM

Silent TEARS

DOROTHY J. NEWTON

PALM TREE PUBLICATIONS

Copyright © 2012 Dorothy J. Newton.

$\mathscr{S}ilent$ TEARS
A TRUE STORY OF BETRAYAL, ABUSE, RECOVERY, AND VICTORY

Written in collaboration with Wendy K. Walters.

Special thanks to Paris Payne, hair and clothing stylist for cover photos.
www.hairloungedallas.com

Printed in the USA

Library of Congress Control Number: 2012930970

ISBN: 978-0-9847653-2-4

All Rights Reserved. This book is protected by the copyright laws of the United States of America. This book may not be copied or reprinted for commercial gain or profit. The use of short quotations is permitted. Permission will be granted upon request. The author guarantees all contents are original and do not infringe upon the legal rights of any other person or work.

Prepared for Publication By
PALM ❁ TREE
PUBLICATIONS
Palm Tree Publications is a Division of Palm Tree Productions
WWW.PALMTREEPRODUCTIONS.COM
PO BOX 122 | KELLER, TX | 76244

Unless otherwise noted, all Scripture references are taken from the King James Version of the Bible ®, Copyright © 1982 by Broadman & Holman Publishers, Nashville, TN. Used by permission. All rights reserved.

To Contact the Author:

WWW.DOROTHYJNEWTON.COM

DEDICATION

To all who have suffered betrayal and abuse.

To all who need deliverance and freedom.

To all who hope ...

I have been crucified with Christ;
it is no longer I who live,
but Christ lives in me;
and the life which I now live in the flesh
I live by faith in the Son of God,
who loved me
and gave Himself for me.

—GALATIANS 2:20 NKJV

ACKNOWLEDGMENTS

TO MY MOTHER, ETHEL (KEEBY)—

You are a strong woman of God and an evangelist, the oldest of thirteen children, a mother, a friend, and sister. You worked hard your entire life and never gave up, even with limitations in education. You taught me perseverance even in the midst of the storm. I am proud that you finally received your High School Diploma in 2008.

TO MY SIBLINGS, GARY, MURIEL, HELAINE, JOHN AND LESLIE—

I ask your understanding and forgiveness. By choosing to privately absorb all the hurt and pain, I denied you the opportunity to lift me up and feel the satisfaction of "being there" for me as you often were gracious enough to let me "be there" for you. After all, we are blessed to be a blessing. You were only allowed to see the part of me I wanted you to see. I thought I was protecting you by not burdening you with problems. I was so wrong. In retrospect, your collective strengths surely would have changed my course and perhaps yours too—bringing us even closer than we already are. Please know how much I love each of you. I give you my word going forward that I promise to depend upon you for all the times that lie ahead—both good and bad. It's never too late to lead an authentic and full life.

IN MEMORY OF—

My Stepfather: Lester Hymes
February 28, 1943—May 10,1983

My Stepsister: Mary Hymes
August 19, 1960—July 30, 1983

ACKNOWLEDGMENTS

TO MY BROTHER, MIKE—

Though we didn't grow up together, we spent time talking on the phone in college. I was privileged to attend a couple of your pro games and honored to be there when you married your beautiful wife, Deidre. When dad was diagnosed with cancer, you took excellent care of him in your home and I enjoyed visiting with you when I came to see him. This was when I really got to know you and it felt as if I had known you my whole life. You are an amazing and intelligent man who always prioritized God first, then family, and then being a professional athlete. Pro football was always what you did, not who you were and I admire this. I do not see you as a stepbrother, you are my brother and I love you.

IN MEMORY OF—

My Father: Horris Lee Johnson
June 25, 1940 — April 10, 2010

CONTENTS

Never think life is not worth living
or that you cannot make a difference.

Never give up.

—MARCI WRIGHT-EDELMAN

Foreword

BY

DEBBIE MORRIS

$\mathcal{O}$ne of the benefits of being a pastor's wife is the people I get to meet. As a pastor's wife for 31 years, I have had the opportunity to meet presidents, movie stars, CEOs, astronauts, professional athletes and racecar drivers, just to name a few. So when I met Dorothy Newton, I could just have added her to my list of celebrities and dignitaries. I knew her as the former wife of famed football player Nate Newton and mother to Tre' Newton, a local football star. But Dorothy's family associations didn't enamor me as much as the woman I was getting to know.

The first time I met Dorothy was for lunch. As we did the "get acquainted" small talk, I began to get a glimpse into the life of an incredible woman. I realized there was much more to this woman than the men in her life. Across the table was a vibrant woman with a story of triumph. When we parted, the one thing I knew was that I wanted to know Dorothy better. A friendship was born that day.

I know the story Dorothy is sharing is not a story she wanted to tell, much less live. It's a story that may be hard to read because of abuse you have experienced, but I pray you push through to the end. You are the reason that Dorothy pushed herself to write this book.

We were friends for a long time before she started sharing bits of information about her life with Nate. In hindsight, I think she was testing the waters to see if I would reject her or not believe her story. I wasn't shocked. As a pastor's wife, I have learned that things are not always as they seem.

One day over lunch, our conversation drifted from the "how's your world?" talk to deep heart issues. With tender transparency, we conversed about hurts and how to walk in freedom. I still didn't know all the details of her story, but I knew we shared a desire to walk above any pain. Even though I couldn't relate to her particular pain, like all of us, I have known hurt, disappointment, shame, fear and rejection. It is impossible to live without experiencing pain.

Dorothy is not content to be defined by her past or her pain. Throughout her whole life she has been redefining her future. When life dealt her poverty, Dorothy worked hard in school and sports to become the first person in her family to graduate from college. When surrounded by abuse, Dorothy made the hard decision to protect herself and her children by escaping.

In *Silent Tears*, Dorothy takes us behind closed doors into the celebrity lifestyle and the shadowy recesses where abuse dominated and destroyed her dream world. In all the years I have known her as well as in this book, Dorothy is careful not to malign her ex-husband and the father of her two sons. This is not a bitter, angry woman attacking her abuser. There is nothing in Dorothy's heart that wants to tarnish Nate or his reputation. Dorothy can see the grace of God on Nate's life.

My friend will become your friend as she graciously takes you into her world. She shares mistakes and victories. She contrasts the voice of abuse, which shouts fear and shame, with the sweet song of freedom and healing. In

Silent Tears, you will be encouraged to not let your pain define you or your future.

I have no doubt that getting to know my friend, Dorothy Newton, through *Silent Tears* will enrich and encourage you.

—DEBBIE MORRIS
Co-author of *The Blessed Marriage* and author
of the upcoming book *The Blessed Wife*

One

THE STORM

*Living is strife and torment, disappointment and love
and sacrifice, golden sunsets and black storms.*

—LAURENCE OLIVIER

September 1965. Tornado sirens wail their warning as ominous dark clouds gather overhead. Hurricane Betsy is fast approaching, promising damage and destruction to everything in her path.

I look around our small trailer. This was home to my mom, stepfather, me and my brothers and sisters. Every room was a bedroom, but only three tiny rooms held the official title. The place was crowded and we took up every square inch of space. I sensed my mother's anxiety growing, but my four year old mind couldn't fully comprehend why. She was packing at a feverish pace, shoving belongings into a few small suitcases. I glanced at the overhead compartments in the hallway. They held precious new pencils, notebooks and art supplies for us to begin school. *Why isn't mother packing these? What about my pillow? Surely we can't leave without my Easy Bake oven! Where are we going anyway?* The sirens seemed to get closer and closer and I covered my ears to shut them out.

I grabbed my mother's sleeve as she squeezed a suitcase and snapped it shut. I asked her about my Easy Bake oven. She paused in mid-fury, attempting to focus calm attention in my direction. She stroked my hair and cupped her hand beneath my chin to explain that we could take only what we could carry ourselves. Tears welled up in her eyes and she closed them for a brief moment and took a deep breath. She quickly wiped them away before they could spill down her cheeks. We didn't have a car, so our only means to escape the storm was public transportation.

Soon we would board a school bus heading for shelter at a Navy Base located in Belle Chase, Louisiana. My mother led the way. My stepfather was a pace behind, his leg in a cast, and four small children under the age of five scrambled to keep up with her while carrying all our little arms could hold.

We huddled closely to my mother, who instinctively herded us together for safety. My fear mounted. I didn't understand the word uncertainty, but I felt its weight that day. The storm took on a personality—it was out to get us. *Will it follow us? When can we go home? Will my things still be there for me to play with?* My mother forced calmness into her tense face and repeatedly told us that everything would be alright. Her eyes swept across the parking lot, searching the horizon for something ... only she knew what.

Finally, the storm did pass. Our family was safe, but we had no home to return to. All that remained of our possessions was contained in those few suitcases. We were homeless. For a short season we took up shelter with various relatives. School was starting up again, but I wasn't excited about it anymore. I was frightened to leave my mother and cried every day, begging her to let me stay with her. She tried to calm my fears and reassure me. Each day she took me to Ms. Stivinson's class. Ms. Stivinson would sit me on her lap, smile sweetly, and tell me in a soft voice how nicely I was dressed or how pretty I was. In time her kindness melted my fears and my discomfort dissolved into trust.

I trusted that my parents would make everything work out okay for us. I was no longer troubled about where we would live. Eventually we did have our own place again and once more settled into a routine as a family. I knew we didn't have all the things that other children had, but I didn't really feel poor. I loved my mother and I couldn't imagine any other way of life.

Those dark hurricane clouds weren't the only storm in my life. Another tempest was brewing, and the damage this one threatened was much more devastating than loss of property. My stepfather drank. And whenever he drank too much, he became violent. He fought with my mother daily, bruising her body, mind, and soul with physical, verbal, and emotional abuse. I shut out the noise. I pretended it wasn't happening. I didn't want him to hurt my mother. I didn't want to feel frightened, but the truth was it sickened me. I had no idea how to escape, but I silently dreamed that we would all fly away from him someday where we could live happy and free.

In spite of the abuse she suffered, my mother was a strong woman and took very good care of us. By now we were a family with six children and no matter how unhappy or trapped she felt, she worked hard to train us with good values, instilling morals into our fragile, young minds.

On Sundays she dressed us in our best clothing and sent us walking down a country road to Pilgrim Rest Baptist Church. Other children fidgeted during service, drew on church bulletins and whispered their way through Sunday sermons. I was different. Church was a haven. It was peaceful. People were kind. I loved to go to church. Ms. Pinkins was my Sunday School teacher and allowed me to read Scripture aloud, sing in the choir, and record attendance. This made me feel special and important. By the time I was eight she taught me how to handle tithe envelopes, count money, and keep records in the church book.

Then it happened again. Another ferocious storm hit Louisiana, Mississippi, and the Gulf Coast. Hurricane Camille unleashed her fury in 1969 and threatened to uproot us once more. This time, though our home and Pilgrim Rest Baptist church were damaged, all was not lost. The evacuation was shorter and it wasn't long before things were repaired and better than ever. I was given more responsibility and a small table was set up front near the pulpit where I served as the new church secretary.

By age ten, I was the narrator for Christmas and Easter plays. I was asked to give the welcome address for Reverend Hardy before he preached his sermons. This bloomed into invitations to other churches to tell Bible stories, read Scripture, and lead the choir with "In The Garden." At times we would travel as much as sixty miles to New Orleans or cross the river to Point La Hache to be welcomed as guests of other churches.

No matter how difficult things were at home, church was filled with joy and fulfillment for me. I was safe there. I was happy there. Scripture took on meaning and filtered through my adolescent mind to influence my thoughts and choices. I understood the importance of prayer and supplication and knew I could bring my requests to God daily. Of course, the one I asked for most was for my parents to stop arguing and for my stepfather to stop drinking.

My relationship with God became the most important thing in my life. His overwhelming love for me would sustain me through all the storms yet to come.

Two

KEEBY'S KIDS

A mother's love is whole no matter how many times it is divided.
—ROBERT BRAULT

My biological father was out of my life for good by the time I turned three. The only daddy I ever really knew was my stepfather, Lester. He married my mother with three small children to care for. In no time, more little ones came along and three children became six. Gary was the oldest, then me, followed by Muriel, Helaine, John, and finally Leslie. Ten short years spanned the difference between the oldest and youngest child, so when we lined up in a row we literally looked like little stair steps.

Each day my stepfather woke up and faithfully went to his job as a crane operator. He made a decent living and for a long season, things were pretty good for us financially. Lester was a man of simple tastes and when

25

he came home my mother always had something hearty and piping hot waiting for him to eat. I fondly remember the smell of red beans and rice simmering on the stove, our little trailer in spotless order, all the clothes washed and ironed, and my mother having everything just so in time for his arrival home.

My mother worked very hard to make sure her family was well mannered and well turned out. In the early days—when money was available—she had our clothing made for us. Everybody called us "Keeby's Kids"—always dressed in neatly pressed matching outfits. Not only that, but we knew how to behave ourselves—mind our manners, be respectful to our elders, and make a good impression wherever we went. My mother would smile from ear to ear when people commented on how well behaved we were in public. We loved seeing her smile and that was reward enough.

Sometimes she would take us to New Orleans to shop for clothes. Those were good, good times. She was so proud to see her children in nice things and it was such fun to take a road trip to the city!

As the oldest of thirteen children, my mother knew how to cook, clean, and take care of a family. By the third grade she had to drop out of school and stay at home to help take care of her brothers and sisters. She didn't have an opportunity to learn how to read and could barely write her name, but she carried herself with such respect and authority. She would take me to the store with her to fill out checks. I thought she was just teaching me how to do it so I could learn.

In the evenings, she would ask me to read Scripture out loud—oh, how she loved the Bible! I never dreamed she asked me because she couldn't read. As I advanced in school I asked for her help with Algebra one night. It wasn't until that moment that I knew her limitations. I was forced to swallow the bitter pill of my mother's illiteracy and I was shocked. She handled herself with such authority. She was intelligent and conducted her business as aptly as any professional woman. She commanded great respect everywhere she went.

An expert communicator, my mother was supremely confident and few knew of her setback. Until I was in high school I never fathomed that she lacked education. In my eyes, she was brilliant. When I became aware of this huge obstacle and realized what she had accomplished in spite of it, it made her even more so to me.

There was never a time when we didn't have what we needed. There was never a time when dinner wasn't prepared or our outfits weren't clean, pressed, and well put together. My mother brought us up with such finesse—she made it seem effortless, though she worked from early morning until late at night.

Like all the women in our family, she was strong—she had to be. Others depended on her and she wouldn't let them down, no matter what. Ours was definitely a matriarchal society. The women established the moral and religious structure for the family. They set the rules, provided the discipline, and taught the lessons. They were the glue that held everyone together, kept our spirits high, and created a community that cared deeply for each other and looked after its own.

Our community was tightly knit and wary of outsiders. It was filled with fierce love and loyalty, steeped in tradition, and guided by an unswerving faith in God.

Eleven of my aunts and uncles lived less than a quarter mile from our home. It seemed the smallest occasion was a reason to gather, make mountains of food, and spend a long afternoon talking and playing with cousins. No one had a large home, in fact most of us lived in trailers ...

to this day I can't quite remember how we managed to get everyone together in one place for a giant Louisiana-style crawfish boil, but we did. It was wonderful! I loved spending time with my family and I felt very special to be part of them. It was the only life I ever knew—a life filled with people who cared about you, shared your joys and your sorrows, picked you up when you were down, and made life worth living. God was in the center of everything. Our faith in Him was solid. The Lord was our Shepherd and we wanted for nothing.

For Christmas we would all gather at Grandma's house. Everyone brought something to eat and we all dressed up in our Sunday best. There was love and laughter and practical jokes and family gossip and drama—it was crazy and crowded and absolutely the most wonderful time you can imagine. I thought all families were like this.

I have always experienced great favor. At church or school, my teachers seemed to single me out for special assignments and grant me special privileges. I got good grades and was popular. My aunts were good to me also—

Auntie Melvina always did parties and made special treats for my friends. Auntie Helen always took the best clothes out of her closet for me to wear. Auntie Dee Dee always called to check on me and sent me letters. Auntie Red always did special things for me or would make me something delicious to eat that she knew was a favorite treat. Every now and then she would give me a gift, just a little something that made me feel special. All of my aunts were really good to me.

Because I was the oldest girl, it was my job to help the younger ones with homework and make sure that everything was taken care of for school. Looking back I suppose it was also because my mother had difficulty reading or writing. My "rank" annoyed my siblings. They called me "Goody Two Shoes" and "Miss Bossy." When they were really irritated with me they called me "Pie Face" or the one I hated the most (and they knew it) was "Miss Princess La-La."

Without meaning to or even understanding why, I pulled away from my siblings a bit. I turned to my aunts, particularly my Auntie Dee Dee who had gotten married when she was just 18 and moved away to California. Even though she was far away, she wrote me letters and encouraged me about school and other things in my life that troubled me. She was my link to a world bigger than our small Louisiana community and I was hungry to discover things outside our little circle.

I knew I was destined for greater things. I believed God had a purpose for my life that was bigger than anything I could yet imagine … and yet, there was a shadow over everything in my life. A dark shadow that cast its coldness over everything warm and beautiful and good.

Three

EVIL DRINK

Wine hath drowned more men than the sea.
—THOMAS FULLER

What makes a man drink? Why does alcohol turn a good man into a violent, raging beast who hurts the people he loves and creates dysfunction that can last for generations?

My stepfather, Lester, was a wonderful, loving man—until he drank. I often wondered if the alcohol revealed his true nature, or if the drink itself was responsible for his horrid, harmful behavior. I have never been able to answer this question, but I know the dark power that alcoholism wields. I have lived through its destructive force and cowered in the corner as it wrapped its cold fingers around my family and threatened to strangle everything beautiful and decent in our lives.

Though I can't remember a single day that he didn't get up and go to work, as I got older, there were fewer and fewer nights that he came home right after work. Instead he went into town and poured himself into a bottle until nothing of his gentle nature remained.

The good times became careful times. The careful times yielded to difficult times and before long, we were in really bad shape. My dad continued working every day, but money stopped coming into the household. Liquor led to gambling. The greater the losses at the gambling table, the more demanding his need for alcohol grew. Late at night (or early in the morning) he would come stumbling home with nothing to share but rage. He was filled to the brim with violent anger and took all his disappointment and frustration out on my mother.

She would try to calm him down—fix him hot food in the middle of the night, fight her fears and try to figure out what she had done to displease him and what she could change to make him better. Before long, evidence of extra-marital affairs appeared and when my mother tried to confront him, things got even worse. It seemed as though the further out of control his life spun, the more he fought to dominate and control the little world at home.

Abuse became a regular, common, every day reality. My mother was inescapably locked in the cross-hairs of his anger and violence.

When there was no longer enough money even for food, my mother began looking for work. Because she couldn't read, I went with her to help her fill out job applications. After weeks of searching, she landed a job as a custodian at our school in Buras, Louisiana. It was the only school in town and everyone from kindergarten through seniors in high school attended. My mother was so excited to have a job and make her own money. She could work during the same hours we were in school, and then be home with us when school let out. She did what she had to do so we could survive.

Because there was so little money, my mother made things stretch by feeding us from scraps she brought home from her job at a school cafeteria. She wasn't stealing, mind you. She brought home only what the children threw away. She would pray over it, cut off the edges with bite marks where they had eaten, and find creative ways to turn this castaway cuisine into something we could survive on. When I first discovered this, I was horrified and disgusted. My mother seemed embarrassed when I found out. At the time I didn't see it as resourceful. I didn't understand how dedicated she was to our survival—no matter what.

Though my stepfather never laid a hand on us, mom knew how upset we all were with the situation, and she felt my brother's anger growing more and more. She was concerned for us, and I think she felt guilty that we were growing up in such an unhappy home. Though it wasn't her fault, she wasn't able to appease my stepfather's anger and she was concerned about what a terrible, tense place it was for children to grow up.

I will never forget the first Christmas after she had a job. We rarely received Christmas presents or birthday gifts and my mother carefully saved a portion of each paycheck until she had enough money to buy something special for each of us. My sisters and I were given monogram rings and the boys each got a bicycle. I'll never know how she did it, but she found a way. No matter how tight money was, how tired she was from working or fending off my father, she always put us first. She found ways to do special things for us and express her love for us tangibly.

Living in a small, close-knit community meant everyone knew everyone else's business. When my stepfather came home in the middle of the night raging, my siblings and I sometimes tried to step in and mediate. On many occasions one or more of us would run outside and plead for help. My brother Gary found his fear melt into anger. He wanted desperately to protect mother, but as a child he was powerless in his attempts to struggle against our stepfather.

Our relatives and neighbors would answer our cries when the fight was on. Sometimes the police would come, but my stepfather held some unexplainable power over them as well. He could always talk his way out of things. It was like a magic spell was woven whenever he started talking. Though the evidence of the abuse was as plain as day and we had been there to witness it all, he seemed to be able to explain it all away.

He was known as a hard worker and was loved and respected by everyone. His behavior toward my mother was so contradictory to the "daytime version" of his life that it left the community just as confused as we were. Somehow, what happened in our home was a private matter between a man and his wife—therefore it should not be interfered with. It was like some unwritten code. There was a deeply ingrained, dangerous tolerance for domestic violence in our community. The women shook their heads empathetically and prayed silently—too many of them had also been victims at one time or another.

Church was our refuge. My mother loved God and was deeply devoted to the church. She found her strength in God. She was active in witnessing God's love to the community and made sure that all her children knew the Bible. She had a heart to serve and was constantly giving herself to and for others.

I threw myself into my school work, carving my place out at the top of my classes. I was involved in everything you could possibly become involved in. Perhaps I did it to escape from the unhappiness at home, I don't know, but Buras High School became a haven for me. I was driven to succeed. I turned my frustration into positive energy and poured it all out in athletics. I competed with focus and my natural athletic abilities brought me to the top of the pack.

By this time, we had even less money to live on and my mother's job didn't allow for any extras. Athletics cost money. Tennis shoes, uniforms, gloves, balls, travel, fees … and we didn't have the resources. I felt guilty having to ask her for money to purchase these things. Because of her good reputation and kindness, people were often willing to lend a helping hand. Sometimes she had to borrow from others or take out small loans to keep us kids supplied. As I grew older I was increasingly aware of our plight and so I often pretended I didn't need anything. I wanted to somehow lighten her burden.

I had a friend named Debra who played sports with me. Her mother was a friend to my mother and was aware of our situation. When we would have out-of-town games Debra would buy me food, or order double portions and pretend she couldn't eat it all and share with me. I was the beneficiary of her acts of kindness all through high school and never once would she allow me to repay her. Her generosity melted some of the hardness that surrounded my heart. God used her to speak to me in this time. She demonstrated His kindness and showed me His love. Over and over again, as the cold, hard knot growing on the inside of me encountered her warmth, it would melt and release—allowing me to trust God and know that I was in His hands.

Sometimes mother couldn't find the money for the things we needed no matter how she tried. I was far too proud to ask my aunts. Besides, they all had kids who needed things too. When it was really desperate, my mom would get a far away look in her eyes, sigh deeply and say, "I guess you'll have to ask your daddy." I'm not sure how or even why he did it, or where it came from, but he always seemed to find the money to make sure I could continue to play sports and be involved in all my academic endeavors and extra-curricular activities.

I played softball. At games I would see my stepfather standing off by himself in the distance. He never came into the stands. He didn't want to be around people, but he was there … watching. When it was my turn at bat I would think, "*Come on, Dot, hit this one right over his head!*" I wanted to make a ball fly over that fence right over his head and get his attention!

Basketball and volleyball were different. You had to play those sports inside a gym. He never came to a single game. I guess the idea of having to come inside and be around people was just too much for him. I sometimes wondered if he wasn't ashamed of himself. I hoped he was. More than anything, I wanted him to stop drinking. I knew he *could* be a good man—he just wouldn't.

There were times when the abuse was momentarily stopped. Maybe that meant he had a winning streak, I never knew. When things were really, really bad, my Uncle Sam could actually put him in his place and cause him to back down, even to express remorse. Still, this would last only for a day or two and then the abuse began all over again. It was like living inside a nightmare that you couldn't wake up from. It seemed normal. We expected it. We got used to it. That's just how it was. There wasn't anything to do but accept it.

The intensity of his physical abuse increased and my mother began to have frequent seizures and was plagued with constant, severe headaches. Several times, it landed her in the hospital for treatment. No matter how we begged him to stop or pleaded for his goodness to return, it never did. The abuse continued and got steadily worse. I honestly feared my mother would die by his hands.

Finally, there was nothing left to do but escape. The only way to do that was to become self-sufficient. I was in the ninth grade by now and my brother Gary and I had begun to chip in, working to help support the family. I worked every weekend cleaning houses or picking bushels of beans. I even worked at a shrimp factory, plucking the heads off the tiny creatures and filling buckets with them. How I hated those slimy things! They smelled horrible and the stench lingered long after I got home and took a bath. It seemed like I could smell them even in my sleep. The outer shells of the shrimp would scrape my fingers and hands as I worked until they were raw. My nails were cracked and the cuticles would tear and bleed. I wanted to throw those horrid little creatures back into the Gulf, not painstakingly fill a bucket with them—but filling a bucket meant earning money, so fill the buckets I did.

During the summer I was granted a very special privilege by the Gulf Oil Company. They had a summer job program they offered to only a small group of select students. Two from my school were given the opportunity to work for them, painting tanks and mowing the lawn— all in the blazing Louisianna summer sun. The job paid well though, and I was very happy to have it. I didn't like the heat, but it was better than peeling those horrible shrimp! My younger siblings worked too. They helped out at the school, waxing and buffing floors or cleaning classrooms. We all worked hard and we worked together.

Everybody gave their money to mama to buy food or save. We all wanted out. We all wanted to be free.

My mother continued saving and announced to me that she was planning a shopping trip to New Orleans. It had been a long time since we had done this, so I was really excited. I knew my mother had to work really hard to save any money, and I had great anticipation for the new clothes and shoes we would come home with.

We took the long bus ride into the city and my excitement grew with each passing mile. She took me to lunch at the Burger King and explained to me how desperate our situation was. I think she was afraid that my stepfather was going to kill her, and then she would no longer be able to provide for us or protect us from him. She talked slowly, and the furrows in her brow deepened. Her shoulders were hunched from the weight of an invisible burden heavier than any woman was meant to carry.

"Dorothy, I know I promised to buy you some new clothes," she began, "but baby we need to use that money to buy a car." She stopped, searching my face to see if I understood. I blinked hard to hold back tears of disappointment. I felt selfish. I had bragged to my friends about shopping in the big city … and now I would come home with nothing … again. How tired I was of not having nice things! Of course I wanted to escape the abuse—I hated it. Even more than that, I wanted my mother to be free. I swallowed hard and shoved my disappointment down deep inside. I looked her in the eyes and my selfish thoughts faded away. Our eyes locked for a moment and I loved her more in that moment than I could ever imagine. "It's time to escape!" I said. She breathed a long sigh and her shoulders seemed to square a bit. "Yes, Dorothy," she smiled, "It is time for us to be free!" She lifted her chin and closed her eyes and I knew that she was praying.

We came home from New Orleans without any new clothes, but now we had a new car. All the way home I wondered how my stepfather would react. I wasn't sure it mattered that much—he was going to be abusive no matter what my mother did, so why not put a plan in place to get free once and for all. I knew she was anxious too, and nervous. She was quiet for the whole ride. At the same time, there was a determined look in her eyes. She gripped the steering wheel of that car as if her life depended on keeping that car in the lane. She could taste freedom. I sensed she was making plans, thinking through things. Every now and again she would wipe a tear that was trying to form, look over at me and smile. Buying the car was the right choice. I knew it was.

Of course, purchasing the car was only one step in the plan. That took all our savings. We couldn't run until we had some money to run with. We would have to find a place to live and have enough money to survive until my mother could secure a new job.

One of my teachers was particularly kind to me. She demonstrated great compassion for how we suffered at home. Her name was Miss Garlington. I often came to class upset, trying hard not to relive the previous night's horror in my head and focus on my work. In fact, Miss Garlington was one of the chief influencers who guided me to pour my energy into academics and sports. She knew about the violence at home and the emotional roller coaster I lived on. She often spoke words of encouragement to me, calming me down, redirecting my energy into positive pursuits, and challenging me to dream of a better future. Her presence in my life was a bright beacon in a sea of uncertain darkness. When she accepted a teaching position in Monroe, I was devastated. How could she leave? She was the one person who seemed to really understand how awful it all was!

As the day for her departure approached, I panicked. I didn't want her to go, but Miss Garlington held out hope to me. On her last day at Buras School she pulled me aside and said, "After I get settled, maybe I can help you all move to Monroe and get away from your stepfather. I could help your mother find a job." My heart soared! Of course she would help us! It was like an opening straight into heaven. Surely this was our answer to prayer. How long had I asked God for an escape and here it was! Miss Garlington wouldn't let me down. Now, I just needed to convince mother …

Ms. Terry from the Church of Christ and Mr. Pat, the assistant principal of our school, had begun helping my mother learn how to read. Their kindness bore fruit and her quick mind readily grasped the concepts. It was like someone turned a switch on inside of her. As her reading level and writing ability began to improve, her confidence soared and her faith grew even stronger. She decided we would begin attending services with them.

I had the promise from Miss Garlington tucked in my pocket, and now mother was learning to read and write. We had a car. All we needed now was enough money to run with. Even with all these little steps moving us in the right direction, we were still caught in the trap. The abuse got worse. My father stopped contributing money to the household altogether and my mother put aside everything possible for our great escape. It was during this time that We ate free lunch at school, and in the afternoon we drank milk from leftover school milk cartons and mayonnaise sandwiches. For the first time in my life I realized we lived in poverty and I felt ashamed.

My brother was much older now and his boyhood anger had turned to hate. No longer able to tolerate the beatings, he sought to retaliate. One night he jumped on my stepfather, hit him hard, then ran away. The next day my stepfather tried to run over him with his truck. Just in time, my brother dropped to the ground and rolled beneath the trailer. The brakes grabbed and the tires locked, throwing a huge cloud of dust as the truck stopped inches before plowing into our mobile home.

If Gary hadn't rolled under the trailer, I was sure my stepfather would have run him down and killed him—he was that angry!

This marked a turning point in our family's dynamic. From that moment on abuse began to filter down to the six children. He still seemed to have a special kind of meanness reserved for just my mother, but it was no longer confined only to her.

Four

FREEDOM

Freedom means you are unobstructed in living your life
as you choose. Anything less is a form of slavery.

— WAYNE DYER

"Mama!" I cried. Tears were streaming down my cheeks. I was frightened … and I was angry. "Mama!" I said again, louder, with more force. I stroked her forehead and cheeks with a cool, damp cloth. She was so still. My stepfather had beaten her again and she had a severe seizure following the attack.

I looked down at her face and thought how beautiful she was, even beneath the bruises. I cared so much for this woman. I loved her deeply. What if this was her last beating? What if she didn't wake up? I shook her gently.

"Mama," I said, softly this time. One of my tears splashed on her cheek and her eyes fluttered open. She grimaced in pain and looked around in confusion. She seemed so small lying there in my arms.

"We must leave, Mama," I urged, my mind racing with fear and distress. "Please?" I begged. "Let's just get in the car and go!"

Her eyes held mine for a moment and I could see she was seriously considering the option. "Please, Mama!" I said again. "We can go to Monroe. Miss Garlington promised she would help us. She's been waiting for us to come. Let's just go!"

And go we did.

It was Christmas break. We packed everything we could fit into the car and the seven of us squeezed in. Nervous anxiety kept us all quiet, each one lost in their own thoughts. *Would we return? What would my stepfather do when he found out? Would he follow us? Where were we going? What about our friends? Would we see them again? Would mother be okay? Where would we live? What about school ...*

Freedom! We could taste it. The further we drove, the more our mood lightened. Someone told a joke in the back seat and we all laughed, releasing the tension. We sang a Christmas carol and our anxiety relaxed into an adventure. A relieved calmness swept over us all and our faces were glued to whatever was forward—no looking back. It was exciting. We had done it. I resisted the urge to let out a yell, and I secretly wished I could see the look on my stepfather's face when he came home in the wee hours of the morning, screaming for his supper and found us all gone!

We made our big escape … now where do we go?

We stayed a few nights with my great-grandmother, and one or two more with a great-aunt, but their homes were quite conservative and seven extra people are difficult to accommodate for any length of time. My mother didn't want us to be a burden, so after we woke up, we would tidy everything up and stay outside during the day. We had to find activities to keep everyone busy and this proved increasingly difficult to do. Staying with relatives was not the answer.

After a few days, my mother decided the only thing to do was head for Monroe and find Miss Garlington. We had no idea where she lived or how she would help us, but we were determined to find a better life, so we set out on another leg of the journey.

We packed everything up again and piled back into our Chevrolet Impala, headed for Monroe. On the trip there my mother began to feel ill. By the time we arrived she was really sick. We checked into a motel, but mother had caught the flu and was too ill to look for work.

We looked up Miss Garlington's telephone number and I called her. I was excited to hear her voice on the other end of the line and I almost shouted that we were here in Monroe. We had come just like she offered! I expected her to be overjoyed to hear from me. I was sure she would come right over and rescue us. The response on the end of the line, however, was not joyful and relieved as I had expected. She sounded shocked, taken off guard. When I told her my mother was ill, instead of rushing in to assist, Miss Garlington was hesitant to help. Her response was slow and in the end proved to be no help at all.

I was crushed. Miss Garlington had promised to help us escape. She had always been a mentor to me and I trusted her. Now, when I needed her most, she did not make good on her word. She left us alone to our own fate. I never felt more alone than I did in that motel room. My heart was broken. I felt betrayed. I was angry and frightened and confused ... and determined not to go back to my stepfather.

Mother grew sicker and sicker and we couldn't afford a doctor, let alone to stay in the motel any longer. Without Miss Garlington's promised assistance, we didn't seem to have many options available. We didn't know anyone else in Monroe. Disheartened, we packed everything back into the Impala and headed back toward New Orleans.

This time, there were no jokes or songs or laughter. The mood in the car was totally subdued. In fact, my mood was blackest of all. I felt responsible for bringing the family to Monroe. The betrayal from Miss Garlington cut through my heart like a knife. My hope vanished like a mirage in the desert. Something inside of me broke. Hot, angry tears streamed from my eyes. How could she do this? What would we do now? I trusted her and she had deceived me.

We made our way back to New Orleans, not knowing how we would survive. We checked into a motel once again, our money all but gone. Mother tried to comfort me. She told me that God would take care of us and that it wasn't Miss Garlington's fault. I was miserable. I had convinced mother to go to Monroe, so I had let her down—I had let the whole family down. My trust was betrayed and I didn't want to trust again.

Sick, but determined, my mother called Ms. Terry, a good friend from the Church of Christ back home. She told her we were out of money and needed to find a place to stay in New Orleans. Ms. Terry called Elysian Fields Church of Christ in New Orleans to share our plight.

These beautiful people came out right away to see us. A dear woman who introduced herself as Sister Rew immediately set things into motion. She quickly found us a place to live near my great-grandmother's house in New Orleans and somehow gathered necessities from the community to help us through. All six of us were enrolled in school, though now instead of all attending the same school together as we had done in Buras, we had to be in three different schools, and I had to go alone.

Each morning I walked Helaine, John, and Leslie to their school and then walked about nine more miles to my school, Francis T. Nichols. My mother carpooled with some people for the long commute back to Buras where she resumed her job as custodian. This required her to rise before 5:00 AM each day to catch her ride by 5:30. The long commute was difficult and she still suffered from seizures and headaches. Her absence meant I had more responsibility to care for the younger siblings and things were different here. We were far away from my aunts and the community of family and friends. Here things were fast-paced and dangerous. It was pleasant not to suffer from abuse anymore, but we couldn't exactly say that things were good either.

In time I made friends. Most of them walked half-way to school, then caught public transportation for the rest of the commute. I didn't have any money, so I couldn't afford to ride with them. I pretended that I liked the exercise, and I was so athletic that no one seemed to question my motives.

Many of my friends skipped school and got into trouble hanging around Bourbon Street. Sometimes these friends offered me rides, but I knew better than to accept. In the back of my mind I was keenly aware of the price my mother had paid for our escape. I knew what she had sacrificed for our safety. I admired her bravery and I couldn't bear the thought of disappointing her or wasting her sacrifice. She wanted us to have a better life. She wanted me to get an education and have better choices. I wouldn't have traded that for anything.

I often walked to the corner grocery store to purchase scraps of meat and other necessities. A nice young boy worked there and we occasionally struck up a conversation. Like others, he too offered to drive me to school, but I declined. When I said no, he decided that he would walk with me and we could work our way up to riding in his car. He seemed very nice and I did like him, but I wasn't ready to trust again. Miss Garlington's betrayal was still fresh in my mind. Even this kind gesture was pressure I wasn't ready to deal with.

The spring semester ended. My mother's health worsened, and she could no longer make the long commute to Buras and back each day. She was growing increasingly concerned about how much time we spent alone fending for ourselves, so she was anxious to find work closer to the family. In time she secured a job at a hotel in downtown New Orleans in addition to another job she had taken to make ends meet. Her body had never really recovered from the abuse she had suffered and the stress of being the sole provider. Living so far away from the family support structure, and working such long hours with so little rest began to take their toll. Mother got sick again and the precarious balance of our life spun out of control. It was unbearable.

Five

BACK TO BURAS

Every tyrant who has lived has believed in freedom for himself.
— ELBERT HUBBARD

$\mathcal{O}$ne day my mother called me into her room and shut the door. "Dorothy," she said, her voice was soft and mellow. "I know how hard you worked so we could leave. I don't think I ever could have done it without you." She paused to gather her thoughts and I felt my stomach tighten. "I am so very proud of you. I want all my children to have the chance for a better life."

"You're so smart," she continued. "I know you can be something and make something of yourself. You are almost a grown woman." Her voice trailed away and for a moment her thoughts drifted to something far away.

She lifted my chin and smoothed my hair with a gesture so gentle you would have thought I was a newborn baby, not a young woman about to enter her junior year of high school. My heart was racing. I looked into her eyes, searching for where she was going with this conversation. Before she even said the words, I knew that they were coming. "We can't stay here in New Orleans anymore," she said. "We need to go back home."

Silence.

I held my breath. I wasn't sure what to feel. Waves of emotion rolled over me like the crazy pattern of the waves you see in the Gulf in an approaching storm. My mind raced. *Home,* I thought. *Is she crazy? He'll kill us!* But I didn't say any of these things out loud. I was holding a handkerchief in my hands and I twisted it round and round, trying to settle my mind. "What is the plan?" I finally asked, breaking the silence. "When do you want to go? What do you need for me to do?"

In the next few minutes, my mother rattled off details like a military general. I could tell she had been thinking through this for some time and there would be no changing her mind. She kept assuring us all that things would be different. She was sure that my stepfather would be so happy to have us all home that he wouldn't want to drink anymore. We were less enthusiastic, but as we packed and talked about seeing our aunts and cousins the mood in our little place brightened. Life had been hard in New Orleans and it was easy to believe that maybe going home would be the best thing after all.

Mother was right. Lester was really glad to see us. I don't know what he and mother talked about, but he was anxious for us to move back into the trailer and he was genuinely helpful getting us settled in.

For the first few months it seemed like a dream. There were lots of big family dinners and it was lovely to see my aunts and laugh with my cousins again. Things felt familiar and safe and normal. The people at our church were overjoyed at our return and they made us feel welcome. My mother jumped right back in her role as Evangelist and she was happy to be back where she belonged. She got her old job back. She looked younger and she smiled more often. My stepfather seemed to want this to work as well. He had missed us. I know he loved my mother and he seemed to love us too. Maybe this would work out after all. The knot in my stomach started to relax.

My stepfather decided it was time for me to learn how to drive. We spent many hours together as he taught me how to steer and use the gas pedal and the brake. It was the most fun I had ever had with him. During my driving lessons with him, I imagined that this was what "normal" dads did with their daughters. The knot in my stomach was gone. Things were different. Everything was going to be okay—this time for good.

3:30 A.M. I awake to a crash in the kitchen. An angry voice chokes the stillness of the night … something about my mother being worthless and why didn't she have something decent ready for him to eat. I squeezed my eyes shut, hoping this was a bad dream.

Another crash and a cabinet door slams shut. My mother is crying now. I can't hear her, she doesn't make a sound, but I know she is crying. The nightmare has returned.

I hear the distinct sound of a hand striking flesh and I feel sick to my stomach. It's as if a giant hand presses me into my mattress. I can't breathe. I can't move. I am bound as surely as if tangible shackles were locked tightly around my arms and legs. "God!" I shout. Another slap. "Jesus!" I cry … sobs begin to build and my pillow is wet with tears. "Please," I whisper. Fear grips me, and anger. It feels like I am choking. "Please, God …" is all I can manage to say.

Morning finally came. I got up for school and headed to the kitchen. There was no trace of the fight. My mother had cleaned everything up like it never even happened. We were all quiet—deathly quiet. Even the birds were silent. No one dared to speak. Mother fixed breakfast without a word, but no one had any appetite. "Eat, children," she commanded, but there was no energy in her words. We dutifully took a bite or two and one by one slipped out for school.

The fairytale had ended. The routine of drunken violence returned as though nothing had ever interrupted it.

Located on our property, sitting parallel to our trailer was an even smaller, vacant two bedroom trailer. One day after school mother announced that we were moving over there. It was crazy. All of us were going to move into that tiny space and leave the larger trailer for my stepfather. It didn't make any sense, but that didn't seem to matter. None of us even bothered to ask my mother why we didn't move him out instead. We packed our clothes and bedding and walked across the yard to our new home.

I continued to throw myself into sports. It was my passion. When I was competing I felt powerful and in control. I was confident. I was safe. I was strong. Volleyball, basketball, softball, track … if there was a team, I was on it.

I studied as hard as I practiced and I got good grades. I ran for Student Council and won. I was heavily involved in the school's drama department and loved acting in plays. Though our school did not have an official debate team, there were many opportunities for public speaking and recitations. I eagerly looked forward to participating in these and enjoyed traveling to competitions. One of my favorites was called "Girl State" where we traveled to the capitol to give speeches, competing for political positions. You had to know politics, have a platform, and be able to give a new speech for each level of advancement. I made it all the way to Secretary of State. It was such fun! My successful involvement in these activities, all while maintaining excellent grades meant that teachers gave me special privileges. At times I would even substitute for them.

I always seemed to get along better with adults than with kids my own age. I always felt the need to be responsible and even though I wanted to fit in, I just couldn't quite bring myself to join the partying crowd. Alcohol was my nemesis. It ruined my life and hurt my mother. I wanted nothing to do with it. I wanted nothing to do with anybody that drank it. It was as simple as that.

My mother continued to cook, clean, and do laundry for my stepfather. They stayed married, but lived in separate trailers. Sometimes he would come home in the middle of the night, drunk, and bang on the door, screaming for my mother to come outside. Those were terrible nights. We kept the door locked and huddled in the dark, waiting for the alcohol to make him sleepy so he would leave. Sometimes he would cry or beg or apologize and my mother would cry too. She loved him. Even though he was terrible, she loved him.

My brother Gary could take no more. He left school and got a job. Before long he was married and ventured out on his own, determined to have a better life, or at least a new one. The physical abuse was less now that we lived in a separate trailer, but the emotional and verbal abuse was disruptive and damaging. Long after the yelling stopped, I could hear it in my head. Over and over, like a broken record playing the same thing without ceasing. I often felt like I lived two separate lives. One life was at home and everything there was mechanical. I did chores, cooked food, washed clothes, took care of my brothers and sisters, and worried about my mother. I felt trapped. I loved my family, but hated how we lived. At school things were different. There I was alive. I made choices for myself and people respected me. I began to think about college and dream of bigger and brighter things. I didn't really have any role models because none of the women in my family had ever graduated from high school. No one had even considered going to college, so I felt lost and on my own … but I was determined nevertheless.

Then, during my senior year, one of my teammates and I qualified for State in track. I was so excited! This meant a trip to Baton Rouge and a chance to compete in front of college scouts who might offer a scholarship. I trained hard. Two teachers were supposed to drive us for the competition. As we started out, the weather turned bad. It was raining "cats and dogs" and it was hard to see the road ahead. One of the teachers leaned over the seat and asked, "Do you girls really want to go to this meet?" I just stared at her and didn't know what to say. *Of course I want to go the meet!* I thought. I had been training and preparing and planning for it for weeks. My teammate started laughing and said, "Not really, why?" Just like that, they headed for Bourbon Street in New Orleans— Baton Rouge was no longer on the agenda. They pulled the car into Pat O'Brien's and shut down the engine. I sat there in disbelief. I wanted to say something, but nothing came out of my mouth. Silently I followed them inside. My feet felt like lead.

The two teachers had a cocktail, then another, then they ordered one for my friend. I was miserable and wanted to leave. The old feelings of betrayal surfaced and Miss Garlington was on my mind. *Why do people act this way?* I mused. Something ugly began to bubble beneath the surface. I was going to talk to the principal when we returned. I planned the conversation in my mind as I sat there listening to them laugh … but I never did. The teachers told the school administration that the weather was too bad to make it to Baton Rouge and had forced us to turn back. No mention was ever made of the detour and the drinking. Once again, my trust was broken.

Graduation! I was the first in my family—first daughter, first granddaughter, and first niece to ever graduate from high school, and my family celebrated in grand style. They were so supportive and we had a giant celebration. I really did feel special.

My mother spoke often about opening a restaurant with me when I graduated from college. I had no real sense of which school to attend, but I was offered an academic scholarship to the University of Southwestern Louisiana (which later became the University of Louisiana at Lafayette in 1999). That scholarship, combined with a Pell Grant meant I could go to college. My hopes soared! I could hardly wait for fall to come.

The college prepared a list of items that incoming freshman needed. My mother guarded that list like it was a priceless historical document. Little by little, one by one, we purchased the items. She was determined to make sure I had everything I was going to need to get an education. She was so proud of me.

"You're going to get a good education, Dorothy," she would say. "Now, don't you be distracted by them boys. What they want won't help you open up your own business anyhow." I can still hear her voice rambling off thoughts and advice as she washed dishes or hulled peas. "You're a strong leader, Dorothy Johnson. You've got a good head on your shoulders. You make sure you find a good church and stay in it! You're gonna be somebody ... ooooh I'm so proud of you!"

That summer flew by. I could hardly wait to start my first semester in college. My life, I felt for sure, was about to begin.

Six

COLLEGE

*College is a catalyst for change, but change
only comes to those willing to embrace it.*

J. ROWAN SAMSON

I pinched myself. *Is this real? Am I actually here ... in
my very own dorm room ... away from home ... a college girl?*
It was real. I felt myself smiling and I looked around,
surveying my new room with satisfaction.

Before my enrollment, my mother made sure we visited
nearby churches that I could attend regularly. We checked
out several and she would fire off questions to the minister.

"Does your church have a program for college
students?"

"Do you provide transportation for them?"

"How often can you pick up my daughter so she can be
involved in your church?"

71

"Do you have a weekday service?"

"What kinds of activities are scheduled for students?" … and on and on she went. She totally overwhelmed one poor little minister. He couldn't answer one question before my mother asked him two more. He just shook his head up and down a lot and showed us the door as fast as he could!

One minister, however, had answers for every single one of my mother's questions and I could tell she was pleased. Whether I liked the place or not, I knew that this was the church where I would belong. Once Keeby had her mind set on something, there was little point in arguing.

I settled easily into the dormitory, but was a little nervous about having a roommate I didn't know. I was used to living in close quarters, but had always been with family … lots of family. Suddenly they seemed very, very far away and I was afraid. I felt responsible for them and I was worried about not being there to help with chores and earning money. There was so much to consider. So much was at stake. My whole family was counting on me to be a success and I did not want to let them down.

As I was enrolling in classes I discovered they had a volleyball team. That was it! I would try out for the team. I didn't even hesitate. I knew sports. I was alive on a court and there was no place that felt more like home to me. My talent soon made room for me and I caught the coach's eye. She watched me play with interest and challenged me to work hard. She was a good coach and under her leadership I grew stronger as an athlete. She encouraged me that if I did well that season, there was a strong possibility of a scholarship for next year. That was all I needed to hear. I worked harder than ever before and was carefully disciplined in my practice regimen, diet, and studies. I knew this was an answer to prayer.

The campus minister my mother had interviewed also watched me with interest. He and his wife reached out to me often. The church had many students among its members, but most of them did not live on campus. The church wanted to launch an on-campus ministry, but they needed someone who lived in a dormitory as a sponsor who could request the use of a student center or appropriate location to meet. I was their girl.

They approached me cautiously, testing the waters to see if I was open to accepting the responsibility. There it was again—responsibility. No matter what, people always relied on me to be the responsible one—to get the job done, to sacrifice, to come through, and to never let them down. I wanted to concentrate on my studies and on volleyball. I wasn't sure I wanted the added duties required to run a campus ministry. I didn't feel qualified. I had long-term goals and I was focused on these. I was concerned that becoming involved in a ministry would result in my grades suffering or not being as committed to the team.

The pressure increased. Before long I was meeting with a group in the student center a few times a week and I was hooked in. I'm not sure how it even happened. I didn't formally agree to anything, it just began to fill my calendar. New people came all the time. Some were just trying to connect and make friends, but many had special needs and looked to me to help them solve their problems. It was a dilemma for me. I too wanted to make friends, and there was a level of fulfillment in helping others, but my classes were demanding and we practiced volleyball twice a day, six days a week. I was tired ... and overwhelmed. Pressure mounted and I could feel the weight of my family's expectations, my coach's expectations, the burden to excel in my classes, and meet the growing needs of the campus ministry. It was too much. I was losing myself.

Just three short weeks into the semester I was questioning everything. *Am I trying to please God or people? Why am I here? Was this the right college? What's my purpose? How am I going to do all this? Did they ask me to lead because I'm capable, or just available? Is this really my calling?* Swamped with obligation and responsibility, joy left me. Duty, not desire drove me out of bed each day. I felt like a robot. I was going through the motions and meeting expectations, but nothing inside felt alive.

It was Wednesday night and I had just finished our second practice for the day. I had been in classes all day and I hadn't eaten. I was irritable and slipped into complaining. I did that more and more. Even when I didn't complain out loud, I complained in my head. I felt sorry for myself and I was frustrated with people around me who didn't work as hard as I did. They seemed lazy to me. The church van was on its way to pick me up, but I was too exhausted and miserable to care. I looked at my watch … *yikes!* I let out a loud huff, then quickly showered and changed and somehow managed to catch the van. I'm glad I did.

That night began like most others, students socializing with each other. There was the familiar buzz of conversation that rose and fell with laughter and stories. I was in the room and just beginning to relax enough to engage with people when a voice cut through the chatter like a knife. "Young men and women, I'm telling you to seek first His kingdom and His righteousness, then all the other things you need will be given to you."

It was the minister speaking the words, but it was God planting them in my heart. Something stirred down deep in my soul. I felt warm inside. I smiled. Was that joy? "Seek God first," the man had said, "then all these things shall be given unto you." Simple.

I never put God last in line again. From that moment I sought Him first and the pressure of obligation and expectation seemed to vanish. I was as busy as ever, but now I was alive. The robot was gone for good. Now I had purpose and every day was new and amazing.

Thanksgiving came and I went home to the family. I felt so grown up. It seemed like a year had passed since I left home instead of a few months. So much had happened in my life. I was different on the inside. Already my perspective had changed and going home was hard. Of course I was happy to see everyone, and you haven't had Thanksgiving dinner until you've had one Louisiana style! It was the best food I had ever eaten—how I had missed this! My aunts couldn't hear enough about my dormitory and my roommate. They wanted to know all about my classes and playing for the team, and my mother was SO pleased that I had become deeply involved with the church's campus ministry. I felt so important. Everyone seemed genuinely interested in all the details of my college life and I was overwhelmed by their attention. It seemed like a brief moment passed at home and all too soon it was time to return to school.

My stepfather drove me for the three hour ride back to campus. It was a little awkward. We began the trip in silence and kept to random, superficial topics for at least half the journey. Finally, without taking his eyes from the road he said, "I don't mean to hurt her." I felt a catch in my throat. "I want to be a better person," he continued. "I don't know why I can't stop drinking and gambling ... I just can't help it." He grew quiet again and I wasn't sure what to say.

"I don't want to smoke, either" he said after we had passed a few miles in silence. "You believe me, don't you, Dorothy? You have always been such a good girl ... like your mother ...," his voice trailed.

"Just stop drinking," I heard myself say, surprised at my own courage to speak. "You can be so kind," I said. "I remember all the times you gave me money for sports and school activities, and you used to come to my softball games. Why can't you just be that person?"

"I wish I could," he sighed, and the silence returned.

Back at school I immersed myself in the world of ministry. I hosted Bible studies, planned activities—all the while drawing in more and more people to meet Jesus. It was no longer a burden. I looked forward to each opportunity and found myself inviting people daily. Within six weeks, attendance had grown significantly. I was planting seeds and seeing fruit manifest so quickly that it was exhilarating. I was excited and my enthusiasm was contagious. It was as if a bright light had been switched on inside of me and people were attracted to the warm glow.

There he was. "Kenny J." He was handsome! I gave him a flyer and invited him to Bible study ... and he came! I introduced him to the campus minister and before long Kenny accepted Christ as his Savior. Kenny was persuasive when he spoke, and when he shared his testimony about accepting Jesus with the group, my heart filled to the brim. By the close of the semester, we were head over heels in love.

I took Kenny home to meet my family and they all fell in love with him too. He fit right in and I found myself beginning to trust him as I had trusted no other. I shared things with him that I had never told anyone else before. I told him about how abusive things were growing up and how scared and alone I had felt. Kenny shared his own challenges with me and this drew us even closer together.

The time I spent with Kenny was magical. He loved God with all his heart. God was everything to us and to a wonderful growing community of believers around us. We spent lots of time together—talking, praying, studying the Word, and just being close. Our feelings for each other intensified and it was the best time in my life.

Kenny was now a senior and I was in my sophomore year. He was looking to his future and ready to make a permanent move to settle down. He began to talk of marriage and I found myself suddenly shy. I wasn't ready for that kind of commitment. I was still bruised from my past and from the betrayal I had experienced time and again. I wanted to give myself completely to Kenny more than anything ... but part of me held back. I was deeply in love, but not ready to commit.

"Seek first His kingdom," was etched in my spirit. *How can I seek God if I am so involved in a relationship?* I thought to myself. I was still at the beginning of college. I was back on a volleyball scholarship and had plans to play for the next three years. What about my family? I promised my mother I would finish school and be the first college graduate in the family! What about the ministry? People were coming to know Christ because of my involvement. *If I marry Kenny, what will happen to those people?* I fought with myself. One day my mind would allow me to leave school and join Kenny in "happily ever after" wedded bliss. The next day I was certain that I had to focus on my goals and accomplish them or I would always be filled with regret that would ultimately spoil my marriage.

Up and down I went, riding on an emotional roller coaster. Beneath it all was my troubled childhood lurking beneath the surface, contributing to the stress, but never allowed to form tangible words to vocalize in my mind. I was determined that I would never allow what happened to my mother happen to me. I was determined to always be capable to survive on my own—independent, well educated, and strong. Fear of betrayal was there—I was just unwilling to acknowledge it. This fear placed an invisible fortress around my heart. No one could come in, and I couldn't come out. Fear imprisoned this part of me. I didn't even realize it, but it was there as surely as if there were real iron bars and a lock encasing my heart.

My Auntie Dee Dee had made plans to go to college, but instead got married and moved away with her husband, Uncle Bubbie, who worked for the government. The responsibilities of being a wife and mother served to complicate things and it was many years before she had the opportunity to return to school for her Bachelor's Degree. During this time she wrote me letters, encouraging me to stay in school and finish my degree—there would be time for marriage later. She spoke of the limitations I would experience without that cherished college degree. I clung to her words as a source of encouragement and guidance. I was keenly aware of the struggles my mother faced because of her lack of education and how limited her choices were because of this. My aunt knew a great deal about the situation surrounding my childhood and her words carried great weight with me. I was thankful for her inspiration and this helped me to realize that God had a plan for my life. I was thoroughly convinced that scholarships were His provision for my education. Why would He have provided the money for me to go to school if it wasn't supposed to finish? It would be wrong of me to waste this opportunity.

I thought often of my siblings and didn't want to be a "drop out" they couldn't look up to. Troubled by my past, absorbed in my present, and confused about my future—I pulled back from Kenny.

I had been the envy of many girls in our campus fellowship. Kenny was irresistible. He was a fine catch—

handsome, well-built, patient, well-spoken, kind, tender, and sincerely good. Kenny was what some would call a "Mandingo Man." Every female wanted Kenny, but I was the lucky one he chose. I was proud to be with him and I felt special that he wanted to be with me.

As his senior year progressed, Kenny became increasingly insistent for deeper commitment and wanted more and more of my time. I was not only active in campus ministry, I was very focused on my studies and also took my position with the volleyball team very seriously. I needed time to pursue these endeavors. It required focus and dedication to keep up my grades and perform well. As a result, we were unable to spend much time together and our relationship grew shaky.

Not surprisingly, another girl saw the opportunity to make Kenny feel special and wanted. She began calling him, inviting him out and spending all her free time with him. This was worlds apart from what I was doing—squeezing him into a few spare moments and even when we did find time to be together I was often preoccupied with responsibilities or just too tired to be attentive. Slowly, unconsciously, I pushed him away.

In my mind I truly wanted to be Kenny's wife. I believed he was the man God had for me. I even dreamed about it, but I believed firmly that this had to be after college. Then (and only then) could I allow myself to become an adoring and wonderful wife. Looking back I know that fear played a larger role in my reluctance to commit than I admitted to myself at the time. I had known the harshness of anger and abuse. I had felt the sting of betrayal by people I loved and trusted and I still suffered from that pain. I just wasn't willing to risk allowing Kenny an opportunity to hurt me in that way. I pursued my goals and pushed him further and further away until one day, he stopped trying to get close.

Kenny moved on ...

Seven

HOME AWAY FROM HOME

It is not so much our friends' help that helps us, as the confidence of their help.

— EPICURUS

$\mathcal{O}$ur campus ministry group had grown to over one hundred strong. The church provided a caring "home away from home" experience for students, and was one reason why the campus ministry flourished so strongly. It was a beautiful expression of the love of Jesus. For students who desired to build a friendship with a local family, the campus ministry facilitated an "adopted parents" program. The college students were paired with a caring family and would spend time with this "adopted" family on weekends. I was blessed with a number of Christian mentors during this time. A lovely woman named Nancy along with her family, the LeDoux's, and Pastor Floyd Kaiser and his wife, Margaret, were particularly special to me during this time. These people proved not only to be great examples to me, but they covered me with love and prayer and offered wisdom and guidance for my life from God's perspective.

On weekends, and most other times I was not occupied, I had a place to go and spend time with people who loved me. They provided me with home cooked meals, transportation, laughter and delightful memories. I often had a cheering section made up of church members who came out to support me during volleyball games. Their kindness overwhelmed me and demonstrated God's pure love for me in a way that changed my life forever.

I knew Kenny was seeing someone else. We didn't really officially break up, but we drifted apart until I knew the relationship had ended. I knew he would bring his new girl to a meeting one day and I secretly dreaded it. I still loved him. The thought of seeing him happy with someone else was painful, even though I genuinely wished him the best and did want him to be happy. *Oh, if only he was willing to wait!* I thought to myself.

One girl in the group that had never been fond of me (at least in my mind) didn't feel as though I deserved a man as wonderful as Kenny to begin with. This girl had quickly encouraged Kenny to move on when my reluctance to commit became evident. "Pursuing Dot is a waste of time," she told him. She introduced him to a friend of hers and encouraged him to ask her out. Real or imagined, it seemed as though she celebrated my loss— perhaps I had gotten what I deserved. Each time I went to a meeting, I could feel her eyes and imagine whispers: "Good for him!" "… about time!" It was uncomfortable and inside I wanted to escape.

The day came. He brought her. I was hurt inside. The old feelings of betrayal began to surface in my mind. It was difficult to push through these thoughts and focus on God and my goals. It was literally as if a wrestling match was taking place inside my soul. I argued with myself, gave myself pep talks, and sometimes cried out to God in desperation. I questioned if I had done the right thing to reject Kenny's offer for a future together and struggled to keep my focus on my studies. Somehow, I found a way.

To further complicate matters, our campus ministry group naturally fostered deep relationships and people began pairing off. We shared meaningful times of worship and prayer together. It was natural for people to bond spiritually and when common goals and common interests were added to the equation, the "coupling" began. No less than fifteen couples formed from this group that went all the way to the altar. I was truly happy for each and every one of them, but something inside me was empty and hollow. *Will I ever know that kind of happiness? Will I ever trust someone enough to walk down the aisle? Will he treat me well? Will he hurt me?* These thoughts tormented me in moments of quietness and I turned them over to God, trusting Him to bring me peace.

Kenny was very kind to me during this time and placed some distance between us before involving his new girlfriend in campus ministry. I appreciated his sensitivity, but being around this girl was enough to drive me to distraction. The disappointment in my soul was intense. I felt neglected as I never had before and had to grapple with my emotions privately so I could find the strength and maturity to be gracious and kindhearted in social situations.

To save face, I continued to study with the group and participate in all the activities. I even encouraged other members of the group to reach out to Kenny's new girlfriend and love her. After all, that's what Christ would have done and I genuinely wanted to be a follower of Christ. To anyone who expressed concern for me or wondered how I was doing, I was quick to tell them I was fine. I would pull out a convincing smile and assure them that the break up with Kenny was not his fault—someone else was just able to give him what he needed now and I wasn't that person. He deserved to be happy.

Many times I was tempted to go to Kenny, apologize, and let him know how I felt. I wanted to tell him how much I loved him and needed him. I would imagine the scene in my mind. It would always end with him asking me to marry him (again) but this time I would look into his eyes and say, "Yes, Kenny!" with enthusiasm and an ardent embrace. Sometimes I even picked up the phone, ready to call him … only to put it back down on the receiver. I just couldn't bring myself to do it. It would be a lie. I wasn't ready to love like that … or be loved like that.

Even with all the love I received from my wonderful church family and the students in the campus ministry, something on the inside was deeply wounded , something that had never healed. I never shared my traumatic childhood with anyone else in that ministry other than Kenny—so no one ever knew the depth of fear and inability to trust I experienced. I was simply not capable of accepting Kenny's goodness, kindness, and genuine love for me. My defenses were built into a strong-walled fortress and I couldn't find the resolve to tear them down and let him inside.

The remainder of my sophomore year and my junior year were difficult and lonely. During this time I met Wayne and Jane Nance. Mrs. Nance became my mentor, and oh, what Divine Providence to bring her into my life. Her influence helped me to grow in Jesus.

I learned the true value of a mentor through my time with her. She was older and wiser and pushed me to be more than I was. She pointed out the good she saw in me and challenged me to reach for God's best in every piece of my life. She helped me see my failures as stepping stones to success and use these for growth and development, not as anchors to weigh me down. She drove me to honor Christ with all my actions and seek His guidance in every decision. I wanted to be like her and in a very short time I had grown remarkably close to her.

She was a true Proverbs 31 woman—strong, dignified, multi-talented, a caring wife, mother, and friend to many. I admired her strength. Like me, she was a woman given to her responsibilities, but they didn't consume her. She managed to live a very balanced life, meeting the needs of others without neglecting her own. She looked to God and sought His will as her primary objective. Her love for Him was obvious and contagious. I longed to know Him as she did. I longed to feel as fulfilled and confident and significant as she was.

Her wisdom and gentleness disarmed me. I found myself venting my closely guarded feelings, fear, and concerns. My defenses fell away when I was with her and I felt safe enough to share my pain. She listened to me ever so patiently and her calmness would wrap around me like a warm blanket. She gently led me down a path that began with inner contemplation and led to tangible actions. She successfully navigated the storms in my soul and helped me chart a course into the calm waters of my spirit—a place where God's love was all-encompassing.

For the first time I began to allow inner healing to take place. I knew that I was on my way to a new beginning.

After six weeks of spending time with the Nances, Jane's husband, Wayne received news of a job transfer requiring them to move to Houston. I was devastated.

"Why, God?" I cried. The same sinking feeling I experienced when Miss Garlington told me she was moving away came back. Just as I had done with Miss Garlington, I had shared with Mrs. Nance all the details of my childhood and my mother's abuse. I had also told her intimate details of my relationship with Kenny and was vulnerable enough to share my feelings about the break up. I had just begun the process of healing and was approaching a place where I could bring closure to these painful events and start anew ... but it was abruptly halted. Just as the shame, embarrassment, and feelings of being unworthy and afraid had started to melt away, they threatened to return like a flood and drown me in their wake.

How could this happen to me ... again? What was wrong with me?

I will never forget the day they left. Completely overcome with emotion, I could not even go to send them off. I wept bitterly, but found no solace in my tears. Once again, a shoulder I trusted enough to cry on had disappeared and I was left alone to cry alone—silent tears.

I was certain I would never be able to trust again.

Eight

GUNSHOT AND GRACE

Above all the grace and the gifts that Christ gives to His beloved is that of overcoming self.

— FRANCIS OF ASSISI

$\mathscr{I}$t was now my senior year of college. It had been a successful volleyball season and I enjoyed traveling with the team very much. I was still committed to the campus ministry and in the off season I remained disciplined in physical conditioning. I was strong and healthy and in the best shape of my life. I was close to my coaches and teammates. I was over Kenny and once again happy in my involvement in ministry. I was going to graduate in December 1983 with a degree in Sociology and Business. I was excited about the future. I was proud of what I had achieved and was ready to make my way out in the world on my own.

One April morning I was sitting in my dorm room studying when I received a call from my volleyball coach telling me she was on her way over. This was quite unusual and I began searching my mind trying to imagine what I could possibly have done wrong that was bad enough to bring the coach out for a personal visit. I could think of nothing, and by the time she arrived I was very anxious to hear what she had to say. *Had something happened at home?* Immediately I felt uneasy and grew concerned that something bad had happened to my mother. *Why else would coach be coming?*

I began to pray earnestly, asking God for strength. I prayed that my mother was not dead. I feared that my stepfather had beaten her to death and I suddenly felt guilty for being away from home. I told God I could handle anything but my mother being dead.

It seemed as though hours passed before my coach arrived, when in reality it was only a few minutes. When I answered the door, there she stood with several of my teammates. My heart sank and I felt my knees shake. Adrenalin poured through my body and my thoughts spun out of control. Clearly this was bad news. I searched the faces of my teammates looking for a clue—everyone was visibly upset.

"What is it?" I asked. "Please? Is it my Mama?"

My coach came inside and we sat on the edge of my bed. She held my hand and slowly said, "Dot, your stepfather has been shot." I stared at her in disbelief.

"He is in the hospital in critical condition," she continued. I let out a sigh of relief. "Oh, Mama," I whispered, tears streaming down my face. "Thank God ..." I'm sure my coach didn't understand my reaction ... how could she? I had never told any of them how my stepfather treated my mother. "I need to go to her," I said and stood up to pack. "Wait, I should call her," and I looked around the room confused, as if I couldn't remember how to use a telephone.

One of my teammates helped me call home and I was still crying tears of relief that my mother was not harmed when she answered. "Dorothy? Is that you?"

"Yes, Mama, it's me, Dorothy," I answered, so happy to hear her voice.

"Baby, listen to me. You need to focus on your schoolwork," she said. "I'm alright." Ever practical, Keeby did not want my studies to suffer, even with a crisis as big as this.

"But Mama," I interrupted.

"Listen to me, Dorothy Johnson," she continued, not allowing me get any further in my protest. "You couldn't get in to see him right now even if you were here. He's in intensive care. Why don't you wait until the weekend? You can come then without missing any of your classes. I'm fine. Really," she said.

"Who shot him?" I asked. "How did this happen? Where was he?" For a moment I felt panic rise and thought to myself, *Oh God, Mama, you didn't pull the trigger did you? Was it self defense? Did he hurt you?* Of course I said none of this out loud, but I was in shock. My feet felt like someone had glued them to floor.

Since none of my friends had any idea about my background, I couldn't really share any of the terrible things that were running through my mind. I wanted to be alone. I was grateful for how much they cared about me, and several of them stayed behind to make sure I was okay, but I was in turmoil and part of me just wanted to be left alone.

I was deeply concerned for my mother. In spite of the horror he put her through, I knew she genuinely cared about this man. She had continued to cook his meals, clean his trailer, wash his clothes, and pay his bills all this time … no matter how he treated her or what awful things he said to her. At last I fell into a fitful sleep, praying that God would watch over my mother and help her through this new storm.

The next morning my sister called, crying. "What is it?" I asked. I knew how she felt about our stepfather, so couldn't imagine that concern for him was the reason for her tears. "What's wrong?" I asked again, this time a bit more forcefully.

"It's Mama," she said and the crying started again. "Dorothy, you've got to come home. Now!" This was too much. I sat down hard, dazed. "She's sick … " more tears, "She's in intensive care."

I stared at the receiver. *Did I hear her right? Mama!* The moment I hung up fierce energy poured through my body. When I heard about my stepfather, my feet turned to stone. When I heard about my mother, it was like fire coursed through my veins. I hastily threw some clothes into a bag and sped home. I didn't even think about the consequences of missing class or practice. I didn't take time to notify anyone, I just knew I had to get home. *Home.* I thought. *Mama is my home. Without her there isn't any home.* The car couldn't go fast enough.

I arrived at the hospital in record time. I had no idea how fast I drove and could barely remember anything about the trip. It was as if I blinked and was there. I was anxious to find out more about her condition and I desperately wanted to see her and know for myself that she was okay.

My mother had suffered a heart attack. I suppose the news of my stepfather was too much for her to bear. Now they were both in intensive care, life hanging in the balance. It felt like I had been kicked in the stomach. No matter how deeply I breathed, there just didn't seem to be enough air.

We received an outpouring of support from the family, our church, and our friends. Everybody knew Keeby and everyone seemed to want to help in some way. All across Palquemines Parish, prayers were lifted on behalf of my mother and stepfather—earnest prayers—and God heard.

In a few days time my mother was moved to a regular room and showed remarkable signs of improvement. We were a people who believed in miracles. We had seen them many times and trusted God for one now. He did not fail.

I made several trips back and forth in the coming days. On my third visit home, two weeks later, my stepfather was also moved out of intensive care and settled comfortably in a hospital room to begin his long road back to recovery. It was a miracle. Not only miraculous that he was alive, but even more because this experience would finally bring him to Christ.

Police officers made several trips to the hospital, asking questions and analyzing details of the assault. A report was filed, but no one had yet gotten to the bottom of the mystery. My stepfather offered up what little he remembered. He had been drinking and gambling at a night club where he frequented. An argument broke out between him and another gentleman which soon escalated. Things got heated until they were completely out of hand. The result was a shot being fired and a bullet landing firmly in his stomach. Rumors flew all around the county and many speculated, but no one actually was able to name a plausible suspect, so no arrest was ever made. My stepfather had been too drunk to remember who he had the fight with.

My mother was just relieved he was alive and thanked God every day. It was amazing to watch how gentle she was with him and how attentive she was to his every need. My siblings and I had mixed feelings about the ordeal. Of course we were glad he was alive, but we were also partly glad that he had tasted the consequences of irrational violence. He had perpetuated pain so often on our mother, his being shot almost felt like justice. Like maybe he deserved it. I wrestled with these thoughts, but in time I chose to look at it as a chance for him to redeem himself and live a better life. God needed to shake him up to get his attention—and now He had it.

People from the community came to visit him every day. Acts of kindness demonstrated God's love to him by caring for a man who had done little to deserve such care. Others were bolder and prayed with him or shared the Gospel, witnessing to him and giving him the opportunity to make a decision for Christ. He was encouraged to trust God to heal his body, to repent, and turn his life around.

God must have spared him for a reason and he better find out what that reason was. Slowly they cracked his shell.

I visited him too. It was the right thing to do. I began to feel a burning desire for him to know Jesus. I had seen so many give their lives to Christ during my time in the campus ministry and I wanted my stepfather to know Him too.

I was sitting there with him one afternoon and a pleasant silence had filled the room. He looked over at me and I saw kindness in his eyes. For the first time I could ever remember in my life, he asked me about myself? "How's school?" he began. I was taken aback. He had never asked me a question like this before. I answered him cautiously, and though it was awkward at first, the more I talked the easier it got.

"Tell me more about this campus ministry you're so involved in," he probed. I looked at him, searching for some sign of false concern on his face, but there was none. I started talking and couldn't stop. It just flowed out. I told him all about my friends and the wonderful church and how families adopted students and mentored them and helped them discover their destiny. I told them about leading others to Christ and how God could change a life—any life, even his. I spoke of repentance and forgiveness and hope and healing and my stepfather took in every word like a sponge.

We lapsed into silence again after a time and I thought the conversation was at an end. "Tell me," he began ... "Tell me about what you want to do with your life, Dorothy." I turned my head and looked at him in amazement. *Was this the same man who beat my mother? Was this the man who came home drunk in the middle of the night, demanding food and shouting obscenities?* I looked at his face and felt God's love surround me. I realized I was looking at a man who had not been touched on the inside before by the character of God. God loved this man ... and therefore, so would I.

Memories began to flood me. My stepfather had often been tasked with the duty of driving me back to college after a visit. We usually went back on a Saturday after he had a chance to sleep it off and sober up. For the long three and a half hour ride it was just the two of us alone together. He often talked about himself on those trips and offered excuses for his behavior toward my mother. He always told me how sorry he was to have hurt her when he lost control. I was convinced that his actions were not premeditated, but that of a man totally lost in pent up rage that came out when under the influence of alcohol. Perhaps one of the reasons I was so intrigued by sociology was my stepfather's behavior. I'm not sure. My stepfather claimed that he wanted to stop drinking, but over and over he denied the needs of his family in favor of his desire to drink. I didn't hate him, even then. I felt sorry for him. He was a loser trapped in a losing cycle, unable and unwilling to break free.

Yet here he was now, surviving a bullet in the stomach shot at point blank range. Surely God must have more for him, and if I could be part of the miracle, so be it. I poured out my heart for God to him and shared how he could know God's love and experience God's peace. I was certain that if he gave his life to Christ, he could be free forever from the grip of alcohol and gambling. He could live a new and wonderful life.

During our visits he told me how proud he was that I was going to earn my degree. He told me he wanted to be at my graduation and I was deeply moved. To pass the time we played games to help strengthen his lungs. The hospital had a cylindrical device with balls in it attached to a hose with a mouthpiece. You had to blow in the hose to see how high you could lift the balls and that helped expand your lungs and kept fluid from building up in people confined to bed. We took turns blowing into the device and his face would contort so strangely that it made me laugh. Of course, being an athlete in top condition, it was no contest, but it was a good time between us.

In the hospital, there was no chance for a drink and he dried out completely for the first time in his adult life. I could see the impact that God's love was making on him. He was a changed man. He was growing warmer and friendlier by the day. I knew he would never be the same again and I looked forward to our visits. I was hungry to be around him. I had never really known the love of a dad and I wanted to experience it. The doctors had nothing but good news to report. In fact, his prognosis was so good that his release was planned in a few days. I felt relaxed when I drove back to school, anticipating that our lives were all about to change for the better.

It had been three days since my last visit. The routine of practice, classes, and campus ministry had blended into my trips to the hospital. I was managing things okay but was beginning to feel tired. The coach asked if she could stop by. She had been extremely supportive over the past weeks, and I assumed her visit was to check on me and knew she wanted to discuss me helping the team next season since I was still in the process of completing my senior year. "Sure," I said easily, and I returned to my studies without any anxiety.

She knocked on the door and I opened with a big smile. Instantly, I knew something was wrong. She had not come alone. Once again she had assembled a group of team members and by the look on everyone's faces, I knew the news was not good.

"Dorothy, honey, there is just no easy way to say this: your stepfather is dead," she said.

"How can that be?" I stammered. "I just saw him! He's getting better. He's supposed to go home today!" I shook my head in disbelief. This could not be true. I looked at my friends skeptically, "This can't be true," I said firmly. But I was wrong. It was true. My stepfather never got a chance to go home. He never had the opportunity to live out a changed life. He was gone forever. Just when I began to hope for a happy home for my mother he was gone …

I was shocked. Angry. Emotions came to the surface and spilled over ... everywhere.

Nine

NOTHING IS
WASTED

*Life's challenges are not supposed to paralyze you,
they're supposed to help you discover who you are.*

— BERNICE JOHNSON REAGON

*T*he night following the news of my stepfather's death,
I lay in bed staring up at the ceiling. Hot tears spilled
from the corners of my eyes and washed down my cheeks,
making my pillow damp. I felt numb inside. *Why God?* I
thought to myself. *Why didn't he get the chance to go home
and live a new life like he was supposed to?*

For the first time, I had an encounter with the Holy
Spirit. In a gentle whisper He told me that my stepfather
did go home—just not the one here on earth. I heard Him
so clearly and the awareness of Him communicating
directly with me changed my life. I *thought* I was close to
God, and I was, but now I realized I had so much more to

learn. When I heard the Holy Spirit speak to me, I realized that everything in my life—the good and the bad—were all being used to help me grow and mature. Nothing was wasted. Even the pain had purpose. I took great comfort in this.

My relationship with God grew tangibly stronger. I studied the Bible with a new hunger, and for the first time in my life I was conscious that I was an eternal spirit—that I would live for eternity beyond my days on earth.

In the days leading up to the memorial service, I called my mother several times a day to check on her and be sure that she was okay. I was deeply concerned for her health. She seemed more fragile to me now than she ever had before. I was sad to have lost my stepfather just when I began getting to know him, but knowing that my mother was truly safe—totally free from danger gave me great peace. I was relieved to know no one would ever abuse her again.

The day arrived for my stepfather's home-going service. My campus minister, Danny, and Mr. Kaiser, the pastor of my college church drove to attend and show their support for me. I don't think they had ever encountered anything like that service before (or probably since). It was not the usual, reserved, dignified funeral service they were accustomed to presiding over. In my father's home-going service, there was such a huge display of emotion and grief. The women cried loudly and sobs shook their whole bodies. On campus, I had easily blended into the culture of the ministry. I don't think anyone even considered I might have come from a different background. Now here they were in this service surround by raw, black, Louisiana tradition—they were clearly uncomfortable.

In spite of the sadness of the occasion, I couldn't help but chuckle as I saw their faces flush and noticed how their quiet, stoic posture made them stand out more and more in the expressive crowd. The harder they tried to seem inconspicuous, the funnier they looked. I was truly touched that they had come for me, but I was actually relieved for them when the appropriate time came and they could finally disappear without being rude. I still shake my head and laugh when I think about how fast they got out of there.

I spent a little time with my family, but I went back to school determined to put all the distractions behind me and finish my semester strong.

Returning to college, my life was truly upside down. Kenny, the love of my life, was engaged to be married to another woman. My stepfather was dead and my mother had suffered a heart attack. Mrs. Nance, my spiritual mentor and friend, had moved to Houston. Then I discovered the campus minister and his wife, Danny and Theresa, had accepted a new ministry position in Oklahoma. Theresa was such fun to be around. She laughed a lot and made me feel warm and welcome every time I saw her. She was special. Everything about her made me desire to go deeper, to gain even more knowledge of God's Word. She was a true spiritual mentor to me—pouring in, encouraging me to grow and experience more of God's grace and power. News of their leaving was a crushing blow.

I had also finished my last year with the volleyball team and my friends were beginning to marry and move off. It seemed as though everyone I had invested time in building a relationship with was moving on to do what God had planned for them. I wondered what he had planned for me.

When the spring semester ended, I went home for the short break before summer school would begin. My mother was spending much time and energy trying to deal with the death of my stepfather. She was grieving without the comfort of knowing who had shot him. There had been so many conflicting statements given to the police. So many people had changed their stories from their original statements that there was not enough evidence to catch or convict the perpetrator.

Even though she wanted to put it behind her, my mother was constantly being dragged back into the ordeal, having to interact with law enforcement and relive the tragic events. The stress was too much for her already failing health. She began experiencing seizures more frequently and recovery from them took her longer and longer. I was powerless to change her situation, and as the time drew near for me to return to school I had to lovingly place her in God's hands to care for. I truly had to surrender my trust to God.

I returned for the summer semester, but things were really different for me. I was now the manager for the volleyball team and the role was entirely different than before. The church was in the process of hiring a new campus minister. Most of my friends had graduated in the spring, and they had moved on. I was not going to graduate until December, but I was and felt eager to begin my post-college life too. I was restless, lonely, and tired.

One evening I received a call from my mother telling me that Mary, my twenty-three year old stepsister, had been diagnosed with Hodgkin's disease and had been taken to the hospital in Baton Rouge. Friends in my church knew some people in Baton Rouge and arranged a place for me to stay on weekends or whenever I needed to be there to care for Mary and my mother.

I dreaded a return to the hospital. I was accustomed to being around young, vibrant, healthy people. I hated hospitals. Hospitals made me uncomfortable. I felt nauseous and would sometimes even vomit. Walking the corridors brought unpleasant memories to the surface— memories of my stepfather's passing, fears of my mother's frailty, and now the uncertainty of my sister's future. I felt powerless in this place, helpless and frustrated. I desperately wanted to do more than offer up prayers and give words of encouragement. But prayers and words of encouragement were all I had to offer—so that's what I did.

Mary looked forward to my visits. She had developed a daily routine in the hospital that included studying her Bible and reading daily devotionals. On the weekends she wanted me to come and read aloud to her. Sometimes family members were present. At other times we were alone, but these were special times for me and I was delighted to bring Mary some joy. Sharing God's Word with her created a deep bond between us.

As time progressed, Mary grew increasingly ill. She showed no signs of improvement and it grew increasingly difficult to watch the deterioration of her condition. Her doctor was a very caring woman. She had grown to love Mary and was doing everything in her power to make sure she received the very best care available. Mary was quite dependent on her visits and clung to hope.

The doctor had postponed her own family's vacation several times, but was now planning to go away with them. This gave me great concern and I followed her out of Mary's room and told her that I feared when she left that Mary would give up and simply slip away. The doctor shared my concerns, but assured me that the physician who would care for Mary in her absence was wonderful and that Mary would be fine.

The next day, she brought the new physician to Mary's room to introduce her. Mary cried. I sat at the end of Mary's bed and cried too. It felt like a desperate moment. The doctor cried also and it felt like a permanent good-bye.

It was so difficult, watching Mary's health deteriorate at such an alarming pace. All the while her relationship with God grew stronger. Over and over she expressed her concern about her children. She didn't want them to grow up without their mother. I looked into her eyes—she was so young ... *Why God?* I thought to myself. *Why?*

That weekend was the last time I saw Mary alive. Exactly two months and twenty-one days after my stepfather died, Mary joined him in heaven.

Once again our family plummeted into sadness and grief. Mary was gone. Death was now an overwhelming reality for me. It was my enemy. But in the loss, I found a deep appreciation for the gift of life. I was determined to make the very best of mine.

Ten

NEW BEGINNINGS

*It matters not the number of years in your
life. It is the life in your years.*

—ABRAHAM LINCOLN

"You're a what?" I asked.

"I've become a Jehovah's Witness, baby," my mother
answered calmly.

"Why? When?" I managed to say. I didn't quite
understand. She had always been active in church. When
we were younger she wouldn't even allow us to speak to
a Jehovah's Witness for fear we would become confused.
She was an Evangelist with the Church of Christ and loved
telling people about Jesus. Her favorite thing in the world
was to lead someone to Christ. I couldn't comprehend what
had occurred to cause her to make this shift.

In fact, it was her zeal to witness and evangelize that drew
her to them. Jehovah's Witnesses emphasize witnessing

and still go door to door to proselytize. Their emphasis on equality of all races and clean moral living were very appealing to my mother. This I could understand, but rejecting the symbol of the cross, not believing in hell, or that Jesus and the Holy Spirit are fully part of the Trinity was more difficult for me to comprehend. Abstaining from celebrating birthdays or any of the traditional Christian holidays further complicated things for me. Though I loved my mother dearly and respected her deeply, I simply could not agree with her new definition of faith and practice. The woman who had been my bedrock and given me a strong foundation of the Bible, the woman who had led me to Jesus had now accepted a version of salvation I could never agree with. This too felt like a betrayal. Perhaps it was brought on by a life of suffering, then the trauma and tragedy of losing my stepfather and Mary so closely together—I may never know. At any rate, it did cause a strain between us. Tensions mounted. I did not want to move back home.

Dallas. That was it. Dallas was the place for me. I had my degree in Sociology and Business neatly tucked under my jacket and it was time to make my way in the world.

Several times my roommate, Sheila, and I visited Dallas while on volleyball trips. Each trip made the desire to move there grow strong. It was like a magnet pulling us there. Dallas was an oasis. It was a big city, filled with excitement and opportunity. Our small town paled in comparison. In Dallas we could expand our horizons, test our wings, and find our futures.

Sheila lived just thirty minutes away from school and she went back home to find a job, gain some experience, and earn some money to prepare for the move.

I did not follow in her footsteps. Home had lost its appeal to me, so I remained in Lafayette. Because of the strong network of friends I had made, I had access to many resources there—friends, places to stay, job opportunities—I immediately found a job as an accountant at a jewelry store. I boarded with a delightful older woman, an empty nester named Ms. Rodgers. Her daughter was recently engaged and we would help each other through our times of transition. I paid rent to her and in return she gave me a loving, peaceful home, companionship, and support. I remained with her for a year, but wanted to experience living on my own and taste total independence for a season before moving to Dallas.

In February of 1986, Sheila decided she was ready for Dallas, but I was not yet ready to join her. I had just signed a lease that wouldn't be up until August and I was working for a wonderful company, Wm. S. Nacol Jewelry. I was gaining life experience and growing deeper with the Lord. It was a good time for me to receive and become strong. I felt sturdy in my independence. I was enjoying every moment, but began to feel a shift coming. Once again I felt a restlessness begin to stir. It was not discontent, but rather an eagerness for something more. I could feel this season drawing to an end.

For months I prepared for my move to Dallas. I was at a fork in the road and it was time to make a decision which path to take. Reluctantly I turned in my resignation to Mr. and Mrs. Nacol. They had been so kind to me and I was as sad to leave them as they were to see me go.

New beginnings are exciting, but new beginnings require necessary endings and these can be painful. Leaving my church family, school friends, and natural family was a difficult thing to do. I was a young, black woman leaving my support structure and comfortable, secure situation to forge my way ahead in an unknown world—no job, no place to stay, few friends, and no real connections—just a dream, a spirit of adventure, and a belief that I was obeying God. Instead of being terrified, I had complete faith in God and was totally at ease in my trust in Him. I knew everything would work out.

Many friends communicated that my decision was inspiring to them. It was quite a risk. It took courage and faith. I honestly felt a great deal of support from them. In the four weeks leading up to my departure, I was literally invited to eat dinner with different friends each night. The love I felt was overwhelming. Part of me was sad at the thought of moving so far from them, and the other part of me was overjoyed that God had expanded my circle so much. I could hardly wait to see what was in store.

The time came to say good bye. I placed my furniture in storage (since I didn't have a home to move into), packed my clothes into my car and began the five hundred mile drive to Dallas. I stopped off in Houston to spend the night and visit with friends. On Sunday morning, I arrived in Dallas—my new home.

I met up with Sheila and we had a joyful reunion. She had been living in Dallas for six months and her lease would soon expire. We decided to search for a place large enough to share. We had a ten day window for me to find a job and for us to find a suitable apartment. That night I prayed that the Lord would bless me with a good job to begin my career. I checked the newspaper and mapped out several places to seek work the next day. At the first place I interviewed, I was asked to return later that same day to meet with some other people in the company. That was a good sign.

I returned in the afternoon to meet with three other people and I knew beyond a shadow of doubt that I would be offered the job. I was amazed at how quickly God had answered my prayer. Amazed, yes—surprised, no. I trusted God.

They did offer me the job and it paid well—so well, in fact, that I could have lived on my own with money left over for expenses if I had chosen to do so. I knew God was in this opportunity so I did not hesitate to accept the offer. I would be starting in two weeks.

I couldn't wait to get to the apartment and tell Sheila the good news. On the way back I praised God and thanked Him repeatedly in my heart. He was so good to me. His favor was overwhelming. Everything was unfolding in such a beautiful order. Every detail was a testament to His care and provision.

Sheila took off work the next day so we could search for an apartment. Another of our close, college friends (we called her Bug, but her name is Vanessa) was also living in Dallas. She and Sheila had already been communicating because she too was looking for a place to stay. We were all good friends with each other, so we decided to look for a place large enough to live together. We found a three bedroom apartment in Valley Ranch, only four miles from my new job, and less than five miles from where my new roommates were already working. It was perfect! By the weekend we had pooled our belongings together and had decorated our new, beautiful, three bedroom apartment.

I came to town on Sunday. I got a job on Monday and found a place to live on Tuesday. It was obvious to me that God's hand was on the move to Dallas. All that remained was for me to find a good church home. Although Sheila believed in God, she had not committed her life to Him at the time. She was very respectful of my faith and open to Bible study. Knowing how important it was to me, she had compiled a list of churches for me to check out before I arrived. While she was looking, she remembered that I had said I was interested in finding a church that had a deaf ministry. This interest was inspired by a wonderful family I had met at my church in Lafayette, Betty, John and Brad. Betty had special needs and was unable to hear or speak. John worked for an oil company and traveled a lot. Brad, their beautiful five-year old son was an absolute joy.

Because I had experienced such sadness in my final term at school, my time with this gracious family had been precious and meaningful. They coaxed me from my grief and helped me to see that joy comes in the morning.

No one at our church in Lafayette knew sign language, so whenever John was traveling, this left Betty isolated. Several people, including myself, decided to learn sign language so Betty wouldn't feel alone when he was gone. I threw myself into learning sign language and before long I was helping Betty learn her way around town. As a result, I became her interpreter whenever she needed me and we spent a great deal of time together. We became fast friends and sisters in Christ. When I left Lafayette, I promised her that I would find a church and get involved with a deaf ministry so I wouldn't forget what I had learned. It was important to me that I would always be able to communicate with her.

Sheila had Highland Oaks Church of Christ on her list, and it was a long drive from Valley Ranch—but turned out to be well worth the trek. There we were on a Wednesday night sitting together at this church far from our home, but I knew this was where we belonged.

Sheila had never accepted Christ into her heart. Her past and her mother's approach to the Word had turned her off and erected a barrier. Yet though she had never formally accepted Christ's invitation, she was one of the most beautiful people I knew. She was kind, filled with integrity, and her values and morals were the same as my own. She had always been comfortable with my friendship, in spite of my strong faith and the fact that I talked about Jesus all the time. She often went to Bible Studies and retreats with me during college. I could tell she enjoyed the service at Highland Oaks and this was more confirmation to me that this is where we should attend.

We went back on Sunday, driving the forty miles passing the time in happy conversation. Sheila had no interest in the deaf ministry, but there were lots of other things there she could get involved with. After church we would fellowship with people and exchange stories and laughter and get to know each other more and more. Every time we left we felt more like family. It was a beautiful time.

Two weeks flew by. I had found a job, an apartment, roommates, and a church home without the tiniest struggle. My life was filled with joy and beauty. I constantly offered praise and thanksgiving to God for His goodness. I kept the lines of communication open back home with friends and family and gave them cheerful updates on my new life in Dallas.

My new job was in healthcare administration. This was very different from accounting, but I found I enjoyed it immensely. The job offered me a great deal of stability and it paid very well. It was a blessing from God. It was clear to me that He had orchestrated and ordained it from the beginning. I had great favor with my coworkers and was easily forming friendships. Life was great! A woman named Janet took me under her wing. We instantly became close friends and I discovered that she was a wonderful person. She was a single mother with two children and was very receptive to the Word of God. Even with all her responsibilities, she went the extra mile to train me, showing me love, patience and kindness. In just three short months I was promoted from supervisor to manager. I was overjoyed.

I became more and more involved at Highland Oaks and was active in church events and ministry.

Invitations rolled in from members and I became deeply involved with their ministry for the deaf. I had a desire to become fluent enough to serve as an interpreter of sermons for the deaf.

Sheila and Vanessa (Bug) as well as one of my other friends started coming to church on a regular basis. It was a long drive, but we visited during the commute and enjoyed the services immensely. I saw Sheila growing close to Mrs. Beachum, the minister's wife, and she enjoyed the services so much that there was no way I would consider finding a church closer and more convenient to attend.

Two months later, Sheila made a commitment and gave her life to Jesus Christ. The day she was baptized was one of the happiest days of my life. We had been best friends for seven years—she was my best friend and I loved her like family. There wasn't a time in all that seven years that I wasn't praying for her or with her and we rejoiced together in sweet celebration of this new chapter in her life.

We continued at Highland Oaks and I knew it was an important time in Sheila's spiritual development, but I began to pray specifically for God to guide us to a church closer to our home where we could be more involved.

One day, to our surprise, a couple knocked on our door. We rarely had guests, and if we did, they were expected, so the knock startled us. We lived on the third floor, so if someone had put in enough energy to climb all those stairs, we knew it must be important. We opened the door to meet Kevin and Sandra Moses. They smiled warmly and greeted us with some literature, inviting us to attend a Church of Christ that was just starting up in an office building nearby. The church was looking to expand and God opened a door once again where I could be fed His Word. The congregation there was small, but filled with sincere people who loved God. There weren't many ministers there, and few activities, but we were eager to assist in building this ministry. For a season we attended there as well as traveled to Highland Oaks, but finally decided to put all our energies into the new church. Once again a new beginning called for a necessary ending.

Eleven

FINDING LOVE

Falling in love consists merely of uncorking the imagination and bottling the common sense.

—HELEN ROWLAND

My life settled into a nice routine. I was happy. I was content. I was filled with God's joy, growing in His Word, enjoying my roommates, thriving at my job, and excited to wake up every morning to greet a new day.

Enter a mysterious stranger.

It was December, 1986. I needed to visit my insurance agent and he was conveniently located in the same building as my bank, Sunbelt Savings. I went first to see my agent, and then to the bank. While there, I noticed a man staring at me. His stare was so intense that I found it unsettling. In fact, I noticed that each time I visited the bank or the agent, he was there, staring at me. Always before I simply ignored him, but today it dawned on me that he was flirting. He was at the counter speaking with a teller, asking the usual questions, but then he started staring at me again. I immediately left the line, feeling nervous and uncomfortable. I went back to my insurance agent's office to wait, hoping he would leave. Then, I thought, I would go back to the bank and conduct my business after he had gone. The stranger's gaze was too much for me. Whatever advances he planned on making, I wasn't interested.

Once inside the insurance office, the agent asked if I was okay, wondering what was wrong. I told him about the stranger and the agent asked me if I knew who he was. I had, in fact, seen him a few times on television and I told my agent that I knew who he was but I wasn't interested. He asked me if I knew the guy was a professional athlete. I remained unmoved. "Not interested," I said and gave him a smile. "I just want to finish my business and hit the road for Louisiana. Tomorrow is my birthday and I feel like going home!"

My agent said, "Wow! Happy birthday!" Then, "To tell you the truth, this guy has been asking around about you and he really wants to meet you." Realization set in. Here I had been thinking this guy kept showing up randomly, by chance, in places where I was. Now it was obvious that it had been clearly intentional. It unnerved me. It angered me. I swept out of the office, "Forget it. I'll stop by the bank some other time!" I headed for my car, never looking back.

When I got to the parking lot, there he was, draped across *my* car, smiling from ear to ear.

"Hi," he said casually, "My name is Nathaniel, but most people just call me Nate. Would you join me for dinner?"

"No, thank you," I said forcefully. "I don't care who you are, I am in a hurry and I need to get down the road."

"Where you going to in such a hurry?" he replied, still smiling easily.

I let out an irritated sigh. "I'm on my way to visit my family in Louisiana if you must know," I answered.

"Well, can I have your phone number at least? I'd like to call you sometime."

I squared my shoulders and faced him. Politely, yet sternly I replied, "I don't give my number to strangers."

"Well, I'm not exactly a stranger, now am I?" He flashed another smile attempting to disarm me, totally undaunted by my rejection.

"I'll tell you what. How about if I give you *my* number and you can give *me* a call when you have a little more time? Would that be alright?" He looked hopeful.

I said nothing. I stared at the ground and wondered how to escape this uncomfortable situation. This big man was blocking me from entering my car.

"Now me, I'm from Orlando, Florida," he began with a different approach. "Now *that's* a drive from Dallas, let me tell you. How long of a drive is it for you to get to New Orleans?" he prodded.

My curt responses never disheartened him. He easily moved from one topic to the next, as if our conversation was a natural exchange between two long time friends. He seemed totally unaffected by how chilly and closed I was to his advance.

"What's the weather like in New Orleans?" He tried yet another approach.

"Okay," I said, "If I take your number and call you, I can answer all your questions then." I had no intention of calling him, but thought that might get him to let me leave.

He looked at me intently, then his features softened once more into a relaxed gaze. "Please, just one more question," he said, "if you answer that, then I promise not to take up any more of your time."

I just stared at him, not believing he still cared to talk to me after such obvious rejection.

"Why won't you talk to me after I've made so many attempts?" he asked.

"Look, I know who you are. I know you play football for the Dallas Cowboys. I'm just not interested in getting to know you, why is that such a big deal?" I said. "My brother is a professional ball player and he told me to be wary of athletes."

"Is that right?" he smiled again. "Your brother is right, you should be wary of professional athletes," he chuckled. He held me captive there for at least another thirty minutes talking about anything and everything.

At last I interrupted him, "Listen, if I don't leave now I'll be late for my birthday celebration back home. Please let me go."

"Is it your birthday?" he said with new excitement.

"Tomorrow. Saturday. The twentieth." I said matter of factly.

He started laughing uncontrollably, then said, "This is definitely meant to happen on this day. I can't believe it. I just can't believe it!"

"What are you talking about?" I said, annoyed, but now a bit intrigued.

"Tomorrow is my birthday, too!" he said.

I must have looked very skeptical because he pulled out his wallet to show me his driver's license as proof. His birthday was in fact the very next day, the same day as mine. The coincidence was undeniable. Same date, same year.

This inspired another thirty minutes of conversation between us. I looked him over carefully and handed his phone number back. He looked surprised.

"If you really want to contact me, call this," I said, writing my number on a slip of paper and handing it to him.

"I will do that!" he said, grinning broadly. I got in my car, giving him a smile and a wave as I drove off, heading home for the weekend.

The truth was that there would be no birthday celebration for me at home. Since my mother had become a Jehovah's Witness, there were no more birthday celebrations. Witnesses don't celebrate birthdays. Still, I wanted to be near my family on my birthday. On the trip home I kept rehearsing the odd exchange between Nate and myself and dismissed the event. *That's probably the last time I'll ever see him,* I thought to myself.

I returned back to Dallas late Sunday night and checked my answering machine. There were several messages from Nate. He was just as persistent with his calls as he had been at our face-to-face conversation. We soon became faithful telephone friends and sometimes spent hours talking to each other on the phone.

This was during the time when William "The Refrigerator" Perry was made famous playing for the Chicago Bears. Nate was larger than Perry and as a result was given the nickname, "The Kitchen." When I met Nate he was a free agent playing left guard for the Cowboys.

Following football camp, Nate religiously asked me out for a date. I refused at first but was softened from his many attempts. I finally told him that I'd be happy to go on a date with him, as long as it was on my terms. I decided that my volleyball tournament that Saturday would be our first official "date." He agreed and came to watch me play. After the game he said that he enjoyed watching me play, but didn't understand why this had to be our first date. I told him that I wanted him to see me when I was hot and sweaty—without any makeup. Then, if he still wanted to take me out on a date, I would go. He laughed that charming laugh and I melted. I really did like him. We left the game and ate burgers and visited with each other for a long time. I went out with him for the first time still wearing my sweaty clothes from the game.

From that point on, we began spending a lot of time together. Nate, or Nathaniel as I called him, was a lot of fun to be with and I enjoyed our conversations. He explained that this was the first year of his professional football career and that he had walked on as a free agent with the Dallas Cowboys. Because he was a free agent he would have to try out with the Cowboys each season and not one season was guaranteed to the next season. He also told me that he had left the Washington Redskins by his own volition, when in reality he'd been cut from the team. Following his dismissal from the team, it had been plastered in the media that he was in a car accident—an alleged suicide attempt.

He had played ball for Florida A&M and he told me that his time in college was not something he was proud of and that he had dreamed of playing professional football. He shared with me that during this season in his life, none of that mattered. He was focused on waiting for the right woman to come into his life. He told me he wanted a Christian woman and that he wanted to put his old life behind him. I thought I had experienced a lot of struggles during my childhood, but I soon realized that Nate was no stranger to trials and tribulations either. We were both carrying baggage.

When I listened to him talk about his past, the setbacks, the mistakes, I felt an enormous amount of compassion for him and I had a desire to share Christ with him. I told him all about who I was and how God was alive in my life and how much I loved the Lord. I remember quoting a portion of my favorite verse found in Galatians 2:20, "I have been crucified with Christ but I no longer live, it is Christ who lives in me." I told him that nothing in life mattered more to me than my devotion to God. I knew He had great plans for my life. I shared the miraculous events of coming to Dallas and finding a great job, a beautiful apartment, and a loving church so quickly. I even asked Nate if he was interested in studying the Bible with me. We had long talks together and grew closer and closer. I shared with him about how God would help him make a fresh start after having been through so much.

I learned that Nate's real mother was an alcoholic and that he was raised by his father. The woman Nate called mom was a school teacher and was his father's second wife. In Nate's eyes, she was his mother. He loved and respected his parents a great deal.

Many of our conversations revealed difficult life experiences and what type of people we ended up becoming as a result. The vulnerability he shared with me made my heart warm up towards him even more. He was so easy to talk to.

Nate was very romantic. Sometimes we would get in his truck and just drive for hours. We didn't really go anywhere, we would just drive and drive and talk and talk. Nate loved driving and we had good times being out on the open road. We laughed about everything. We laughed about nothing. It was wonderful to enjoy each other's company. I felt at ease with him. He was kind and seemed to love me for who I was.

Still, I had some reservations. Nate was not a Christian man. He didn't pretend to be a Christian. In fact, he definitely knew about God, but had this twisted belief that you had to be a good person first—before you could come to God. Since he didn't think he already was a good enough person, somehow he wasn't qualified to be a Christian. I honestly thought I could change this point of view. You can't be a good person without Christ—none of us can. You don't have to be a good person to know Him in the first place. You can't truly be a good person until you know him.

I brought up the possibility of us doing Bible study together once again. I knew I didn't have all of answers, but I believed that I could help him along the way. I was sure that what had worked for me would work for him too. I wanted so desperately for him to understand what I understood about the love of God and how fulfilling and peaceful his life could be.

My brother, Mike Johnson, was an intelligent, professional athlete. He played ball for the Cleveland Browns. I had met Mike for the first time when I was in college. In fact it wasn't until college that I even began to get to know my biological father. I sought him out and we began to form a relationship while I was in school. Mike was one of my siblings by my biological father, so naturally, I wanted to meet him too. As we got to know each other, Mike and I talked often about our passion for sports, but more importantly, we talked about the higher purpose for our lives. When he spoke I always listened because he was extremely wise. I quickly developed respect for him and when I talked about life to him and God's plan for our lives, Mike always talked about love, not football.

I told Mike all about Nate and he encouraged me to stay true to who I was and not to be easily influenced. He urged caution in developing a relationship with Nate, knowing too well the lifestyle that many professional athletes live off the field. I constantly reassured him that I loved the Lord above all else and that nothing could come between me and God. I admired Mike and trusted his perspective because, though he loved the game of football, he was never *in* love with it.

Mike's life didn't revolve around football. He had an exit strategy in place for when the time came to leave it behind. I heeded his warnings and told him that Nate and I were only friends. I viewed my relationship with Nate as an opportunity for me to share Christ with him. I really believed that God put Nate in my path to minister to him and I could not walk away from it.

As time went on I could no longer fool myself. I eventually realized how much I loved Nate—not just because I wanted to share Christ with him, but I was in love with him. I believed that within time he would truly come to know the Lord and all his struggles and problems would be in God's hands. We spent a lot of time talking about God and the word of God and Nate constantly told me how much I'd influenced him in a positive way. I knew that he wasn't perfect and that it was going to take time for him to change. He asked me for my patience. He confessed that he had not been the best person in the past and that he knew he probably wouldn't be the best person in the future. But he promised to do whatever it took to refrain from living like his old self. He wanted a new life, to be a better person. He wanted us to be together and grow together in love. I believed he was open to Christ, there was evidence that he was softening. I trusted that he wanted to become a Christian.

There was negativity all around. Nate had experienced a lot of difficulties during the mini football camp with the Cowboys in the spring. He was extremely overweight and the media was right on top of it. His poor showing at the mini camp made headlines on the newspaper sport pages and on every sports channel there it was: "Nate Newton, Battle of the Bulge" … "The Fat Guy" … "He's too fat, he can't move." It seemed like every time we picked up a newspaper or turned the television on, there were quotes and comments about him, all unfavorable.

The more Nate became aware of it, the harder it was for him to accomplish his goals. When we were together, he would ask me to pray out loud. I was there with him and for him through that difficult time. He was always so fascinated by my relationship with God and he had begun to pray a lot more than he had in the past. He asked me to pray out loud so he could hear me. He wanted to know how I was praying for him and what I was saying.

I prayed that Nate would see God personally and not just through me. I wanted him to accept God into his heart and see that nothing was impossible with Him.

We spent the entire spring season working out together. I was in great shape and enjoyed the discipline of exercising with Nate. We exercised our bodies and trained our minds. By the time June came around, and it was time for him to attend training camp, Nate had reached his conditioning goals.

He not only met the weight requirements, but he was also in the best shape ever. He gave credit to God for what He had done for him. He started to believe in himself and believe in the power of prayer, at least in the power of my prayers on his behalf. Nate made the team that year, and landed a starting position as an offensive guard for the Dallas Cowboys.

He told me he understood that being cut from the Redskins was part of God's plan for him to play with the Dallas Cowboys—his dream team. Being on that team was something he and his best friend, Tony Hayes (T. Hayes), had always dreamed about. Now it was a reality. He was a free agent—signing a contract with incentives as a starter. We celebrated his accomplishments. I gave praises to God and thanked Him for His faithfulness. I began to see Nate as a man with a lot of courage, hope, and faith. I admired him. He never gave up, and he worked hard to press on. I was proud of him. I was happy for him. I was in love with him.

Twelve

NATE NEWTON'S GIRL

Love is an endless act of forgiveness.
—PETER USTINOV

From the time I was a little girl, my mother made sure we were in church every Sunday. She taught us that being in the Lord's house and fellowshipping with His saints was a priority. No matter what else was going on, we always took the time to go to church.

I loved going to church. I loved to sing and worship the Lord. I looked forward to being fortified with the Word through sermons, and visiting with people who loved God was always a treat. I was deeply involved in church life for as long as I could remember. It was as natural to me as shopping for groceries or going to school. Church was an integral part of my life.

Now Nate was in the picture. The Cowboys played on Sundays and Nate wanted me there for him—needed me there for him. I loved watching him play, it was thrilling. It felt good to be in the stands and know that Nate Newton cared that I was there watching him. I felt like part (even if only a small part) of the Cowboys organization. This was *my* team too and I wanted to support them. Nate needed me.

I sat in the stands beaming with pride. I was Nate Newton's girl! Nate introduced me to his best friend, Tony Hayes, and we would sit in the stands together and cheer Nate on. Tony was a Christian and it comforted me that Nate's best friend was also a witness to him. I felt better knowing that Nate had chosen Tony, a good Christian man, as his best friend. Sometimes a wave of guilt would wash over me because I was there in the football stadium instead of in church, but the next minute something exciting would happen in the game and I was swept up in the heat of the moment.

At first I tried to juggle things, but there wasn't a way to be actively involved in church on Sundays and still go to the games. I began to compromise. Slowly, my involvement in church decreased. I justified it because I was very diligent to read my Bible on my own and I prayed all the time. I was Nate's personal witness and I desperately wanted Nate to know the Lord.

The Cowboys were not playing well that season and it was a difficult time for the whole team. I saw my role as an encourager. Nate often asked me to pray for him and for the Cowboys and he seemed very sincere in his requests. He believed my prayers made a difference and that God was in control, sorting things out for him. He called me a woman of God.

People sometimes asked if I was afraid Nate would get hurt or if injuries would end his career. I was never— not one time—worried about Nate getting hurt. I was so completely confident that God's hand was on him. In my mind he was a powerful giant and the thought of him getting hurt never even crossed my mind. Watching him play was exciting. I respected him as an athlete and admired his dedication to the sport.

With each passing week, I fell deeper and deeper in love with this man—it was intoxicating. He was meeting deep emotional needs for me and I was growing to trust him more and more. I found it increasingly difficult to balance my love for Nate and my love for God. I always wanted God to be first, but Nate kept slipping into that first position and I was in a constant state of unrest.

It bothered me that Nate had not yet accepted Christ as his Savior, even though he clearly believed that Jesus was God's son and that salvation was the way to heaven. I couldn't grasp why he wouldn't give his life to Jesus since he obviously believed in God and in the power of prayer. It just didn't make any sense to me, and it frustrated me. I often asked Nate to come to church with me, but he never wanted to attend. He was not involved at all in any aspects of spirituality. He was completely fine with me going to church, reading the Bible, praying, even talking to him about God—he was more than fine, he was supportive. He just wasn't interested in a relationship with God for himself. Mine was good enough for Nate. As long as he had me and I was close to God, that was close enough for him.

Because of this, I tried to slow things down in our relationship. Media attention was growing, and this time it was positive. Everybody loved Nate Newton—they just couldn't get enough of his charismatic personality. But the more positive attention he received, the less the subject of God came to the surface in our conversations. Now that Nate was on top, he didn't seem to need my prayers. God was reserved for the low times. Everything had changed and I knew it. Still, I loved him. I couldn't deny it. I wrestled with this over and over in my mind, praying that Nate would accept Christ. I decided I needed to be patient with him and not nag him about it. I was sure if I spent time with him and my life was full of God's love, then eventually Nate would come to the decision to accept Christ on his own. God was important to me, surely Nate would recognize this and be drawn to experience the same intimacy that I knew.

At times I was deeply concerned that Nate had not accepted Christ, but I pushed those fears down—deep down. I didn't want to think about it. Nate was such a great guy and he made me feel special. How could it not work out? I just needed to give him some time.

It was wonderful to be fascinating to someone. Nate was never bored with me. He listened to me talk and if I got quiet, he asked questions to draw me out. He complimented me and made me feel beautiful. He encouraged me to be myself and he never tried to persuade me to be someone I was not or do things I was uncomfortable about doing. He never tried to stop me from attending church, though he was really clear about wanting me to attend every game. He was not pleased if I missed even one.

Other than this, Nate was very supportive of me. He was interested in my job and encouraged me to talk about my day, my friends ... anything that was on my mind. In my whole life, I had never met anyone this interested in me. People had always sought me out, sharing their problems with me, asking for my advice or wanting me to pray for them. I loved doing this and always felt like God was using me to touch them. I had many friends, but very few people ever asked me about how I was doing, so Nate's interest was more than flattering, it was fulfilling. It awakened something down deep on the inside. I felt valued when I was with him. I felt precious to him and I liked the feeling.

He was generous with his time and his personality. Nate made people laugh and he had wonderful manners. He was a gentleman—respectful of authority, respectful toward me. He was a leader and an influencer. People were naturally drawn to him and this quality was very attractive to me. I imagined what a powerful influence he could be if only he would finally yield his life to Christ.

Nate made me feel safe and this was no small thing. For the first time in my life, I felt like I had a protector. I didn't feel like it was up to me to handle everything, I knew he would never let anyone harm me. He wanted to be with me. He enjoyed spending time together and I was overwhelmed by his attention. Even on days when I felt ugly, Nate would look me in the eyes and tell me that I was beautiful, inside and out. He put me on a pedestal, and it was fun being there.

He pointed me out to others and made sure they knew I was his girl. He made sure everyone showed me the proper respect and was open with others publicly about how much I meant to him.

Family was important to Nate. He treated my family well and he was very kind to my mother. This touched me deeply. I could imagine raising a family with him—a modest house somewhere near Dallas with a few children running around on the lawn, going to Cowboys games together, and having people in for the holidays. It was a beautiful picture in my mind, far from the dysfunction I had grown up with. It was a dream that I wanted very much to make a reality.

Nate listened attentively when I talked about my relationship with God. He never tried to stop me and he somehow knew that my connection to God was what made me special. He was interested in Christianity, and asked questions about this too, but he did not feel like he was good enough to become a Christian. He knew that if he gave his life to Christ, there were a lot of things he enjoyed doing that he would have to give up, and he just wasn't ready for that. I appreciated his honesty. In fact, I took it as a good sign that he was willing to listen to me and not pretend. I never stopped communicating or spending time with him because of his reluctance. I didn't want to seem judgmental and knew that if I pulled away, it would hurt Nate. He was so open and accepting of me, my beliefs, and everything that was important in my life, I wanted to return this level of openness and respect to him.

The more time we spent together, the more Nate let his guard down. His language went from being always respectful, to an occasional slip of the tongue, to regular use of profanity. He drank beer too much and too often. He sometimes said mean things. I had never experienced him that way before and I didn't like it. Warning signs were flashing red in my mind and my spirit, but somehow

I always managed to shrug this behavior away. No one changes over night, after all. It takes time. I decided to be patient with him and believed that if I could continue being a good influence on him, it would make a difference. I encouraged him to be better, to be his best. I wanted him to be better so badly. I believed that he sincerely wanted to improve himself and adjust the bad things in his life. When he behaved badly, I told myself he was wrestling with his old nature, that it had a firm grip on him that would release when he committed his life to Christ.

I wanted Nate to know God's fullness and not change for me—because of me, but because Jesus had done a work inside him. My patience with his behavior slowly slipped into compromising my own standards. Little by little, Nate was changing into someone I no longer recognized, and I was excusing his behavior away and always expecting that a change was coming soon.

Every time a black cloud hovered over the relationship for me, Nate found a way to make the sun come out again. No one could brighten a room or lift the mood like Nate could. He always apologized if he behaved badly and would make it up to me by going out somewhere with me, my roommates, and Tony (we called him T. Hayes). We would drive somewhere and have dinner, laughing the night away. He was so much fun to be with. If Nate was there, it was a party!

Nate wanted to spend time with me every spare minute, and I wanted to be with him too. He never took me to clubs or movies where I would be uncomfortable, we would just get in the car and ride. We saw lots of Texas that year. Driving was how Nate relaxed. When he was behind the wheel of a moving vehicle, his head cleared, his defenses lowered, and he was open for honest conversation and genuine communication.

As time went on, this open free-flowing communication began to dwindle. I could tell that something was bothering Nate, but since he wouldn't open up to me about what it was, I couldn't seem to help him through it. His behavior seemed to be growing more reckless and he was beginning to be agitated and angry more often, and even when we were alone together, he was growing short with his words. Where he once shared all his most personal thoughts with me, and took me into his confidence, he now seemed guarded. I assumed it was the stress of so much publicity and the growing pressure to perform well at every game. It was true that Nate was changing. The change was apparent to everyone—it was like he was speaking a completely different language. The change troubled me. I was as supportive as I knew how to be, and Nate seemed calmer when I was around, so I took this as a good sign.

Thirteen

LOVE IS A
WONDERFUL
THING...

*When a heart finds another, what's a cloud more
or less in an otherwise beautiful sky.*

—WOLF & PAGE

$\mathcal{N}$ate and I were better than ever. We were meeting each other's friends and getting to know each other's family. I believed that he was the one I would spend the rest of my life with. More and more I could look at the future and imagine growing old with Nate Newton at my side. Still, I was plagued by a nagging unrest that Nate had not committed his life to the Lord and I was uncertain about where he was in his relationship with God. I knew he believed in God, but when the conversation turned to salvation, Nate would bring up that he wasn't good enough yet. He hated hypocrites and vowed never to be one. He didn't want to pretend he was a Christian, and since he was straddling the fence with one foot securely in the world, and the other uncomfortably entertaining the possibility of being a Christian, he wasn't ready to accept Christ.

Over and over I tried to explain to Nate that God takes us as we are. He doesn't expect us to ever be "good enough" for Him. In fact, we can never be good enough—we have a sinful nature from the day we are born. Even before we commit one sin, we have a sin nature. It is only by the grace of God, through the blood of His Son, Jesus, that we can be acceptable to God. It isn't by any works or deeds that we do, not by how much money we give, how clean our language is, that we don't smoke or drink or gamble—none of that makes us "good enough" for God. We come to God naked, bruised, filthy and with nothing to offer Him but our heart. He takes us and covers us in His righteousness, accepting us simply because we are His children and His love for us overcomes every evil thing inside of us. It is only by a work of grace that takes a sinful man and redeems him. Becoming "good enough" is a progressive work that takes place after we come to Christ, not before.

For Nate, this explanation was not sufficient. He believed he had to clean up his life before he was worthy of God's salvation. In his mind, he was too sinful to be acceptable. This worried me.

I had rededicated my life to God, vowing to keep Him in first place. This was truly my heart's desire. I loved God deeply and wanted to please Him in everything I did. There was a tug of war in my heart. When I was alone with God, I was totally filled with peace, secure in His love for me. When I was alone with Nate, God receded to the background in my thoughts, and my connection to Nate increased my physical attraction and all I could think about was sexual intimacy with him.

When I was just a young girl, I made a conscious decision that I would wait for sex until I fell in love. My mom talked about being equally yoked and I felt strongly about waiting for sex until I got married. Nate felt differently than I did, but he respected my position. Nate thought it was okay—even good for dating couples to engage in sex. I believed it was wrong. I had remained pure. Now here I was, deeply in love with the man I believed would become my husband, still a virgin. I was beginning to feel guilty for making him wait when I was the one who wasn't ready to walk down the aisle yet. My resolve was wavering.

I made a decision—to go on birth control pills. I didn't want to make Nate wait any longer and my attraction to him was very strong. I decided that if I was going to betray my morals, the last thing I wanted was to bring a baby into the equation, so I visited the doctor to start the pill.

My doctor was a very wise, kind, Christian man. He offered counsel for me to wait, even as he reluctantly wrote me a prescription for the pills. He was filled with gentleness and his brow furrowed as I took the script from his hand. Even there in the office I wavered, having second thoughts about this decision. Going on the pill was deciding to have sex outside of marriage. I was making a conscious decision to sin.

Nate and I planned it. It was anything but a spontaneous burst of passion. It wasn't a magical night where we lost control, threw caution to the wind, and were swept up in the heat of the moment. In truth, "the moment" had been building for months. The tension was enormous. Looking back, it is strange for me to reconcile that I wasn't ready to commit to Nate in marriage because he had not yet made a commitment to Christ, but I was ready to commit to the acts of marriage with Nate. It no longer seemed important to wait until the wedding bells rung. I was an adult after all. I was in love. We were in love. Wasn't that what *really* mattered?

Nate and I were playing house. It was like a trial run to see if marriage would work out. I never wanted to be in a situation like my mother, financially dependent on a man and unable to escape if things went wrong. As much as I loved Nate, I wasn't ready to walk down the aisle and commit my life to him forever. I needed some measure of control. I didn't want to be married. Things were good just like they were for now. Nate seemed content to be with me on these terms and in my mind, this left me freedom to walk away should the need arise.

I often traveled to be with Nate for away games, and sometimes his family would join us. One weekend they came in for a home game, arriving on a chartered bus from Florida. I went to the hotel with Nate to greet his family. I had met several people from his family at previous games, so I was excited to see them again and interested to see who else might have come along to see the game that I had not yet met.

To my great surprise, a woman traveled with the family—some long, lost girlfriend had come to town to see Nate. I was shocked. I had a hunch that something was wrong with Nate and wondered why he had grown closed with me, but never in a million years would I have expected him to be involved with another woman!

Nate's family seemed embarrassed by the situation. They apologized to me profusely and seemed genuinely concerned with how this affected me. They knew that Nate and I were close. They knew how important I was to Nate. Why this woman had chosen to come along, knowing I would be there is a mystery I have never understood. Of course, this all happened the day before the game—*after* the Cowboys had sequestered all their players in the hotel to keep them focused on the task at hand. They didn't want their star athletes distracted by anything that might hinder their performance in the game. So Nate was not available to see me in my misery or answer my questions. He wasn't there to face the music, own up to his deceit, and explain his lies.

I felt so betrayed. I thought I was special to him. I knew I had been totally faithful to him. He was the only man I had ever given myself to, and the thought of him being with someone else made me feel as though I had been kicked in the stomach. I felt ill.

Nate's family was sensitive to my struggle. I could tell they were sincere in their concern, so I dug down deep, found every ounce of kindness I could muster and pressed through the game rituals, pasting a smile on my face, visiting with people and supporting Nate. I don't remember much about the game. In my mind, I was working through all the things I wanted to ask Nate on the way home. The more I thought about it, the more I realized that this was an opportunity to make a clean break and get out. I recognized how much I had lost my focus on God, my personal career, and even family goals. I had become totally absorbed in Nate's world, Nate's future, Nate's needs … and had lost myself in the process.

After the game, Nate's family said good-bye and loaded back on the bus for Florida. It was time for Nate and I to have a heart to heart talk. I decided I didn't want to have anything to do with him anymore. I had been with him for almost two years and he never mentioned he had a girlfriend during the same time he was dating me. I was hurt. I was angry. I didn't want to talk about it—wanted no explanations, I just wanted to make a break from Nate and move on. I should have done it long before, and this was the jolt I needed to wake me up from my fairy tale and enter the land of reality.

Instead of confronting Nate and asking him to explain his deception, I chose to distance myself from him. I refused to accept his phone calls. I wouldn't answer my door. I was devastated by his betrayal. Falling off a pedestal is a lot harder than stumbling on the ground. Nate hurt me deeply and I built walls of protection around my heart. Betrayal and disappointment were companions I knew too well.

I decided that this might be a good time to move back home—return to Louisiana. I gave three month's notice at my job, packed all my things and placed them in storage. I would use only the bare essentials in my apartment until my lease expired and I was free to move home. I hadn't made any plans about where I would go in Louisiana, where I would live, or where I would work, but I was focused on this new course of action and determined that everything would work out just as it should.

I stopped taking the pill. I regretted that I had ever gone on it. I regretted surrendering my virginity. I determined that I was through with Nate Newton ... for good!

Nate kept dropping by my office and coming to my apartment trying to talk to me. He was doing everything he possibly could to stop me from leaving. I felt like he was stalking me, every time I turned around, there he was!

I knew his football schedule, so it made it easier for me to avoid him while I did the things I needed to do. I was irritated by his persistence. Why would he keep coming around when it was so obvious that I no longer wanted him in my life?

After four solid weeks of Nate dropping by the apartment, I relented and let him in one night. I wanted him to see that I was serious. I thought that if he saw my apartment bare and knew I was resolute in my decision to move away from him and on with my life, it might make him realize that our relationship was over.

Nate asked me to just listen to what he had to say. He was in such earnest that I didn't have the power to refuse. He told me that he had not been spending time with the young lady and had not been seeing her for a very long time. They had bought a house together and he was helping her out financially. He told me that they were no longer in a relationship and that her showing up at the game was a surprise to him as well. He told me how sorry he was that I was hurt—that he had hurt me. He seemed desperate for me to believe him and forgive him.

For days he kept coming to my apartment and stopping by my office, and each time he always seemed to have just the right things to say. To put me at even greater ease, he communicated with the woman on the telephone in my presence, so I could hear what he said and be assured that there was no relationship between them. I wavered.

Nate produced receipts to show me that he had given this woman a lump sum of money to help her out. He assured me over and over again that it was *me* he wanted. It was *me* he wanted to be with, to spend his life with. He was so sincere and took such extreme measures to prove himself to me that I couldn't help but begin to soften. Maybe my past had made me super-sensitive to betrayal. Maybe I *had* jumped to conclusions. Maybe I wasn't being fair to Nate.

I took my things back out of storage and weighed my options. What should I do? Before this incident with the woman, our relationship had seen ups and downs, but I had experienced nothing like this—nothing that had made me lose trust in him. Nothing that made me feel betrayed. I still loved Nate, and part of me wanted to forgive him and move on. Was my love strong enough to overcome the pain? Could I trust Nate? Would I stay in Dallas and give our relationship another chance or move home to Louisiana and forget all about Nate Newton?

I decided to stay. I withdrew my resignation from my job and they were thrilled for me to remain. We started seeing each other again on a regular basis. Things were good again. I forgave Nate and he went out of his way to make sure he didn't hide things from me again. He knew I was serious enough to leave my job and move away from him and this had a profound impact on Nate. He didn't want to jeopardize what we had and he grew more determined for us to be a life-long partnership.

Nate agreed with me that God was the only way our relationship would work. Though he wasn't ready to go to church, he consented to a Bible study with me and another couple from my church. I was still shaken from the incident with the girl from Florida, but I saw it as an opportunity for us to strengthen our bond, establish trust, and for Nate to finally commit his life to the Lord. I knew that total forgiveness was required from me, and I gave it.

Still, at times I would catch myself looking in the mirror and wondering who it was that was staring back at me. I didn't recognize her completely. Once confident and bold, I was unsure of myself. I missed my close relationship with God. I still knew Him, I still trusted Him, but I was no longer deeply intimate with Him. The sense of loss was overwhelming. I felt God calling me to return to Him.

Nate invited me to take a trip with him to Atlanta. Road trips were the best with Nate. When we were on the road together it was magic. We shared a special affinity together on the road. It was as if we were the only two people in the whole world. Nothing else was important. It was just us. Maybe this was just what we needed right now.

It was a beautiful drive. We were never in a hurry. We took our time to stop and see anything that captured our interest. We talked comfortably about everything and were totally at ease with one another. We met up with friends of his and shared the most beautiful four day weekend together.

Our first night together on the road, I reminded Nate that I had only been back on the pill for one week. He brushed it off, reassuring me that nothing would happen, that I should trust him. We were both aware of the risks, but neither one of us thought for one moment that I would conceive. The pill was our magic shield against responsibility.

From then on, we were sexually intimate on a regular basis, so I don't know exactly when it happened. I felt safe on the pill and never once had even a fleeting thought that I might become pregnant.

Early in February my family came into town and I was feeling a little sick. I complained of nausea and I just felt a little off. My mother looked me right in the eyes and said, "Dorothy, you're not pregnant are you?"

"Mama! No!" I exclaimed. "How can you say that?" Being pregnant never entered my mind. I felt safe on the pill.

A full two months went by before I realized it, and I was stunned. I couldn't believe it! How could this have happened? We never used any extra protection because I was taking birth control pills. 98% effective sounded like pretty good odds. I had denied God's way for my own selfish pleasure. I had denied God's plan for Nate's pleasure. I made a choice. I knew what I was doing. Though I felt protected from the risk, I was willing to take it. In those moments of passion and intimacy, God was the last thing on my mind.

It is ironic. My fears of being unequally yoked in marriage didn't translate to the danger of creating a soul tie with this man and the possibility of creating a baby in the process. It would certainly change my life forever.

Fourteen

SHATTERED DREAMS

"For I know the plans I have for you, not to harm you but to give you hope and a future."

—JEREMIAH 29:11

God's best for my life was all I had ever wanted. Now that didn't seem possible. I stared down at the pregnancy test in disbelief. I read the instructions once more, hoping that maybe I had done something wrong to make the test inaccurate. But there was no denying it. I was pregnant.

I sat there in shame, tears rolling down my cheeks. I looked in the mirror and felt sick. The woman who stared back at me was a stranger. She looked lost and confused and totally without hope. The sadness in her eyes was unbearable. I turned away and crumpled in a heap on the floor. I had never felt so lonely in my entire life. What a mess! What was I going to do? What would my family say? *Oh, Mama!*

I grabbed a towel and hugged it into my chest, squeezing it until my knuckles hurt and my hands were shaking. My mind went to all the people I had studied the Bible with in college. I thought about everyone that I had witnessed to and how many of them had come to know the Lord. I could see their faces. I felt as if I had personally let every one of them down. I was a fraud. How could I have been so stupid? These thoughts overwhelmed me with grief and sorrow. At last I let my mind turn away from other people and imagine what God must think of me, how I had turned my back on Him… sobs shook my body. I don't know how long I lay there crying, but I cried until there were no tears left inside. I was disgusted with myself. What had I traded for temporary physical fulfillment? *Oh, what had I done?*

I grew cold lying there on the floor. Shame and fear gave way to pity, and depression settled in like a dark, ominous cloud. For the first time my thoughts wandered to Nate. *What would he think? How would he react?* I didn't really blame him, I was too filled with blaming myself. *How would I tell him? What would he say?*

I avoided him for days, not sure how to break the news. I was miserable. Doubt, fear, frustration, anger … my emotions were boiling just beneath the surface and I found it hard to concentrate on anything.

I went back to see my doctor and he confirmed that I was, in fact, pregnant. He seemed sad for me and asked about the father. I told him who it was. In a very kind gesture, he invited me to come have dinner with him and his wife in their home. I was so desperate and alone that I accepted. They prayed over me that night, and I learned that we attended the same church. They were supportive and encouraging without one hint of judgment. I was overwhelmed by their kindness.

Later I called Sheila, my college roommate and best friend, and asked to meet her. Even though we were both wrapped up in our own separate lives, our bond was still close and I knew I needed to tell her in person. I dreaded telling her. I had hired her and was now her boss. We were very careful at work to keep things professional, and this was such a major event I knew I couldn't tell her about it at the office, so we decided to visit after work.

"I'm pregnant," I blurted out, not sure how else to begin. Sheila is such a beautiful person—inside and out, I knew she wouldn't judge me. She hugged me tightly and held me with such kindness. Her voice was tender. "Dot, I saw you drifting away. You were so in love that I didn't want to interfere."

Tears rolled down my cheeks, I felt so ashamed of myself. I was grateful for her friendship at this moment. Sharing my burden with her was such a relief. "What should I do?" I said ... not really expecting an answer, just lifting up the same question I had been asking myself for days.

"Don't worry," she smiled, "We're going to get through this."

After talking to Sheila, I knew I needed to call Bug—the mother hen in our little trio. At first she fussed at me, "I could see this coming. You haven't been the same person since Nate ... I tried to tell you ..." and on and on she went. Then, her voice softened and her affection for me came shining through. "Everything is gonna be alright. Everything is gonna be okay. Everything is gonna work out just fine. You'll see." We talked for some time and I felt less alone. Now, I just needed to tell Nate...

I gathered my courage. It was clear to me now, the people who loved me *would* be disappointed in me, but they would still love me. It would be the same with Nate, I was sure.

Nate and I had dinner plans to visit with Lynn & Kelvin (K-Mart) Martin on Friday night, so I decided that I would talk to Nate on Thursday. He came by the apartment as usual, and since I had been avoiding him for a few days things were a little tense. We were usually together every day, so this break in the routine had him on his guard.

"What is wrong with you?" he asked.

"Nathaniel …" I looked at him, hoping he would just guess the trouble and I wouldn't have to actually say the words.

He looked at me intently, sensing I was about to tell him something important. I could see the muscles in his neck tighten and his face was a mixture of concern and frustration.

"Nathaniel, " I began again … "I'm pregnant."

"You're what?" he said. "You *knew* I didn't want any kids!" he shouted.

I stared at him, shocked at his response.

"You knew what we were doing, Nathaniel Newton!" I answered, suddenly angry. "It wasn't like I was trying to trap you or something. Having a baby wasn't part of my plan either."

We argued for some time, angry words spilling out until Nate walked out, cursing and slammed the door behind him.

I hadn't been prepared for such an outburst of rage. I didn't expect him to be overjoyed, but I never dreamed he would be so angry … and so angry with me.

An hour passed. I sat alone, numb. My mind couldn't seem to make two thoughts line up in a row. Random bits of information flooded my mind, none of it making any sense. Then there was a noise at the door and Nate returned. He was still mad.

"Why are you so upset?" I asked.

"What about *me*?" was his response. "How do you think *I* feel?"

I just stared back at him, not sure how to answer. He walked across the room, sat down, sighed deeply, then told me he already had two children and didn't want any more.

I was stunned. I don't know how long I sat there trying to take in this new information ... *did I really even know this man at all?*

"Why didn't you ever tell me?" I managed to ask.

"What does it matter to you?" He said.

I shook my head and tried to wrap my head around the fact that Nate had children out there somewhere. *Who were they? Where did they live? Did he see them? Who was their mother? How old? Boys? Girls?* I couldn't stop the questions in my mind, but I didn't voice a single one of them to Nate. I didn't dare.

I had taken the next day off from work, knowing I was going to tell Nate that night and somehow sensing that it might not go well. This only increased his anger toward me.

"Why didn't you save the vacation day so we could take a trip?" he asked. Nate loved nothing more than road trips and during off season he had much more free time available than I did, so I saved all my vacation days for trips with Nate.

"I thought this was important," I answered, hurt that he was being so selfish.

Nate answered with a barrage of insults and accusations, blaming me for the pregnancy. I answered with indignation, blaming him for his lies. The argument continued, escalating until Nate left again, hurling profanities at me as he slammed the door on his way out.

I didn't hear from him any more that night. The next morning I woke up, got dressed and went into the office to clear my head and take care of a meeting. Nate showed up.

"I thought you were off?" he asked, accusation was thick in his voice.

"I just came in for a one hour meeting," I answered. "I'm getting ready to go now." Nate nodded and we walked out together in silence. He had his arm lightly on my elbow and directed me toward his truck.

"Get in," he said while calmly opening the passenger door for me.

I slid in my familiar place, closing my eyes and wishing I could make this nightmare end.

Nate walked around to the driver's side, opened the door and climbed inside. He sat there quietly for a few moments then reached over and took my hand. "We'll work it out ..." he said, his voice soft and low.

I felt my muscles relax and I let out a long sigh. This was the Nate I knew. I leaned over and melted into his embrace. It felt good for him to hold me. I didn't want to do this alone.

We sat in the parking lot for some time and Nate told me he still wanted to go to the Martins together that night. He wanted to tell them about the baby. This was encouraging to me. Maybe everything really would work out okay. Maybe Nate would be just fine about it after all.

We went to dinner as planned. Lynn and K-Mart were good friends and being with them felt natural. Nate told them the news and I was surprised at how upbeat and nonchalant he sounded. Surprise, surprise! Lynn and K-Mart had news for us too ... they were expecting! Suddenly, it was a party! We learned that our due dates were very close together. Lynn and I had lots to talk about, and Nate seemed to be growing very excited about the prospect of having a baby. I was never so relieved! That night I slept soundly. I was thoroughly exhausted. I hadn't slept well in days, worrying about how Nate would respond, worrying about everything …

The next day I decided it was time to call my family. There was no point in putting it off any longer. I called my mom first. "I knew you were pregnant, Dorothy," she said. "I could tell the moment I saw you. I have been wondering when you were going to call."

It felt good to talk to mom. She was so understanding and I knew she would be there for me, no matter what. I knew she would love me no matter what. "Dorothy," she said, "you be smart about this. Don't settle. No matter what happens, don't you get rid of that baby. If Nate doesn't want it, we'll take it. Don't you even think about getting an abortion. That isn't a solution." Her words struck me. I wasn't even aware that I had considered the possibility of aborting, but her strong warning suddenly shook me. At least part of me measured this option. It certainly would solve the problem. In the back of my mind, I had played with the idea that abortion might be a way out. Of course it wasn't!

There was no way I was going to deal with one sin by committing another. Just like that my mind was resolved. I would not abort. I would not give up my baby. I would keep it. It was mine. Nate or no Nate, this baby was in my life for good. Something broke inside of me and love for this child began to swell. Suddenly I was filled with overwhelming love for the life that grew inside of me. Selfish pity for my plight turned into a desire to protect and defend the little one who was now part of who I was.

I began telling my friends about the baby. I was overwhelmed by the responses of love and support. I didn't feel judged. I didn't feel an outcast. I felt genuine kindness coming from them and my heart was filled with hope.

I began reading about pregnancy and babies, learning everything I could. I carefully calculated my savings and took a long look at my financial situation to make sure I was prepared. It had been three weeks since I first told Nate the news and the excitement he demonstrated with the Martins had steadily waned. This bothered me, but I assumed he was just working through things in his mind.

He came by my apartment one night and he was unusually quiet. "I know this isn't your fault." He began. "This is our problem."

I looked at him cautiously, wondering where he was going with this.

"It's my responsibility. I want to take care of this. I have thought about it a lot since you first told me you were pregnant." He paused. I held my breath.

"I think you should get an abortion. I'll pay for it. I'll take care of everything. I just don't think having a baby is the best thing for us right now."

Nate breathed out slowly. I could tell he had made up his mind. All I had to do was say yes and the problem would be solved. I sat there in silence, wrestling with my emotions. I thought I had settled this already.

Deep down inside, I was still struggling at how I had failed God. I was struggling with shame and guilt. I was still angry with myself for compromising. I was angry that the birth control pills hadn't worked. I was angry that Nate wasn't treating me the same anymore. He had grown cold—there was meanness in him toward me that I had never before seen and it scared me. I didn't really want to have Nate's baby. I wasn't even sure I wanted to have Nate anymore. I wavered.

"I'll think about it." I said.

Nate looked at me and started to say something, but the look on my face must have stopped him. "Fine," he said. "Let me know when you make the appointment and I'll take care of it."

I got some literature and went to a clinic to ask about an abortion. I even made an appointment … but I couldn't go in. I sat outside in the parking lot. *"Before I formed you in the womb, I knew you …"* The words of Jeremiah 1:5 played over and over in my head. God already knew this baby. This baby was already His child. I just could NOT make another bad choice. No. I was not going to give this baby up just to make my life less complicated. It had done nothing to deserve being erased. The child was innocent. The child had no choice, even if I did. Abortion was not the answer. I drove away from the clinic and never gave abortion another thought.

Nate came by and I told him I was going to keep the baby. He was very angry with me. He argued and cursed.

He insulted me and made me feel selfish, but he could not persuade me. I didn't care how angry he was. I didn't care if he left me forever. My mind was made up. I told him he didn't need to worry about anything. I had no expectations from him. The decision to keep the baby was mine. I would take care of the baby. I would raise the baby. I would pay for the baby. I wanted nothing from Nate Newton. He didn't need to worry about anything. He was free to go.

Fifteen

ULTIMATUM

The one who loves the least, controls the relationship.
—DR. ROBERT ANTHONY

Nate was not happy with my decision to keep the baby. He gave me an ultimatum. "Have an abortion, or we're finished."

I was surprised at his behavior. I knew he had two children already, but I now learned that they were from two different women. Both were little girls. One was seven years old and the other was just about to turn seven. My disappointment was bitter and my heart was broken. I thought Nate truly loved me. He was the one who wanted to get married and live happily ever after. How could he leave me over a baby—his own baby? It didn't make any sense.

I begged him not to leave. Truthfully, I was scared to have a baby on my own. I didn't want to be alone. Maybe, just maybe if Nate stayed we could work things out. "I am keeping the baby," I told him. "If you feel you need to go, then go. I am keeping this baby." He told me he would try to stick around, but would make no promises. I let out a long sigh … if he left, he left. I had made up my mind and there was absolutely nothing Nate could say or do that would make me reconsider.

The lease on my apartment was coming to an end and I was trying to position myself financially to prepare for the baby to come. Nate didn't have his own place at the time. He lived with friends, Thorton and Karen Chandler. They offered for us both to move in with them to help us until we could decide what we wanted to do about a place to live. Nate came to see me and was persistent that this was a good solution for our immediate future. He appealed to my practical side by pointing out that this would save money until we figured things out. In my mind I was still resigned to raise the baby on my own, so saving money for the time I would have to take off work was the right card for Nate to play.

The Chandlers had a nice sized home and were sincere in their desire to help us, so I accepted. I put most items in storage, then moved my personal things in with Nate at the Chandlers' home. Things were cheerful for the first few days, and it was nice not to feel alone, but after that, Nate was never around. He would tell me he was coming home, but then he wouldn't show up. I was restless and worried about him. I was angry and frustrated.

He became distant. We grew further and further apart. We didn't talk like before. We didn't go on long drives or laugh with friends anymore. He would go away for days at a time and then show up with no explanation of where he had been. Finally, he disappeared for nearly three months. When he was in town for mini-camps he called occasionally, but seemed disinterested in me or the baby. I was coming to terms with the fact that I was going to have this baby on my own. I cried. I prayed. I planned. I made a strict budget. I cried some more. It was a very dark time for me. I felt betrayed again. Nate's rejection hurt me deeply.

I grew increasingly uncomfortable staying with the Chandlers. Even though they were always kind, I felt like an intruder. I was used to being independent. Nate was gone more than he was around, and this embarrassed me. I felt like a burden and I didn't like the feeling. I didn't belong there with Nate's friends, I wasn't even sure I belonged with Nate. I started thinking about leasing an apartment on my own again.

One day I went out to my car, had a dizzy spell, and fainted. I was out cold. When I woke up, I found myself in an ambulance on the way to the hospital. I have no idea who called Nate, or how he knew, but he showed up at the hospital concerned that I was alright. When I was discharged, he took me back to the Chandlers and disappeared again.

I called my family and they reached out to me. They promised their support every step of the way. Friends from college and friends from church also came to see me in person and extend their love. These gestures reminded me that God still loved me. He hadn't given up on me and I shouldn't give up on myself.

Fortified by the love of family and friends, I decided to move back into a place by myself. I asked God for wisdom and guidance. I asked His forgiveness over and over. Though I knew He had already given it, I had trouble receiving it. I felt ashamed. Still, I could feel His presence and His love. I was grateful to Him. I wanted more than anything to be right with God again. I wasn't quite sure how to do that because my life was in such a mess, but

I believed with all my heart that He loved me and that I could still be useful to God. I wanted to serve Him. I took my things out of storage and once again moved into an apartment on my own.

The time came for Nate to go away to training camp. While he was away, he called often to check on me. Our conversations were tender and kind, like old times. He was concerned about making the team and as before, reached out to me for support and asked me to pray for him. The players were not allowed to leave camp, so I knew Nate would not pop in unexpectedly. I used this time to separate completely in my mind. I was sick often and had dizzy spells, sometimes fainting, but I was determined that I would be stable on my own. I had insurance to take care of me if anything happened—my bills would be paid. I was frugal and careful. I didn't need Nate.

One afternoon the phone rang. It was Nate. "When I come back from camp," he began, "I want to know what the sex of the baby is."

"Why?" I asked. "What difference does that make?"

"Well, if it's a boy, then I'll try to work things out with you. If it's a girl, then I don't want to have anything to do with you," he said matter of factly.

I listened in horror. *Was he serious?*

I had no idea what the sex of the baby was, but I felt my heart hardening. I said coldly, "Well, it's a girl, so I guess when you get back from camp you can just go on with your life and I can go on with mine."

I fell into a routine of work, doctor's appointments, and restless sleep. I stopped going to church. I was too ashamed because my stomach was swollen with the life growing inside. I was pregnant and not married. It felt like anyone who looked at me was judging me and it added weight to my shame. But even then, even in my doubts about the future, I was overwhelmed with love for this little child. I read books about pregnancy and children, wanting to learn all I could about being a good mother. My prayer time sustained me and I took comfort in praying for other people and ministering to their needs.

Football camp ended and Nate called again. He wanted to know how I was doing and when the baby's due date was. He told me that during camp he spent time in deep reflection and had undergone a change of heart. There was great compassion in his voice and he seemed genuinely concerned about how I was feeling and how I was getting along during the pregnancy.

A few days later, Nate came to my apartment and apologized to me for his behavior and for being selfish—thinking more of how the baby affected him than me. He told me he was going to live up to his responsibilities and wanted us to raise the child together. He told me that something evil had awakened inside of him when he found out I was pregnant. Something ugly that he hadn't dealt with had been lurking deep within. It rose up and expressed itself in anger.

"Dot," he said, "I'm sorry, baby doll. I am truly sorry. I didn't mean to hurt you. I want to take care of you. I want to be with you. I want to take care of the baby. Please forgive me."

I looked at him standing there, apologizing to me in earnest. Compassion for him rose. My fears about how to raise a child by myself were there, just beneath the surface of my emotions. I searched his eyes, looking for some sign that he meant what he said.

"I am going to take care of you," he said. "I will be here for you and the baby," he continued, "... whether it's a boy or a girl."

I stood there, stroking my stomach and wanting so badly to be loved and cared for. I felt terribly alone. In my mind I was already living in sin. My world was in total chaos. My life was a mess. I knew living with a man was wrong, but what difference did it make now? I had already slept with him. I was pregnant with his child. Maybe letting him move in and take care of me was a good idea after all. At least I wouldn't be alone anymore.

"Alright," I said, letting out a sigh.

Nate flashed his characteristic smile. "You'll see," he said. "Things will work out for us." He pulled me into an embrace and for just a moment I stiffened, then relaxed and let him hold me. "I love you," he said. I was tired. I needed someone to love me and Nate would do.

There was a shift in our relationship. By now I knew I was having a boy but I didn't want to tell Nate. I wanted to see if he really wanted to be with me regardless of the sex of the baby. He was calmer now. He had made the team again and he wanted to spend time with me. He was gentle again and more like the man I had fallen in love with. *Did I only imagine the other things?* I would wonder to myself. It seemed like I knew two completely different people. One was kind, funny, and attentive. The other was self-centered, brutish, and mean-spirited. *How could both of these be Nate?*

Wherever we went together, Nate was relaxed and completely at ease. He seemed ready to commit for the long term. He seemed excited to become a father. He was proud of me and introduced me as his wife, even to the media. I didn't correct him, but I didn't want to get married either. I wasn't sure how long the fair weather between us was going to last. Some part of me didn't believe Nate would stay around forever. I kept waiting for something to happen that would set off his anger and make him disappear again. I did finally tell him that the baby was a boy, and this made him very happy.

September came and the days were beginning to shorten as the oppressive Texas heat at last lifted. I was having frequent dizzy spells and had become anemic. My doctor advised me to stop working. I was prepared. I had a good job and had always been frugal. I had saved and planned and always lived within my means, so I was covered. I didn't worry about things financially. Nate was around, but I didn't need him. It was important for me to be able to provide for myself.

Football season was now in full swing. Even as I drew nearer to my due date, Nate insisted that I come to all of the Cowboys' games to watch him play. I went faithfully, but it wasn't as thrilling as it once had been. How I wished things were different. *If only I hadn't gotten pregnant,* I wondered to myself. *What would things be like in my life right now?*

One Sunday night after a game Nate was in an exceptionally good mood. He asked me if I wanted to go with him to the State Fair. He was full of laughter and in high spirits and it sounded like fun. I was getting very close to my due date and feeling restless.

We went to the fair and I ate any and everything in sight! I just could not stop eating! Nate was making fun of me and seemed to be enjoying buying me more food and was amazed when I ate more. Before long I was totally miserable. I told him I wanted to just go home and rest. I had eaten too much and didn't feel well.

Nate took me back to the apartment and told me he was going to go out for awhile, but would check on me while he was gone. Just then I felt a sensation like a needle pricking me in my right side. "Ouch!" I complained. Nate poked fun, "You just don't want me to leave, do you?"

"Go on," I said, "get out of here!" and I meant it. I was so full of food I didn't care if he came or went—I just wanted to lie down. There it was again. "Ouch!" It felt like a needle jabbing me. *Why did I eat so much?*

Nate came back a little later and I felt the sticking pain again. He decided to hang around just in case I needed him. The needle pricks kept returning. It didn't seem to fit the description of any labor pain I had heard of or read about, but I decided to call the doctor just in case. While I was on the phone with my physician, it happened twice more and he told me to come in immediately—I was in labor.

We drove from Coppell to Medical City in Dallas. On the way there I could not seem to get comfortable. I kept squirming around in my seat and then it felt like someone would jab me in my side with a needle. When I arrived they examined me and I was already dilated. Within one hour, Nathanial Newton, III (Tre') was born.

October 15, 1989—God blessed me with a beautiful baby boy. It was the most precious gift I had ever received. For the first time in months I felt the sun come out in my soul. I was deliriously happy when I held that little bundle in my arms. It was a turning point. God revealed Himself to me there in my hospital room. I felt Him whisper my name. I felt Him wash my sin and shame away. I knew I would love this little boy for the rest of my life. As surely as I knew I would never leave this little baby, I knew God would never leave me. As much as I knew that little boy could never do *anything* that would make me stop loving him, I knew God would love me forever, no matter what. I understood that His love was perfect and there was nothing I could do to cause Him to take it away from me. It was like receiving a warm embrace—I *felt* God again, and it felt good.

The whole hospital seemed to celebrate. Nate Newton just had a baby boy ... a son! He pranced around the hospital cracking jokes and shaking everyone's hand. He bought pizza for the entire floor. Nate was on top of the world. He had a son! I was laying in my room thinking, *Wow, he's really happy!* Then, just as soon as that thought came, another took its place, *I wonder how long this will last?*

It was almost like I wasn't even there, the whole place was buzzing around Nate, congratulating him, slapping him on the back, asking for autographs—I was just part of the background scenery, but I didn't care. I had Tre'. Tre' was the world to me now. I looked into his eyes and I melted. If I didn't have a single soul in the world, I would have this child to love. That was enough.

I had prayed for this little baby every day, no matter how sad I felt or how much fear, doubt, and shame I experienced. I prayed that he would be God's son. I looked at my little boy and tears welled up in my eyes. One of the nurses was watching and expressed concerned that I seemed so sad. She didn't understand. I felt like I had a chance to make things right in my life again. It was like turning over a new page with no mistakes on it. I knew Tre' was special. I was proud to be his mother. I was overwhelmed that God had trusted me with his life. I kept quoting 1 Samuel 1:27-28, "For this child I prayed; and the LORD hath given me my petition which I asked of him: Therefore also I have lent him to the LORD; as long as he liveth he shall be lent to the LORD."

I felt totally forgiven and had complete reassurance that things would be okay. I truly felt God's love again—it was tangible. I hadn't felt His presence in so long.

"Oh God, I love you," I whispered. "I can feel how much You love me. Thank You. Thank You … thank You for giving me this peace. Thank You for giving me something so wonderful in the midst of something so bad. Thank You for this baby boy..."

The tears kept softly flowing, but they were not tears of sadness, they were tears of release. Several nurses hovered nearby and as they checked my vital signs they were concerned at my tears. All I could say to them was, "I'm overwhelmed with love."

My dear friend, Lynn Martin had also come to the hospital to have her baby that night but was sent home for false labor. Before leaving, she came up to see me and little Tre'. Just five days later she had her son. In years to come, our friendship would prove to be a steady beacon in my life. Our sons would grow up to be friends and in dark days ahead, I would lean heavily on the Martins for support and strength.

Sixteen

UPS AND DOWNS

I am so accustomed to being unstable, that the only stability in my life is being unstable.

—JOSH LUCAS

The rest of October and November was beautiful. My family came to help out with the baby and I found a great deal of comfort in spending time alone with God and Tre'. I pushed it to the back of my mind that I was living with Nate not married. I was focused on taking care of Tre'. Feeling God's presence again in my life was so fulfilling that I didn't want to deal with anything that might hinder the reconnection I felt. I knew I would have to deal with it sooner or later, but later was better.

December came and Nate and I shared another birthday. The day after we celebrated it was like someone had flipped a switch. Nate was a different person again. He started coming in late at night, or not at all. He started drinking more and his language was growing increasingly coarse.

Sometimes he would come in at 2:00 or 3:00 in the morning and demand that I get up and fix him something to eat—and not just a sandwich, but he wanted me to cook a complete meal. I was exhausted from taking care of the baby, but to refuse him meant an argument and I didn't want him to wake up Tre'. Once or twice he grabbed me hard and shoved me against the wall. It frightened me. Nate had always had a temper, but he had never physically hurt me before. I told myself we were all just really tired from taking care of a newborn.

I still had one more month of maternity leave and I was trying to figure out child care. The thought of leaving Tre' with someone terrified me, but the thought of becoming financially dependent on Nate terrified me even more. Nate's early morning rants were bringing up very bad memories in my mind and I was determined not to find myself in the same position my mother had been. I wanted to hold onto my job. Nate wanted me to stay home with his son. He begged me to stay home and take care of Tre'. We argued about it, but my arguments were half-hearted because I really didn't want to leave Tre' with anyone else.

I wanted to take care of him. I wanted to protect him. I wanted to raise him.

I gave in and turned in my resignation. I had saved enough money that if I was careful, I could live for up to a full year without needing a penny from Nate. This fact gave me comfort. For the first two weeks, Nate was thrilled that I agreed with him and would stay home with Tre'. In short order, however, he began complaining that I was dependent on him. He grew irritable and argumentative and insulted me often. He stopped coming home at night. The Cowboys were not playing well and that made his mood even blacker. The season ended early which left Nate with lots of free time and little obligation. He would disappear for several days at a time, then reappear as if he had just stepped out for milk.

I had no idea what to expect from him. I didn't know what kind of relationship we would have ... or should have. Nate came and went as he pleased without explanation. Whenever there was a mini camp, I knew he would be there at the apartment. There was no commitment, we just sort of acted married whenever it suited Nate. He still loved to go on road trips and he loved showing off Tre'. He took me to Louisiana to visit my family. By the time Tre' was four months old we were taking trips as long as three weeks at a time visiting family members and friends... Louisiana, Florida, North Carolina, Georgia... we traveled a lot. I didn't mind because things were good when we traveled. He beamed with pride whenever he introduced Tre' to someone. He was very proud of his son.

The time was approaching for another training camp. This one would be in San Antonio. Every time he had a day off he would insist that I come down and bring Tre' to see him. Lynn Martin's son was just five days younger than Tre' and K-Mart was also at camp, so we would drive down together to visit. I realized how different everything was now. My relationship with Nate was that I was there for him—whenever he needed me or wanted me, I dropped everything and made myself available to him. Whenever he didn't need me or want me, I receded into the background to wait patiently until he needed or wanted me again. He didn't treat me badly, but it wasn't about loving me or being with me, it was now about Tre'. He was proud of having a son and I was his son's mother. I didn't have freedom to make plans on my own because I needed to always be available to Nate whenever he called. Wherever we went, Nate introduced me as his wife. People naturally assumed that we were married. We acted married. We had a son. I think even our closest friends assumed we were married. I fell into this unofficial role, not really sure of what else to do.

As camp drew to a close, Nate was confident he would make the team, so he didn't need me to pray for him anymore. The season opened and I dutifully came to all the games, supporting him. When not on the field, he was cussing and drinking more than ever. Things in our relationship really began to go downhill. I often felt like we were strangers. I had been at home with Tre' for a year and was seriously considering returning to work. I had promised Nate that I would not go back to my career until Nate was at least two and I did enjoy being home with him. My lease came up. I had to decide if life with Nate was "good enough" to maintain. *What did I want? What else would I do if I left him?* Sometimes I looked in the mirror and saw my mother staring back at me, but I shrugged it off. This wasn't like my mother and stepfather. Nate didn't beat me. I could leave if I wanted to.

When my lease had expired, it was up to Nate to decide what to do. Since I didn't have a job and wasn't making any money, finding a place to live was his decision. I didn't feel like I should weigh in much since I couldn't contribute. He had talked often about having a house with a yard for Tre' to play in and a house sounded nice to me. There was a little place Nate was interested in near Coppell Deli, a favorite stop for the players on the way to the airport for away games. It was small and in much need of repair. This didn't matter to me though, I wanted Nate to understand that I was with him because I loved him and because we had a child together. People called our little place "Newton's Shack" and poked fun of it, but I didn't care. Living in the little house never bothered me. It seemed to please Nate that I didn't care about money. He was satisfied that I loved him for who he was and not his celebrity status.

We moved into the tiny house and I went to work making it a home for Nate, Tre' and me. Things got worse between us. Nate stayed out late all the time and didn't communicate his plans. He didn't talk to me much at all. A woman accused him of fathering her child. He denied it flatly, but he had an attorney involved. I never had any proof, but I was always suspicious that he had paid her off. I knew he was sleeping around, many of the players were—it was part of the life. He was careless with receipts and how he talked about other women. I knew he was unfaithful.

When Nate was drinking his anger boiled over and he said dreadful things to me. I was growing desperate and would sometimes shout back, "Why am I here, Nathaniel?" Or in frustration I would say things like, "I should have kept my job. I should have stayed in my own place!" This would make Nate so angry that he would hit something—not me, but a wall or cabinet or something. His anger was explosive and when he hit something, he hit it hard. It scared me, but he never touched me. I was sure he wouldn't go that far.

I was always very careful to make sure that Nate was taken care of. I was like a domestic goddess—running all the errands, cooking, washing, ironing, packing his bags. I even got involved scheduling his appearances and researching his endorsements. I was now totally financially dependent on him and he was totally emotionally dependent on me. He was used to having me at his beck and call.

Nate spent more and more time in clubs and on the streets. He would roll in at 3:00 or 4:00 AM demanding full course meals. If I refused he would threaten me or hurl profanities. I usually found myself doing whatever he asked to appease him.

One night Nate stayed out all night and came home at noon the next day. Finally, I had enough. I was tired of being disrespected. I was tired of being yelled at. I was tired of the other women. I told him I couldn't live like this anymore and asked him to put a deposit on an apartment for me so I could move out. He cursed at me and yelled, "You're not going anywhere!"

He moved close to me in a hot rage and I was scared. I thought he might actually hit me this time, so I went into another room. Satisfied that he had won the argument, Nate got undressed to take a nap. I decided I would wait until he was asleep, then I would run out of the house. The only problem was that he was in the bedroom, so I couldn't take any clothes.

As soon as I was sure he had nodded off, I went out to my car and put nine month old Tre' into his car seat, I was leaving for good. As soon as I put the key into the ignition, Nate came running out of the house wearing only his underwear. He shouted, "Where are you going? You better not leave!"

I put the car in gear to back out and in a split second Nate's fist crashed into the windshield, shattering it on the driver's side. I screamed.

Our driveway was in plain sight of a busy street, visible for all to see. People stopped and looked, but no one called the police. No one attempted to intervene. I was terrified. I backed out of the driveway, shaking, glass shattered on the seat and in my lap and Tre' crying loudly. *Where should I go?*

I drove to a nearby park and sat there in shock. Who should I call? Who would believe that Nate could do such a thing? I had met a lot of Nate's teammates and their families, but I didn't really know any of them.

I thought about calling Lynn Martin. They spent enough time with us for her to see that I wasn't always treated well. I remembered one night when we had been at their house ...

K-Mart said to Nate, "Hey Time. Big Time (K-Mart's nick name for Nate) ... you got you a son!"

"Yeah," Nate had replied, "that's my baby boy alright, but I got me another son, too."

Lynn, K-Mart and I just looked at each other that night, but none of us said anything to Nate. I shut down completely for the rest of the night. Later on I questioned Nate about it to learn he had a son he had never seen, but was paying child support for. It was on his mind that night because the woman was trying to get her new husband to adopt the boy and Nate had to sign papers so the adoption could proceed. Once again, I was devastated.

I felt like Lynn would understand how afraid I was that Nate had gotten angry enough to damage property. Still, Lynn never did abide sadness or excuses of any kind. If you tell her a problem, she would speak praises over you, tell you who you are, remind you of your destiny, and tell you who you need to be. She never wanted to hear details or any sort of gossip at all. I imagined that if I shared with her, she would look at me with concern, but her response would likely be, "You're a strong woman. You can get through this." I knew she wouldn't let me be a victim and I didn't want to be a victim.

I put the car in gear ... I started to drive to her house, but I changed my mind. I realized that telling Lynn was not going to work. I was afraid of what she would tell her husband—and I couldn't imagine what would happen if

Nate found out that I had talked to Lynn and K-Mart, exposing his violent temper.

I called Sheila, my college roommate. She answered the phone full of cheer. She was with her husband and sounded so happy. I knew if I told her what had just happened she would drop everything and come to my rescue. I just couldn't tell her what happened. I hung up the phone and stared through my broken windshield. *What now?* I wondered to myself.

I'll call T. Hayes, I thought. *Maybe he can talk some sense into Nate.* T. Hayes always had time to talk to me. He sensed what was going on in our home and seemed concerned about the situation. I was sure I could trust him.

I had rushed out of the house quickly, not taking anything with me but Tre' and a purse. I decided I would spend the night in a hotel, but then would have to go back and get some things. I didn't have a place to stay. My family didn't live close. I didn't have a job. My mother's face flashed before my eyes … I shuddered. *How had I let this happen to me?* I would go back to Nate and begin looking for a job. I would prepare so I could leave.

I went back to the little house the next day, preparing for the worst. Nate came home like a flipped coin. He was a completely different person. He apologized. He was so ashamed of himself. He begged me not to leave. I told him I would stay, but I was going to get a job. He begged me to think of our son, Tre', and not go back to work. I should stick with the plan. He brought up God and said all the right things. I told him I wanted him to take me home to Louisiana. I wanted to see my mom. Inside I was thinking I would tell her what was going on so we could figure out what to do. Maybe I would just stay there with her and not even come back with Nate.

Nate felt so bad about what had happened that he agreed to take me to Louisiana, but as usual, once we got there he painted himself to be the good guy—treating everyone to dinner and handing out money until they were all under his spell. He made sure I was never out of his sight. He eliminated any chance for me to tell anyone about what had happened. For the entire three days we were there it was like I was wearing a leash attached to Nate. He never left me alone for one minute. I quickly gave up all hope of talking to someone there. I knew it wasn't going to happen and no one in my family had even the faintest clue that he was mistreating me. To them Nate was a hero and a gentleman, I was his lucky celebrity wife, someone to be envied not pitied.

When we left we didn't head west back to Dallas, instead Nate started driving South. We ended up in Orlando to visit with his family and friends. I did my best to fake good spirits, but deep down inside I was miserable. I played through the last year in my mind like it was a broken record. One bad choice *(to go on the pill)* led to another bad choice *(to have sex)* which led to a bad *situation (getting pregnant and not married)* that led to another bad *choice (live with Nate, leave my job, etc. etc.)* If only I could go back in time and fix the first mistake! One decision had led me down a detour of winding, bumpy, difficult roads—away from my dreams, away from my destiny. I felt trapped.

We spent three weeks on the road traveling from place to place, visiting people. Along the way we did talk about what had happened and Nate assured me that things would be different when we got home. He promised to get control of his drinking and his temper.

Before leaving, Nate put the car in the shop to have the windshield fixed. When we got home he even switched cars with me because he didn't want me to think about what he had done when I was driving. He grew attentive again. He was kind when he spoke to me and once again things improved between us. I let my guard down and started to think that we had turned a corner.

Everywhere I went, people were star-struck with Nate Newton. The moment they knew I was his "wife" (at least they all believed I was his wife), out came the special treatment. Even at church people often brought me items and asked me to take them home for Nate or other Cowboy players to autograph. It was frustrating. Instead of being interested in me, it seemed like belonging to Nate was the most interesting thing about me. I was losing who I was. My whole world was wrapped up in Nate.

Seventeen

SETTLING

The first and worst of all frauds is to cheat one's self.
All sin is easy after that.
—PEARL BAILEY

---

ies have a way of compounding, like interest on credit card debt. Before long you are totally engulfed and it is hard to distinguish the truth from the lies. I knew that Nate was cheating on me, and it was increasingly difficult for me to be intimate with him, knowing that I was just one of many. He always denied it, but he stayed out late all the time and sometimes didn't come home until the next day. Sometimes when he had too much too drink, he would empty his pockets and a scrap of paper would fall out with a woman's phone number or address scrawled on it. I scooped them up, determined to learn who he had been with, but didn't go through with any investigative work.

A friend of mine and her husband had come into town and contacted me for a visit. She came to see me and wanted to know all about the lifestyle of being married to a professional athlete (even my friends thought we were married because Nate always referred to me as his wife in the media). I looked her straight in the eyes, told her Nate was cheating on me and that I wanted to leave him.

"Do you know for sure?" she asked.

"No. I don't have proof if that's what you mean, but I know he is cheating. I have something I want to check out. Will you go with me?" I asked.

She was very reluctant, and I could tell she didn't want to go, but I didn't want to go alone and persuaded her to tag along. We went to an address that I had seen fall out of Nate's pocket one drunken night. Jackpot! Nate was there! Not only was he there, but he was sitting outside, snuggled up with the woman in plain sight. I had suspected this all along, but seeing it with my own eyes was a shock. Reality set in. I saw red. I made a scene so he would know I was there, I wanted to make sure he saw me, then I took my friend back to her husband. I felt terrible. Not only was I disgusted with Nate, but I was upset for dragging my friend through the ordeal. I didn't know what else to do but apologize to her. I was truly sorry that I had involved her.

When I got back home, Nate was waiting for me. He begged for my forgiveness, but I was too angry to accept. I pleaded with him to give me enough money for an apartment and daycare, just until I could get on my feet, then I would never bother him again. I just wanted to leave. He obviously didn't want me, why should I stay?

Out came Nate's broken record, singing the same old tune, but this time he added a new note. "Everyone has always abandoned me, Dot. I need you. You are the only person in my life that I can count on, that has never let me down, has never left me. I need your help. You can't leave me."

My heart was hardened. I might have even told him he was forgiven, but I certainly didn't mean it. Instead, I started planning. I had received payment for some of my work scheduling Nate's appearances and endorsements and I was expecting an income tax refund of $1,400. It wasn't much, but I was going to use the money to get out. I knew it would be four to six weeks before the check came, that would give me enough time to find a cheap apartment and decent daycare for Tre' while I found a job. My hope was in that tax refund.

I didn't have much time to fellowship with other believers, but I spent time in the Word. It was just me and God—I felt disconnected from my family, disconnected from my friends, and I even felt strangely disconnected from myself. On the outside people assumed that things were good. Only T. Hayes knew there was trouble because Nate would confide in him whenever he really messed up. My best friend from college had just gotten married and I didn't want to worry her with my problems. My family was totally blinded by their admiration for Nate and he piled on the gifts and the charm whenever they were around. His family certainly had no idea I was unhappy.

I had my eye out for that tax refund. It was time to escape. I went to the mailbox and my heart skipped a beat when I saw an envelope from the IRS. I ran back into the house and tore it open, but there was not a check inside. Instead there was a notice saying that the refund I was expecting had gone to pay property taxes in my name and that I owed an additional $700! My disappointment almost crushed me. Stuck again! I didn't even know about the property. I had no choice but to tell Nate and ask for his help. I called my mother to ask about it and she said that she did have property in my name, but she had paid the taxes. There was no way to clear it up quickly, it was going to take some time to sort out. Nate graciously paid the remaining balance and I thanked God that he was willing to help, but I was still unhappy that I was financially dependent on him. I made a choice that it was time to position myself for independence. It was time for me to get a job.

Nate was becoming more of a figurehead in the media. The Cowboys were playing really well, and every time sports were on, it seemed like he was being interviewed. He was jovial in conversation and people loved him. We were always portrayed in public as a happy family. I started going to church again and Nate was supportive of this. I was always happier when I was involved in church and Nate knew this. He told me, "I want you to do the things you enjoy the most. I never want to take you away from that," and he meant it.

I started attending a Bible study during the day while Tre' was in a Mother's Day Out program twice a week. Things settled down between Nate and me for a season.

He was home more. We argued less and it felt calmer around the house. Nate decided it was time for us to move into a little bit nicer town home. It was modest and nice but no yard for Tre' to play in. We stayed there for just six months.

During this time Nate came home from work one day extremely angry and we got into an argument. He slammed his fist down on the tray of Tre's high chair and broke it. At that moment I was determined that I would get a job whether Nate liked it or not. I would never be free to make my own choices unless I was financially independent.

A few months later we moved into a nice little house with a yard.

While Nate was in training camp, I secured a job. I worked for First Coppell Bank. Linda Carter owned the bank and took a special interest in me. She and her husband also owned the Dallas Mavericks, and NBA organization, so she was never mezmerized by Nate's celebrity status. She invited me to lunch occasionally and to her home to visit. She never talked about Nate, so I knew her interest was in me as a person, not my status as a celebrity wife. It was refreshing—different from how most people treated me. She was my friend. I really enjoyed working there and things at home were really getting much better. Nate and I fought less and less and things smoothed out.

Time went by and Nate and I had came to terms with things. We found a place of happiness. It was consistent. I was more at ease because I was earning income, so I didn't feel trapped anymore. I could stay or I could leave. I couldn't shake my guilt about living together and not being married, so I started praying about our relationship. I looked back across the past ten months and realized that things had been calm and even. In fact, things were good. I enjoyed being with Nate. He was a good father to Tre'. I had no more excuses not to marry him. I approached Nate about getting married and he was open to it.

I told him that I had been spending a lot of time in prayer and that I could no longer continue living together with him in sin. I told him that if the way things were between us now was the real deal, then I would be happy to become his wife.

My objection to marrying Nate had been because he wasn't saved. Nate reminded me that he still wasn't a Christian. I knew this, but he always encouraged my walk with the Lord, and I justified Nate's lack of devotion to his hectic football schedule. I told myself that when football was over for him, he would accept Christ once and for all. The New Year was fast approaching and I wanted to start if off right.

Eighteen

I DO...

Between a man and his wife nothing ought to rule but love.
—WILLIAM PENN

"Do you, Nathaniel Newton, Jr., take this woman, Dorothy Johnson, to be your lawfully wedded wife?" asked the Justice of the Peace.

"I do," Nate answered.

"Do you, Dorothy Johnson, take this man, Nathaniel Newton, Jr., to be your lawfully wedded husband?" he asked me.

"I do," I answered.

In a simple courthouse ceremony after a couple of years spent living together, we were married. T. Hayes stood up with Nate and Sheila stood up with me. We drove to see my family in Louisiana to tell them we were married. We sent out announcements to all our friends and everyone was shocked—they all thought we had been married since Tre' was born.

1992 was a good year for us. The Cowboys won the Super Bowl and Nate went on to the Pro Bowl. We spent lots of time together, just the three of us. Nate communicated with me differently now and I felt more secure. At Easter he was asked to speak at church and he surprised me by saying yes! We never prayed together, but he would often ask me to pray about things for him. He encouraged me to spend time with the Lord and be active in church. Whenever I asked him to come to church with me, he was always clear that he had too much respect for God to play with Him. He would say to me, "When I get myself completely together I'll start going to church, but right now I'm just not good enough."

Fall of 1992 came and the new season began. I was very busy scheduling appearances for Nate and making sure he was prepared, packing for him and attending both home and away games. As the demands on my time increased, I was having to miss work more frequently and didn't feel like I could give my job the focus it required. I resigned my position at Coppell

Bank. I prioritized my relationship with God first and everything else followed—including Nate and even little Tre'. I had made the mistake before of putting Nate first and didn't want to do that again. No matter how tired I was or how inconvenient, I found a way to attend church weekly, either before or after games, depending on what time the Cowboys played. I now had a network of believers I was spending time with during the day and was not easily distracted because I was anchored in the Word. I was stronger in my faith than ever before. I was determined that I would live a good life. I was married now. My priorities were straight. I had a son to take care of.

The Dallas Cowboys were off to a great season. They were winning almost every game and with every victory, the media focused more attention on Nate. He was their darling. He always gave an entertaining interview and there was not a sports station on television that didn't want their moment with him. He had more opportunities for endorsements and appearances than ever before. He had become a hot item overnight.

I was consumed scheduling Nate's calendar and organizing his wardrobe for appearances. I had quit my job in October because taking care of Nate was a full time endeavor during the week. I spent the weekends entertaining family and guests. The more attention Nate received, the more the old Nate surfaced. He started drinking too much and once again he stayed out late or didn't come in at all. He stopped communicating. Once again he would show up at 3:00 AM and demand meals or sex. The more this old pattern emerged, the more fearful I grew. I thought to myself, *this cannot be happening again ... we just got married!* But before long Nate was talking down to me again, demeaning me and shouting insults. I reminded him of his promise that things would be different. "Dot," he said, "I'm not perfect, but I promise to do the right things. If you wanted a perfect husband you shouldn't have married me."

We argued constantly and his temper was increasingly violent. He sometimes shoved me or grabbed my throat when he was angry, but he would always apologize later. I didn't like the way things were going. Once again I was acting as his wife, maid, and secretary all rolled into one, making sure absolutely all his needs were met. The only time we spent together as a family was at public appearances—he always wanted Tre' and I there when the cameras were on, but as soon as the lights went off, he disappeared.

He was drinking all the time. I was alarmed at how much beer he could consume and not seem drunk. I knew he was drinking and driving, but if I said anything the least judgmental it started an argument, and the arguments were growing physically violent. Once he crossed the line, it seemed easier and easier for him to do. The abuse got worse.

Nate had a routine. On Wednesday he went to work. He would call to see if he had an appearance and what time. If nothing was on his schedule, he would tell me what he wanted me to cook or pick up for him and when I should have it ready. He would usually arrive around 7:00 PM and eat dinner, then he went to his media room and watched movies until he fell asleep.

On Thursdays it was the same thing, only it was much more likely that he had an appearance. He usually wanted Tre' and I present for all his appearances. We weren't on camera, he just wanted us to be there supporting him.

He loved to get tickets for people, but he liked waiting until the very last minute before deciding to give the tickets away. On Friday before a game, he stayed home, or came home early. He would invite people into town to see the game and it was my job to entertain them. He would be jolly on Friday night, looking good and being gregarious. By Saturday morning, Nate would be detoxing and treating me like a servant. I had to make sure Tre' made absolutely no noise, fix Nate exactly what he wanted to eat, the way he wanted to eat it, and serve it when he wanted it.

I was also supposed to keep all his guests entertained and out of his way. People stayed with us every weekend there was a home game. By Saturday afternoon, the Cowboys sequestered their players in a hotel to keep them out of trouble and I could relax a little—whether the game was home or away, the Cowboys made sure their players were all safely tucked into a hotel where they could keep an eye on their assets. I didn't mind. Nate was gone and that meant I had a respite from his temper. Each weekend, I knew he would call me from the hotel and demand that I drop whatever I was doing and bring food or his music or some other item he wanted.

On Sunday morning, if it was a home game, he would come home from the hotel, no matter what time the game started. He would come home and I had to make sure that the house was kept in complete silence and that no one disturbed him. I wasn't supposed to do anything but be in the room with him keeping everything perfect. He didn't want the phones to ring or Tre' to bother him and he always asked, "Did you pray for me?" Sundays were always stressful.

On his way to the game, Nate would call me with instructions and his ticket list. I was then supposed to contact everyone he had gotten tickets for and organize everything. I was supposed to see to it that his guests arrived comfortably at the game and that I was there with Tre' as well. It was impossible to make it through the weekend without angering him in some way.

T. Hayes would call me to give me a heads up if he knew Nate was angry with me. He would say things like, "I talked to that boy and I can tell he's not gonna be in a good mood." T. Hayes also called to check on me often to make sure I was okay after he knew Nate had been angry. I would sometimes ask him, "Why don't you talk to Nate?"

He answered, "Nate's trying, Dot. He's trying, I don't know what's wrong with that boy."

T. Hayes knew what was going on. If things were really bad I would call and tell him that Nate was hurting me. I was afraid to go to the police because everyone we met was star struck by Nate. If any trouble arose, Nate charmed his way into a conversation about football and that was that. It reminded me of how people treated my stepfather. Even knowing he abused my mother, they never intervened.

After games we always went out to eat with family and friends. After we ate dinner and visited with everyone, Nate would come home to change clothes. For the next hour he would drill me on every play of the game. Asking me questions and going through the whole game. So, I had to pay close attention when I was there, not get distracted visiting with other wives. Then he would hit the streets. Sometimes he came back late that night and sometimes he didn't. It didn't matter, whenever he did get home, there would be an argument. I tried my hardest to ignore it, but that didn't work very often. I knew he would come home sometime insisting that I make him food or have sex and I didn't want to give him either. I started to hate him. My heart got harder and harder.

In public Nate seemed to care for me and Tre', but behind closed doors we meant nothing to him.

It was an exciting time for the Cowboys. 1993 saw another Super Bowl Championship for the team. I worked for Nate as his local agent, scheduling appearances and endorsements and reviewing contracts for commercials. This was now my full time job. Tre' and I attended most of the appearances to watch him sign autographs or appear on television or commercials, but in between we didn't see him. He turned cold and distant.

I remember one night Nate grabbed me by the hair and pulled me around the house. I was so hurt and angry. I was upset that Tre' was in the house. I wanted to call the police ... I just knew it wouldn't make any difference at all. Nate always got out of trouble as quick as he got into it. He could charm his way out of anything.

Nate spent lots of money on people. He was always the life of the party. He made people laugh. He gave liberally to my family—vehicles, money ... they all loved him, but it made things worse for me. If one of them made him mad, he took it out on me. If I tried to keep him from giving them things (because it would blow back on me) they got angry with me. They didn't understand and thought I was selfish, trying to keep Nate from sharing with them.

I was still friends with Lynn, and we did lots of things together with our kids, but she didn't want to be involved in any of Nate's drama. "Don't let this get the best of you," she would say. I shut down completely. I lived two completely separate lives. One life was inside my home—frightened, abused, angry, and alone. The other was outside my home—functional, normal, a celebrity wife.

A close friend of mine came to me one day, telling me that Nate had come to her apartment, coming on to her for sex. I was furious and confronted Nate about it. He threatened me, abused me, and choked me. I knew she was telling the truth, but Nate accused her of coming on to him.

I felt isolated and alone. Part of me wanted to confide in someone. I desperately wanted help but several things stopped me. First, my friend Lynn was leaving. K-Mart had signed with the Seattle Seahawks and they were moving far away. Telling her seemed pointless. How could she help from Seattle? Then, each time he abused me, I convinced myself it would be the last time. It sometimes felt like I had done something wrong and needed to pay back the debt. I honestly believed that when I had been sufficiently punished, then the abuse would stop. I was also genuinely afraid that if I went to someone about Nate they might confront him and make things worse for me. Finally, I believed that if I had to go through all of this in order for Nate to receive Christ, then I was strong enough to do it. I was willing to live through it.

So, I told no one. Just God. I cried all my tears in silence. I poured out my grief and believed I was suffering as a result of bad choices I had made long ago. I somehow deserved this treatment because of my mistakes. Someday I would pay it all back and this hard part would be over.

I remember watching the other wives and wondering about their lives. Were they happy? Were their husbands faithful? Did they struggle with abuse like I did, or were their homes peaceful? I just wondered if my life was a picture of what other celebrity wives went through, or was there just something wrong with my life?

Nate didn't allow me to hang out with the other Cowboy wives. I wanted to get to know them, but Nate didn't approve. He didn't want me to know them. He forbid me to socialize with them. He would pick and choose who I should hang out with. Every game, the Cowboys were sequestered in a hotel and Tony Tolbert was Nate's roommate, so he encouraged me to spend time with his wife, Tasha. We worked out together, but for the other wives, I was constantly coming up with excuses for why I couldn't join them.

During home games, Emmitt Smith's seating tickets were right next to mine. I always longed to know Pat Smith. She was beautiful—poised and graceful, and always stylish. I wanted to get to know her, but Nate wouldn't allow me to spend time with any of the player's wives. She demonstrated a desire to be friends, and I felt embarrassed, wondering what she thought of me because I didn't reciprocate her kindness. I was never permitted to reach out to her or accept her invitations. I wasn't allowed to accept invitations from the other wives either. I longed to experience that part of football, but it was not to be.

Michael Irvin's wife, Sandy, was also a beautiful woman—inside and out. She loved kids. Whenever I saw her, she would come over and hug Tre' and love on him. I wanted to know her better. She wore the most beautiful clothing. I wanted to dress just like her. She was always kind and never flaunted anything. I was attracted to her gentle spirit. Although I never confided in her how things were at home, our relationship blessed me. Her attention to Tre' warmed my heart.

The one exception was Tasha Tolbert. Her husband Tony was Nate's roommate and he encouraged me to spend time with her. I enjoyed her company so much, and she was such fun to be around. It was God's grace that Nate approved of this relationship—I needed her in my life. We worked out together and I felt close to Tasha and her family. Whenever her parents came into town, they included Tre' and me. Tasha and her family are very special people and have remained good friends over the years.

I longed to be more active with people, but my activity was limited. Nate had to approve. One thing he did allow was for me to attend Bible study. He was always supportive of my relationship with God. John and Gina Gesek held a daytime Bible study in their home for the player's wives. This was a joy for me and gave me some outlet for fellowship. I was sad when they changed it to a couples' study in the evenings because I was no longer able to attend, and I so appreciated the opportunity to know Gina Gesek.

I never wanted people to experience the pain I was walking through. I didn't want to be a burden to anyone. I was blessed when people came to me when they were going through something difficult. Maybe it was because Nate was in trouble often and I stood by him, demonstrating strength. I don't know the reason, I hoped it was because they could see Christ in me. I was genuinely filled with compassion for people. I would minister to them and pray for them, but they had no idea what I was living through. I felt like I was strong enough to handle me. Even in the middle of this bad situation I felt close to God. I felt like I needed Him and Him alone—like no one else was capable or cared. I memorized loads of Scripture verses and I would recite them in my mind when Nate was ranting. They comforted me. They were my escape.

I couldn't wait for the season to be over. I wanted to disappear. It was getting harder and harder to hide the physical abuse, but I knew I had to—if anyone had an inkling of what was really going on, I believed Nate would have killed me.

If I asked him any questions about anything at all he became enraged. Outside of his fabulous football life, Tre' and I didn't exist.

After the Super Bowl, the Pro Bowl came around. We went to Hawaii. Nate was completely relaxed and for once I didn't have to worry about extra people, appearances, schedules, or endorsements. It was the nicest time I had experienced in years.

We returned home and the appearances started up again, and so did Nate's antics. His bad boy image was turning the media against him. He was constantly in trouble with women, DUIs, and general bad behavior. As the media attention turned negative, his reputation suffered. They were destroying him. The worse it got in the media, the more he took it out on me physically. There were times he beat me until I was lifeless, unable to move. It was happening more frequently and it was getting more violent. The morning after a beating, Nate would either act as if nothing had ever happened the night before, or he would be extremely nice to me.

When he wanted to go out or to be with friends, I was expected to come along as though our marriage was perfect. In front of people, he treated me well. He loved to entertain and we had out of town guests frequently. I was happy to have guests because I knew Nate would be nice, but taking care of all their needs and keeping up with appearances was extremely stressful. I also knew that the minute they were gone, Nate would find a reason to be angry and the abuse would start all over again.

I hated my life. It was a roller coaster. I never knew from moment to moment what to expect from Nate Newton. Sometimes I thought I would go to sleep and it would be my last moment alive. Nate was such a people person. He loved having people around all the time, and when there was an audience he acted like I was the most wonderful thing that had ever happened to him … sometimes he was so convincing I almost believed it myself. There were no outward signs for anyone to ever think anything was wrong. My fear of repercussion rendered me powerless to share my secret. *Who would believe me?*

Nate was a darling. Everyone loved him and it was easy to excuse his indiscretions because he was so much fun to be around. He was a celebrity, after all, and the rules for celebrities are different than they are for the rest of us. He always picked up the tab, no matter how expensive the bill was. He lavished people with really, really nice gifts. He set the stage to always be the nice guy, the hero. People envied me and thought I lived a picture perfect, golden dream life. Nothing was further from the truth.

Tre' was now attending a Montessori School and I was working, trying to keep up with my commitments to Nate. The Cowboys continued to do well and I was extremely busy taking care of Nate and his calendar. The arguments and beatings never stopped. I just accepted it as part of life. Whenever he was upset, he abused me. Then he would come and apologize and want to make things "right." Each time I would think to myself, *this is the last thing I'll have to go through* ... and of course I was always wrong. I know it sounds crazy, but I honestly thought I deserved the treatment as punishment for my sins.

There always seemed to be another woman involved. It hurt my feelings and damaged my self esteem, but I just came to accept that this was part of life when you were married to a football star.

I never knew how much money Nate had, and I never cared. I knew he spent lots and lots of money—he had an obsession with cars and dogs—I knew he didn't spend it on me. He used only one credit card, American Express. The bill went to his agent in Florida each month, so I had no idea how much he spent or what he spent it on. I received enough money from him to pay our household bills and he gave me some money for organizing his events and appearances. Since I wasn't allowed to have many friends or hang out with other Cowboy wives, I didn't need much money.

On one occasion, he had so overspent that the agent forwarded the American Express bill to the house for Nate to review and make sure no charges were a mistake. I saw this bill and saw charges to Louis Vuitton and other fine jewelry stores ... none of the items, of course, were for me. I wondered about the woman it was for, though. I wondered if she knew about me. I never shopped lavishly and any spending money I received had come from my job while working for First Coppell Bank, and now from from scheduling Nate's appearances. I knew that if I had asked for something, Nate would have given it to me. He was generous with everybody. I didn't want to ask.

One Thursday night I was sitting in the passenger seat of Nate's truck and we were arguing about that credit card bill. I asked him about the charges and who the items were for. He took his hand and hit me in the face over my left eye. "It's my money, b_____! You better not ever question me ... You have no right to question me how I spend my money, who I spend it on, where I spend it ... just because you're my wife doesn't give you a reason to question my business!" The blow left a visible bruise. I knew I couldn't miss a game without serious consequences from Nate, so I put on big sunglasses and went to the stadium. Sandy Irvin came over to me and after she was done loving on Tre' she said, "Dot, can I tell you something?" I looked up at her, wondering if she could see my bruise. Fear gripped me, *Can she tell? Can she see it?* I felt the lowest I had ever been.

"Dot, you are a beautiful person," she said, "you are just so beautiful!" I wanted to burst into tears. It was as if God had sent her to me to remind me that He loved me.

Every time I summoned the courage to leave him or go to the authorities, it seemed like Nate would get into trouble with the law. I felt like I needed to stay and see him through whatever present crisis he was in and *then* I would go. Each time I would see him through he would be grateful and things would get better for a little while.

Nate told me that every relationship he had ever been in was awful. I felt like I owed it to him to see things through. I felt responsible that he had not yet come to know the Lord and that it was my assignment to see him through to salvation. After he beat me, I would think, *This is the last thing I'll have to go through and then it will be good. If it means Nate will come to know the Lord, then this will all be worth it.* I felt like I was keeping it hidden from Tre'. I would send him to play in his room or start a movie for him. I never wanted him to be frightened. I knew Nate would never ever hurt Tre' ... I just wished he felt the same about me.

Tre' was growing up. He was almost five. I was being exposed to new people through Tre's school, Tae Kwon Do, etc. Nate was not part of this circle. He was too absorbed in football, and because my activities surrounded Tre's needs, he wasn't upset for me to participate. He wanted the best for his son. He trusted me when it came to Tre'.

I found myself with a world outside of football, away from the torture of my home life and it was wonderful and refreshing. Nate didn't know any of these people. When I left the house, I left the tattered, abused Dorothy at home. When I got into my car I was a totally different version of Dorothy—I was a healthy, happy, normal Dorothy. I spent as much time away from home as I possibly could. I ministered to people and it gave me joy. People shared their problems with me and I was happy to help out in any way I could. God was using me and I felt alive again.

It didn't matter if things were terrible at home, out here I was free. The more I carried refreshing water to the souls of others, the less thirsty I was. I survived by serving others. I was making a difference. I could see that my life was valuable. I could see there was good in me in spite of how bad things were at home.

I was completely at the end of my rope, exhausted— mentally, emotionally, physically ... I didn't have the strength to live through one more argument, one more beating, I just wanted it to end. I went to my prayer closet one night after Nate had pushed me around, cursed and yelled at me for hours. I was at my lowest point. I cried out to God. I poured out my heart to Him and poured out all my sorrow and grief. "Lord, I'm ready to be with you. I don't care if I live or die. I know I need to live. I have to live so I can teach Tre' how to love you."

I hugged my knees to my chest, wishing for one moment that I might die and be with God forever. Then in the same moment, I wanted desperately for Tre' to know this same love that I had for God—how I felt like He hugged me during all these times. "God, let me live," I whispered. "Let me live so I can teach Tre' to love you like I do." In that moment, more than anything, I wanted to live. I wanted to survive so I could be the one to teach Tre' to love

God with all his heart, soul, and mind. I couldn't bear the thought of any other person teaching Tre' to know God. I wanted him to grow up strong and healthy and become a godly man. It didn't matter what else I had to go through if it meant that Tre' had what he needed.

Nineteen

THE GOOD LIFE

Success makes life easier. It doesn't make living any easier.

—BRUCE SPRINGSTEEN

Little Tre' was now five years old. The Cowboys were at their peak and Nate was in his prime. As a professional athlete, he was at the top of his game. He was popular and had grown wealthy. We were still living in the modest house in Coppell and one night Nate spotted a rat. That was it ... time to move!

He decided he wanted to build his own home, but he was not willing to stay in the house where the rat had been, so we moved into a town house in Coppell while the new house was under construction. Nate wanted land and privacy—a respite from everything that had to do with the Dallas Cowboys.

Nate gave me a budget to work within and he wanted to pay for everything with cash—no mortgage, no debt. He didn't really care about the design of the home or the furnishings, he left all that up to me. As long as I stayed inside the budget and the house was comfortable for entertaining, Nate trusted me to take care of all the details. I was excited over the project. It was wonderful to have the freedom to make decisions. Planning and working with the builder made me feel important and I enjoyed the process. Shopping for furniture was hard at first, because I wasn't used to spending money or having the freedom to just pick whatever I liked, but it got easier and easier as time went on.

It was one of the nicest things Nate ever did for me. Once he set the budget, he gave me the money to work with and trusted me to decide everything. He never once complained about anything I chose. He seemed genuinely excited as the house took shape and he enjoyed listening to me ramble on and on about the details of the build. Focusing on the project was a good diversion and for the most part, things went well between us.

We had a wonderful builder to work with, and he was around us often enough to see us in unguarded moments when things were not so nice between us. He never witnessed any outright physical abuse, but he seemed to know that things were not all they appeared to be and he was extra gentle and kind with me.

On one occasion, I wanted the front of the house to be a certain way but the builders did something else. I decided I could live with it, but when Nate found out about it he was very, very angry with me. He did not want me to settle. We scheduled a meeting with our builder, but before going in Nate threatened me that I better fix this—handle my business and insist they fix it exactly like I wanted it in the first place without any change in the price. I was horrified. I didn't want to make a fuss with the builders, but I also didn't want to make Nate angry. I went into the meeting to discuss the problem, but before the meeting was over I was yelling and actually got mean with them. I felt so terrible about the whole thing. As I left the meeting, I asked God to forgive me and hoped that the men would know that wasn't who I really was. I was upset about it for days afterwards.

At last the house was finished and we could move in. The rooms were not all furnished yet, but the home was lovely. It was time for Tre' to begin kindergarten, so we moved into our beautiful new home. It was really important to me that Tre' be in a Christian school where what I taught him at home was reinforced. I wanted Tre' to have a loving, solid foundation. Even though Fort Worth Christian School was an hour drive from the new house, it was important to me to keep Tre' there. It was a good school and right for Tre'. I didn't mind the drive at all because being away from home was good for me too.

One of Tre's teachers at school, Mrs. Gleghorn, became a grandmother figure to Tre' and a tremendous blessing to me. She spoke words of wisdom into my life all the time without even realizing it. She poured out her love in tangible ways, always filled with Jesus and always filled with joy. Though she was excited about Nate, her focus was on Tre' and on me. It was lovely to have someone interested in us because we were special, not just because Nate was famous.

My dear friend, Sheila, was moving to Atlanta and I knew I was going to miss her. I was making new friends at Tre's school, but as usual, most people were interested in becoming my friend more because I was Nate Newton's wife and less because I was Dorothy. Within a week of Tre' starting school I met Ingrid at Tae Kwon Do. She noticed people flopping all over me, bringing me things for Nate to autograph or wanting to talk about football, and she kept her distance. I noticed her because she was not seeking me out, so I introduced myself to her. We were giving Tre' a birthday party at Texas Stadium with 500 people in attendance. I invited Ingrid and she was shocked that I would do this since I didn't know her, but there was just something special about her and I sensed that she was genuine and believed we would become friends. We started driving to Tae Kwon Do tournaments together and before long we became very close friends.

Nate was gone a lot and Ingrid's husband, Monte, was an executive who also worked a great deal. Both Tre' and Ingrid's kids were in school, so we had more time to spend together. She went with me to pick out furniture for the house. We would do all her errands together one day, and then do all my errands together the next day. I loved being with her. Little by little I began to open up to her about my life—the good and the bad.

When things were really bad for me at home, I would talk to Ingrid about it. She listened to me with such patience and gentleness. She listened to me talk about the abuse, and I must have sounded like a broken record, but she listened to me every time like it was the first time she had ever heard me. When Nate would apologize and promise that things would be better, I would tell Ingrid that he had turned a corner, and she listened. Then, when things would get bad again and the abuse would start over, she listened and never judged me. Sometimes I talked to her about wanting to leave, but didn't have any access to the money—it all belonged to Nate. She listened to me. She validated who I was and promised that she would stand with me and do whatever it took. I made her promise to never say anything to her husband and she swore she never would.

I believe she kept her promise, because when we did things together as families, I never saw Monte treat Nate differently or seem to suspect anything. They came to games with us, Super Bowls, Pro Bowls, etc. I loved having them in my life. Nate loved being around Monte and Ingrid also, though he always preferred large groups to more intimate gatherings.

I didn't always tell Ingrid when things were bad. It was just good to get up, get out of the house, and have someone to be with who loved me and treated me well. I didn't want to spoil things all the time by complaining about life with Nate. Ingrid always allowed me to be myself. We talked every single day. I could not imagine my life without her in it. We spent a great deal of time together and became the best of friends. We exercised together, ran errands together, did Bible study together, went to school functions and our children's special events together, she traveled to some of the Cowboy games with me... One of my best memories is when she got baptized, I was truly overjoyed. Ingrid was just like family.

In 1994 Nate got into some trouble with the law. He received six months probation after pleading guilty to reckless conduct. He had been in a car accident while under the influence of alcohol. Of course this brought negative press attention to Nate and a public trial, but I stood by him, supporting him and offering encouragement. This touched Nate. He knew I was sincere in my support and he really did try to adjust his behavior and become a better husband through the ordeal. He started spending more and more time at home and doing things with Tre' and I as a family. Things got calm between us and Nate even agreed to see a counselor with me.

We asked around and someone from the Cowboys recommended a counselor to us. It turned out to be a complete waste of time—the man seemed bored in the session and I could swear at times he actually dozed off and fell asleep. We only went to two sessions with him. It was doing nothing for Nate or me so we stopped going. Things were pretty good between us again so it didn't seem like we even needed a counselor. I was happy that things were calm, but I remained uneasy. I couldn't relax. I had given up hope that things would ever really be permanently good. I was always waiting for something bad to happen and start things up again.

Nate was more open to church now, though he had not given his life to Christ. He sometimes spoke with ministers and he seemed to be making positive changes in his behavior. It did make a noticeable difference in the way things were at home. I prayed diligently for him, and I asked God to help me see him through His eyes because I still felt cold inside and was still waiting for something bad to happen.

It was difficult for me to trust people. When someone reached out to me for friendship, it seemed they were more intrigued by Nate's public persona. They were excited to learn about the life of a professional football player and about the world of football and everything that entailed. I would visit with someone and go to lunch, but the conversation always turned to football. Even when I wanted to spend time with a minister to talk about something, inevitably, the conversation turned to football. It was frustrating. I would go to church and leave with multiple requests for autographs. People brought me photos and other items asking me to take them home for Nate or other Cowboy players to sign.

Once during a time when things were bad, I went to a minister and told him I was in danger. I didn't even have the opportunity to share any details, but I really wanted to talk and needed him to pray with me. Immediately he began making excuses for the lifestyle Nate was living and told me that most of what I was experiencing was probably a result of the unique issues that a celebrity has to deal with. Without missing a breath, he turned the conversation back to football and other athletes. He seemed very pleased with himself ... I didn't even need to be in the room, he carried on the whole conversation by himself. I sat there listening, wondering if he had any idea how much courage it took for me to even think about coming to him with my problems. Nate was such a celebrity with a reputation for being a great guy, it made it all the more difficult to share what was going on at home. There was no use in trying. The rules seemed to be different for celebrities.

I was hurt that people's interest in me was all about Nate, so I began to withdraw. I still went to services, but I would sneak into the back after the meeting had started and slip out just before it ended. I distanced myself. I continued to attend regularly, but I felt disconnected—like a spectator.

On the other hand, Nate seemed to be making forward progress. He had always loved to read. He read almost every night before he went to bed. Now, instead of just reading books he was interested in, I noticed that he often picked up the Bible. I was very encouraged by this. He began spending time with the Dallas Cowboys' minister as well. He would come home excited after talking with him and share with me what had been said. He didn't go into great detail about his personal relationship with God, but his actions spoke louder than his words could ever say.

Nate was changing. He was living a life that was pleasing to God, honoring Him. He was better towards me. It had been a long time since there had been any physical abuse and Nate began talking about wanting another child, reminding me that I had always said I wanted two. I was not ready for this. Too many times I had been up and down on the Nate Newton Express and I was still holding my breath for another frightening drop. I couldn't even think about complicating things by bringing another baby into the picture. I continued faithfully taking my birth control pills, not wanting another child.

Nate's behavior was steadily improving, but still he had some occasional relapses into old habits. He was charged with a misdemeanor assault, accused of fondling a woman in a bar. He was found not guilty and the matter was dropped. There were no repercussions from this at home, and the rest of 1995 came and went without incident. The Cowboys had won another Super Bowl and Nate had gone to the Pro Bowl again. Throughout the whole year Nate was gentle with me. He was more responsive to Tre' and he seemed to be consistently working on improving himself and becoming a better man.

We spent time together in prayer and fellowship with some church leaders from Tre's school. Nate asked me to forgive him for his rocky past and how he had treated me. I struggled with fear and doubt, but I did forgive Nate. I opened up my heart and asked God to give me the strength to see Nate as he was meant to be, not as he had been. I wanted to give Nate a chance to truly change.

My heart began to soften around the edges. In time love's flame began to flicker again. God was dealing with me, speaking to me about betrayal and deception. He gently whispered my name and beckoned me to be whole again. I heard His call, but something inside of me was closed off. Painful memories I didn't want flooded my mind when I wasn't guarded. I wanted to let it all go, but I didn't seem to have the power to do it. I wanted to love Nate completely without any reservations. Things had been good for a long time, but part of me remained unresponsive and closed down.

Twenty

A NEW DAY

Though no one can go back and make a brand new start,
anyone can start now and make a brand new ending.

—CARL BARD

When Nate was angry about something he could argue for hours and hours until he was too tired to prove his point any longer. This same tenacity was present when he felt strongly about something and was operating from his convictions. It was now 1996 and Nate was better than ever.

Nate came to me one day and held my hand. He told me he knew he had done a lot of wrong things to me in the past—terrible things, unthinkable, and inexcusable. He told me I didn't deserve to be treated that way—that I had never deserved to be treated that way. He brought up all the times I stood by him when I could have walked away and told me that it meant a great deal to him.

255

"Dot, I'm sorry," he said, holding my hands tightly and looking me right in the eyes. "I'm so sorry. I love you and I have to change. I know I tell you all the time that I'm not perfect, but this time instead of telling you that I'm not perfect, I'm telling you that I want to be who God wants me to be. I want you to help me become that man. You have been through enough … Oh God, Dot, I'm sorry … you have to believe me …"

He sat there gripping my hands and never breaking his intense gaze. I could see that something was different. I had forgiven him and things had been good between us for some time, so something must have occurred inside for him to come to me with such a heartfelt plea for forgiveness. I believed him. I believed him with all my heart.

I took a deep breath, wanting desperately for him to be free from who he was. I didn't want to judge him by his past anymore. I didn't want to be afraid that the old Nate would surface again and spoil the peace.

I was grasping his hands tightly too. "I forgive you, Nate," I said, and I meant it. "I want you to be free. I want you to be a Christian—the man God wants you to be."

We hugged each other tightly and I cried tears of release. Hope stirred inside me, something I hadn't felt in a very, very long time.

I called T. Hayes to see if he knew what had happened to bring such an earnest conversation about. I don't know what happened, but T. Hayes confirmed that Nate was a changed man. He was communicating differently to everyone. He just wasn't the same guy. I began thanking God every day for Nate. I couldn't believe that things were finally good between us—permanently good.

One day I asked Nate for a new wedding ring. I didn't want any memory of how bad things had been. I wanted to forget it all and start fresh. Nate was very happy to do this and he bought a beautiful, expensive ring. I cried tears of joy, letting all the memory of physical abuse, other women, alcohol, and bad times fade away.

In July Nate came to me and said, "Dot, you always told me you wanted to have two children. I don't blame you if you don't ever want to have another child, but what do you think? What do you think about having another baby?"

I couldn't help but laugh. I knew he had been working this out in his mind before he ever came to me. Nate always had things figured out before he brought them up. Tre' had always wanted a brother or sister. He prayed and asked God about having one all the time. I had been taking birth control pills since Tre' was born, so he had seen me take them regularly and naturally asked me what they were for. I did my best to explain, but in Tre's mind, I was taking "birth pills" so I could get pregnant and have a baby. Sometimes he would come in my room and ask me if I had taken my pill so he could get his baby brother.

Things were good at home. Nate was a changed man, and I was a changed woman. Our marriage was strong. We spent time with other believers and there hadn't been any trouble with affairs or late nights or abuse in a long, long time. When Nate came to me and asked if I was ready to have another baby I didn't even question it. I didn't waver at all. "Absolutely!" I told him. It seemed infinitely clear to me that this was the right thing to do.

I stopped taking birth control pills, which worried young Tre'.

"Mommy," he would say, his little brow furrowed with concern, "If you don't take your pill I'm not going to have a brother or sister. You've got to take your pill!"

Before long I conceived and when I gave the happy news we all celebrated. We were excited about the prospect of a new baby. Nate was ecstatic. As soon as he was sure he was immediately on the radio telling everybody, "My wife is pregnant!"

I was so sick during the first trimester. I was nauseous and tired every day. It took a great deal of energy to keep up with Tre', but no matter how I felt I still made sure that everything Nate needed was taken care of. I couldn't wait each night until I was finally able to just crawl into bed and pray for a little sleep.

When I was three months pregnant, I started getting phone calls from a girl who said she was having an affair with Nate. I didn't want to believe it. At first, I just hung up on her, thinking that she was making crank calls or maybe wanting money out of Nate.

She continued to call the house, only now she was giving me details of her time with Nate—intimate details. I listened in horror, realizing that she must be in a relationship with Nate and here I was, pregnant and ill.

I confronted Nate about her and he blew up, furious. For the first time in a very long time, Nate got physical with me again. He shoved me against the wall and grabbed my throat with both hands, squeezing until I was gasping for air. He cursed at me and shouted and threw things. It was horrible … a nightmare. I couldn't believe it! *Again? How could this be happening again?* I crumpled into a heap on the floor sobbing. All the past rushed in like a flood, drowning my hope and reminding me that I was a complete fool for trusting this man.

The calls continued. Nate started staying out late and drinking. He was sullen and irritable whenever he was at home. I knew better than to say anything to him, but I was so disgusted and tired and angry that it would build up inside of me and I would blurt out something stupid like, "Who is she, Nathaniel?" and this would provoke a night of violent anger.

The days began to run together. When I was five months pregnant, Nate came stumbling in during the wee hours of the morning, demanding that I get up and make him something to eat. I was exhausted, too tired to move out of bed. Nate shoved me hard, making sure I was awake and couldn't ignore him. I had to get up early to get Tre' ready for school and make the hour drive, and I didn't want to get up. I sat up in bed and told Nate I was too tired. He pushed me off the bed and onto the floor, "Make me somethin' to eat!" he shouted. I was too tired to argue back. I got up in silence and went to the kitchen.

A few nights later he came in again. This time I didn't answer and I didn't open my eyes. I just laid there, clutching the covers, refusing to acknowledge him. This just frustrated him more. I squeezed my eyes shut and started to pray, and that made him *really* angry. It was a bad night.

This continued on a regular basis. Some nights I would get up and cook just to keep the peace. Some nights I was too irritable and started yelling back. In fact, I was beginning to yell at Nate all the time. I could barely stand the sight of him. I was furious that he waited until I was pregnant to have a relapse. I was angry with him and angry with myself for trusting him again. The abuse was back in full swing and there were nights I thought I would literally die. I worried about Tre'. I worried about who would take care of him if I died. I didn't want to leave him alone with Nate. I talked with Ingrid about it and she swore that she would make sure Tre' was taken care of if anything ever happened to me.

Tre' was old enough to understand what was going on now. It broke my heart that he could hear us fighting.

It scared me that he saw Nate shove me or choke me. I felt like a complete failure and just wanted to escape this horrible situation.

I told Nate one night that I was leaving him. I just couldn't live through this again. Whatever change he had made was totally erased and I didn't have the strength to live with him anymore. This made him furious. Nate threatened me. He told me if I dared to leave him, he would kill me. The look in his eyes was so severe. The hatred and disdain was palpable. I believed him. I believed he would kill me if I tried to go. I was frightened. It felt like ice water was running through my veins. My stomach was quivering and my hands were shaking.

I was desperate now. I cried out to God as I had before. I meditated on the Word and prayed for protection and strength. I prayed for a way of escape and that God would protect Tre' and help him to forget the horrible things he heard and saw.

"The Lord is my Shepherd. I shall not want."

God, I do want. I want to be free. I want to be safe. I am Your child. You promised to protect me.

**"He makes me lie down in green pastures.
He leads me beside still waters."**

*Yes, Lord. Please take me to green pastures. Please bring me
to still, peaceful waters.*

"He restoreth my soul."

*My soul is weary, God. My spirit is alive and filled with You,
but my flesh is totally spent and my soul cries out in despair.
Deliver me, God. Restore my soul.*

**"He leads me in the path of righteousness
for His name's sake."**

*God I need you to show me the path. I know there is a path
of righteousness for me even in this situation. Lead me there.
I'll go.*

I digested every sentence, trying to glean every bit of
meaning from David's psalm.

**"Yea, though I walk through the valley of
the shadow of death, I will fear no evil."**

*But I am afraid. I am so afraid of this evil. I feel as though I
am right in the center of death's dark shadowed valley. How do
I walk through it?*

"For thou art with me, thy rod and thy staff they comfort me."

Yes. You are with me. When Nate hits me, he's hitting You. You are with me every moment, with every breath. You see it all. You hear it all. You care for me. You comfort me. You must have a plan for me ...

"Thou preparest a table before me in the presence of mine enemies."

Is Nate my enemy, Lord? Or is Nate tormented and controlled by my real enemy? Your table is my provision ... even when I am in captivity and surrounded by betrayal, lies, deceit, violence, anger, and abuse. Your table is my protection, keeping me safe, keeping me alive so I can care for Tre' and protect my unborn child.

"Thou anointest my head with oil,"

God, I need Your healing. My mind—my head—needs to be healed. It is broken and bruised and weary and sad. Please let Your oil of gladness flow over me. Let Your healing balm flow. Anoint my head, Lord Jesus, anoint my head.

"My cup runneth over."

Yes, You have given me much to be thankful for. My cup runneth over with love for Tre' and the baby who is not yet even born. My cup runneth over with the goodness of friends who care for me. My cup runneth over with Your love. God, I love you. God, how I need you ...

**"Surely goodness and mercy shall
follow me all the days of my life:"**

Your goodness overwhelms me. Your mercy is never ending. Help me to understand. Help me to see, Lord. Let me feel your goodness and mercy and grant me many days to my life ...

"And I will dwell in the house of the LORD forever."

Yes, Lord. I will dwell with You forever and ever. I will never leave you. I will never forsake you. I will always call upon Your Name. You are my hiding place. You are my shield and my deliverer. You are my song. You are my strong tower. You are my refuge ...

I meditated on this passage daily and took strength from its words. I poured out my heart to God and gave Him all my sorrow and grief, doubt and fear. I fellowshipped with God in my suffering and I found comfort in His presence and in His care.

I never once blamed Him for what I was going through. I never once felt like He wasn't protecting me. I felt like I had placed myself in this situation—over and over again

I had made bad choices and the consequences were pain, suffering, and abuse.

Each day I drew comfort from God's Word. Each day I asked for His protection over my life, over Tre', and over our baby. My energy was totally spent. I knew if my situation was going to change, it would absolutely take God's intervention.

Twenty-One

THE LAST STRAW

*It is devastating to be abused by someone you
love and think loves you in return.*

—DIANNE FEINSTEIN

Nate had not come home for several nights. He was
not at home as I stood over Tre's bed, watching him sleep.
He was so peaceful, lying there with his little hands
cupped under his cheek. *Such a handsome boy,* I thought to
myself. Love for him welled up inside of me and I reached
down to stroke his head. Just then the baby kicked me, as
if he was jealous of the attention I was giving his brother.
I patted my stomach and admonished him, "Stop that,
now. I love you too little one. Don't you ever think Mama
doesn't love you with all her heart."

Tre' rolled over and his brow furrowed. A moment
before he had been totally peaceful, but now his face

looked troubled and he was restless, as if he was having a bad dream. I knelt down beside him, remembering how many bad dreams I had known in my childhood. I knew what it was like to be afraid for your mother. I knew what it was like to wish your daddy would stop yelling, stop hurting her …

I ached inside. I never wanted my children to know the fear I felt as a child. I never wanted their dreams to become nightmares. I crawled into Tre's bed and held him close, tears streaming down my face.

"God," I prayed, "watch over my children and protect them from harm. Let them learn to love you with all their heart, soul, mind, and strength. Show me a way of escape. Keep me from the bondage of unforgiveness. I belong to you, Lord. Nate belongs to you. This isn't right. This isn't your plan for us. Guide me now. I don't know what to do. I need You … "

I laid there praying off and on throughout the night, stroking my stomach with one hand and cuddling Tre' with the other. Remarkably, the night passed in peace. There was no argument with Nate, no demands, just God's peace—a respite from the storm. I didn't know how, but I knew God was going to take care of us. I knew this suffering would not last for always.

I was concerned for Tre'. I knew what he was going through all too well. I knew the deep fear and anxiety that came from watching someone you love battered and abused. No child should have to feel like they are on guard, watching and waiting for something bad to happen, never knowing what will trigger the abuse, never quite feeling safe. I wanted him to know that prayer had the power to change things. I wanted him to know that kneeling at the feet of Jesus would always give him the strength and power to do whatever needed to be done.

On our long commute to school each morning, I prayed with Tre'. I talked to him and tried to give him a safe place to vent what he was feeling. He was free to talk about anything and everything. I was strong for him. I did my best to explain things and share how God protected me and watched over us. I sometimes felt guilty that I had put him in a position to experience this pain, but I was so proud of how he handled things and how open he remained with me. We developed clear communication with each other and a lasting trust was established. During this season, our relationship grew strong and deep—a relationship that would last forever.

I was still working for Nate arranging appearances and things. As Nate's popularity increased, I needed to work more closely with Valerie, Nate's publicist. She was a nice, sweet Christian lady and I enjoyed working with her. We talked often coordinating Nate's calendar and keeping the schedule straight. In a moment when I was vulnerable, I confided in her that things were bad at home. She was kind and understanding and tried to reassure me that it didn't have to be that way. She thought it might help if she mentioned it to someone inside the Cowboy organization. She was sure they would intervene and make sure that Nate got the help he needed and that I would be protected. Suddenly I was frightened that I had told her. What if it got back to Nate? I told her that she could tell no one. She might think it was going to help me, but it would only make things worse. I regretted telling her. I hadn't meant to, it just sort of came out. I wasn't myself these days—tired, bruised, swollen ... being pregnant was compounding things and I wasn't as young as I once was.

It had been a bad night. Nate had come home very late and the abuse was worse than usual. I dropped Tre' off at school and sat in my car for a moment, wondering about what I should do next. When Nate first woke up, he was not usually violent. In fact, even if we had been through a bad night, he often didn't seem to remember what had happened. I was never quite sure what to expect, what it would be like. I was exhausted beyond belief and my body was sore all over—like one giant bruise, so I put the car in gear and headed for home. Nate was still sleeping so I went into Tre's room to lie down. I set an alarm just in case I fell asleep, wanting to be sure I had enough time to shower and dress before I left again to pick Tre' up from school.

I felt better when I woke up and the sun was shining as I pulled out of the driveway headed for Fort Worth Christian. *Why do I put up with this?* I asked myself. *Why don't I just leave him? Once and for all ... leave him? It isn't my fault that Nate beats me. It isn't my fault that he sleeps with other women. I don't deserve this. Tre' doesn't deserve this. I can't bring another baby into this horrible situation. I can't!*

271

Just then my cell phone rang and it startled me. It was Nate. I stared at it, frightened that Nate knew what I was thinking. I swallowed hard and answered, "Hello."

"Where you at?" Nate said.

"I'm on my way to pick up Tre'," I replied. It was silent on the other end.

"Nate," I said …

"Nate, why are you treating me this way? Why are you doing all this?"

It was as if something had uncorked inside of me. "I can't do this anymore. I won't do this anymore. I'm leaving you. Don't worry, I'm not gonna run to the media or anything. I won't tell a soul what has happened, but I have to go. I just have to go …"

"Nate," I said firmly, but my body was shaking, "I want a divorce."

Nate was furious with me. He started shouting. I couldn't believe I had told him what I was thinking. It's a good thing the route was so familiar, because I know I wasn't paying attention to the road, it was like the car was driving itself.

Nate ranted for a few minutes and then told me we would talk when I got home, and I *better* come home. He was yelling and cursing, "Who did you go tellin' my business to?"

I froze. *Oh God,* I thought, *did Valerie …?*

"Don't make me come and find you. If I have to, I will. If I have to come find you, I'll kill you," Nate snarled and hung up.

I was terrified. I picked up Tre' and thought about just driving away, but I was too afraid. I knew Nate would never lay a hand on Tre', at least I didn't think he would—he had become such a wild card, but I was certain that I was in for a very rough night ahead. I knew if I didn't go home he would find me.

I called Valerie. "Did you tell anybody?" I asked. "Who did you tell?"

Valerie was stunned. She was very upset. She felt like someone needed to reach out and help me. She meant to help. She didn't realize how desperate my situation was.

Without thinking I drove to Ingrid's house. She would know what to do. I arrived a total mess. She could tell I was upset. We sent the boys to another room to play. I wrote a letter that if I turned up dead, it was because Nate had killed me. I made her promise not to read it, but if anything happened to me she had to take it to the police. She promised and I watched her put it in her safe. I was scared that I was going to die. I was afraid of what would happen to Tre' if I died.

"Ingrid," I said. "You must promise me that if anything ever happens to me you will raise Tre'. I don't want him to grow up with Nate if I'm not there."

She promised me that she would take Tre' and raise him. I was worried that since she had never told Monte about my situation he might not agree to take Tre' from Nate. I knew how charming Nate was to everybody else and I could see him telling Monte that I had gone crazy or something and I was sure Nate would get his way. I made Ingrid write it down that she would take him. I made her sign it and give me a copy and then I watched her put her copy in the safe. I let out a sigh of relief. Tre' would be okay.

Ingrid didn't cry, but her countenance betrayed her sadness. I knew she was scared for me. I sat in her home, thinking that if my family knew what I was going through, they would risk everything to protect me, but they didn't know. I thought about my aunt in Virginia, I knew she would help me, but she didn't know either. Sheila, Bug, … many names came to mind, but no one knew I was in danger. I hadn't told anyone and now it was too late. Nate was going to kill me, I was sure of it.

"You promise me you will take Tre'," I said to Ingrid.

"Yes, yes of course I will," Ingrid said, her eyes were completely sincere and her face was filled with concern.

"You should not go back there," she said. "Stay here. Don't go home."

"I have to," I said. "I have to go back, you don't understand."

"You don't understand," I repeated, "I have to reassure him that I have not gone to the police. He told me I have to bring Tre' home. I have to go …"

I collected Tre' and drove back home. I tried to prepare him.

"Tre'," I said.

"Yes, Mama?" he replied.

"When we get home, I want you to stay in the car until I come back outside to get you okay?"

"Why?" he asked.

"Listen baby, I'm going to turn on some music for you. You just put your little headphones on and pretend like you're driving the car. Can you do that? Your daddy is really upset about some things and I don't want you to come inside until he calms down."

"Okay," he said. It was like any other day to Tre'. He was used to daddy being angry and mommy getting hurt. He had learned to hide and be quiet and wait until the storms blew over. It was sad.

We were almost home. An icy calm settled over me. I expected the worst. I didn't even mind except that I cared so much about Tre'. If Nate killed me, I would be with Jesus and no longer suffering … if only Tre' … I couldn't think about it or I would break down and cry. I felt the baby kick and I was sorry I would never get to hold him in my arms … so sorry …

I put the car in park and took the keys out of the ignition. I got out Tre's music and his headphones and told him to wait for me in the car, not to come inside. I looked at him and hugged him hard. I kissed him on top of the head and slipped out of the car. Slowly I walked through the front door, not knowing what to expect. *Would he beat me?*

Would he shoot me? I didn't even think we had a gun in the house, but there was one in the guest house.

I walked into the kitchen, shaking. I was frightened. I didn't know what to expect this time, but I knew it was different than before. Nate was already there.

"What the f____ are you doing?" he shouted.

"What do you mean?" I answered.

"You know what I mean. If you *ever* tell *anyone* my business *ever* again … I'll kill you."

I sat down at the table, preparing for a rant. "I'm tired of this, Nate. I want to be free from you. Can't you just let me be free from you? Free to go on?"

"The only freedom you're ever gonna get is if I kill you!" he said, and I saw the gun lying on the counter. It was the rifle he used to shoot snakes when he was out with the dogs.

I just stared at the gun. Nate followed my gaze and his lips curled into a snarl. He wanted me to be afraid.

He started shouting again and moved toward the table. The table was custom made from heavy, beveled glass. I was sitting at the end of the table in front of the large picture window in the dining room. Nate grabbed the edge of the table and shoved it toward me. Pure instinct made me scoot back as fast as I could, fearing the table would plunge into my stomach and hurt the baby. The table just grazed my stomach as I scrambled out of the way. It came crashing to the floor, breaking the granite tile as it struck with a heavy thud.

I stared at the table in disbelief. He could have hurt the baby. Explosive anger welled up inside of me. Adrenalin rushed through my body and hot, angry words came to the surface.

"You're sick!" I shouted at him, looking at the mess on the floor. "You are sick, Nathaniel Newton! What is wrong with you?"

Nate glared at me and started walking toward the counter, toward the gun.

"Enough is enough," I screamed. "I am going to the police. We have a child together, Nathaniel. We have another child on the way. Do you want to hurt the baby? What do you think you are doing? I am going to the authorities … do you hear me, I am calling the police!" I was still sitting in the dining room chair where I had scooted to avoid being hit by the table.

Quick as a flash Nate had the gun in his hands, pointed at me. I froze.

"What are you doing?" I asked, shaking.

"I'm going to kill you, that's what," Nate said, leveling the gun right between my eyes.

I held my breath, waiting for him to pull the trigger. *Oh God,* I prayed silently, *don't let Tre' find me here like this ...*

Nate held the gun pointed at my face. I don't know how long he stood there, but neither one of us said a word. I was shaking all over, tears streaming down my face. I could hear my heart pounding in my ears and I felt like I was going to faint. I wanted to run but my feet were glued to the floor—I couldn't move.

Nate kept the barrel pointed steady between my eyes, then he moved the barrel a few inches to the right and pulled the trigger, smashing a bullet through the window behind me, shattering it into a million pieces.

I screamed and fell to the floor, grabbing my ears. "Nate!" I screamed.

"You won't call the police. I'll kill you first," he said and rushed out the door, jumped in his vehicle, and sped off.

I don't know how long I knelt on the floor, but I suddenly panicked, wondering where Tre' was. *Did Nate take Tre'?*

I went outside and Tre' was not in the car. *Where was he?* I ran back in the house. *Did he see anything?* I called for him, "Tre'!"

"Tre' come here!" I shouted.

Tre' came running toward me and I scooped him up and held him tightly. We got in the car and drove away, glass was shattered all over the place. There was a gaping hole where the window should have been. I shuddered as I put the car in reverse.

I called T. Hayes and told him what had happened.

"Are you okay? Are you hurt?" he asked, concern thick in his voice.

"I'm fine," I said, convincing no one.

"Don't stay there right now," he said. "Why don't you come here for awhile?"

Dutifully, I obeyed. I didn't have the energy to make any decisions on my own. His wife, Lisa, was also expecting a baby and I knew if I went there I would be safe. Sooner or later I knew Nate would call T. Hayes, he always did.

Tre' was quiet in the car beside me. I don't think he saw anything, but he must have heard the shot. He didn't say a word and I didn't trust myself to speak to him about it.

I called Randy, our builder and said as nonchalantly as I could, "Randy, can you go over to the house and take care of something for me?"

"Sure," he said, "what's up?"

"There's some shattered glass at the house … " I took a deep breath, "… in the kitchen…" my voice broke.

"You okay?" he asked.

"Uh-huh," I managed, "thanks, Randy." I hung up and drove to T. Hayes' house.

The next day Randy called. "Are you okay, Dorothy?" he asked.

"I'm fine," I said.

"I found shot gun shells on the floor," he said. "Are you sure you're okay?"

"I'm fine," I said again. "Are you at my house now?"

"Yes, I'm just finishing up. I have taken care of everything good as new."

"Is Nate there?" I asked.

"No, ma'am, he isn't," Randy replied. "Do you need something?"

"No ... no, I'm just fine, Randy. Thanks for everything," I said and hung up. I didn't want to go back to the house until T. Hayes had heard from Nate. He would know when it was safe.

I took Tre' to school the next day and called T. Hayes before driving back to the house. The window was fixed like nothing had ever happened. There were two shotgun shells sitting on the counter. Randy had put the table back up on the pedestal and the only visible evidence of the trauma was a chip in the granite floor where the table had fallen and another chip missing from the beveled edge of the table where it had struck the floor. An uneasiness was in the air, thick and foreboding. I prayed and thanked God that I was alive. I asked for His guidance. I knew I couldn't stay with Nate anymore. From T. Hayes I gathered that he had cleared out, so I knew I had a little time to think and figure things out.

I looked around my house—our house. We had known happiness here. It hadn't been that long ago that things were good between us. I thought about Nate's excitement when I announced I was pregnant and the tears came pouring out—silent tears that no one saw or heard but God.

Twenty-Two

HUMILIATION

Grace grows best in the winter of our soul.
—SAMUEL RUTHERFORD

*I*t was three weeks before I saw Nate again. He turned up to tell me he was going to Florida to train with a bicyclist there to get in shape before training camp began. I didn't care. I was glad he would be gone and I could figure out what to do. I didn't have any money of my own and didn't have access to any of Nate's money—I didn't even know how much he had.

I found out that he was seeing another woman in Florida but the news didn't shock me. The woman who had been calling me to tell me about her affair with Nate started calling again, but now she was different, angry with Nate.

I don't know why, but I contacted Nate in Florida and told him, "I don't know what's going on, but I think you are about to have legal problems with this girl."

A week later, Nate came home and apologized to me for his behavior. He wanted to work things out between us.

"No," I told him, emotionless, "I really just want you out of my life. The sooner you go to training camp, the better, that way I don't have to see you."

Nate apologized again. "We can work this out …" he began.

"No, Nathaniel, we can't." I said. "I'm leaving you. I don't care if you kill me. I have it worked out so Tre' will be taken care of. I am prepared to die. If you hurt me again I will go to the authorities and get help. I have already spoken with an attorney and you are going to be served with divorce papers. You can take whatever you want—I don't want anything from you, I just want out! You can kill me if you want to, but I have already told the attorney that you plan to do that, so go right ahead, the police will know it was premeditated."

Nate was enraged. He pushed me up against the wall and struck me. I crumpled down, crouching on the floor to protect my stomach and Nate kicked me. "I'm having to deal with enough right now, b___!" he shouted. "I can't be bothered with you too, do you hear me?"

"This girl is trying to threaten me. I need you now, Dot. Just when I need you, you think you gonna leave? No … you're not gonna be there? You gonna walk away from me like everybody else?" he shouted.

I packed some things for Tre' and I left. I headed to Louisiana. Nate didn't try to stop me. I had obviously not called the police or the media, so I guess he figured I wouldn't say anything to my family either. He was used to me keeping my mouth shut and remaining the dutiful wife. I always came back.

I contemplated telling my family. While I was driving to see them, I rehearsed my story. When I actually got to them, I couldn't go through with it. I don't know why, I just couldn't do it. Everyone kept asking about Nate and wondering how he was doing—they all loved him. Why wouldn't they? He had always been so nice to them … they had no idea that he was a different person behind closed doors. I couldn't seem to make myself tell them I was in trouble, even though I desperately wanted their help.

While there, Tre' became ill. He got so sick that I had to take him to a hospital in New Orleans. We were there all day and when he was discharged I took him to my mother's place in Buras, sixty miles away. Nate called and I told him about Tre'. He told me the woman was filing a lawsuit against him, accusing him of rape. He begged me to come home. He pleaded with me, telling me how much he needed me. He promised if I would come home and see him through the trial he would give me a divorce.

I wanted that divorce. I was paying an attorney $250 per hour and I didn't know where I was going to find the money if Nate contested. Holding out the divorce was the right bait for me. I wanted it and if Nate was willing to set me free, then I would go home and deal with whatever I had to in order to buy my freedom.

The media was stirred up. The woman accused Nate of sexual assault and it was embarrassing for both of us. It made the national news and I was humiliated. I went back home and Nate disappeared to escape the media frenzy. I don't know where he went, but he wasn't around and I didn't care. I was growing closer to term and my focus was on taking care of Tre' and the baby.

I hardly heard from Nate the last few weeks of my pregnancy. I was so sick, it seemed like all my energy was used up going back and forth to the doctor. I was scheduled to be induced on July 15th. Nate called the weekend before and asked about when I thought I might go into labor. I had no idea whether he would show up or not—it didn't matter to me. I didn't care if he was there or not. I wanted Ingrid to be with me in the delivery room. She was a steady, constant, loving force in my life and I wanted her by my side. When I was with her my heart was lighter, my troubles melted, and I felt strong and free. I wanted my mother, too. I needed her support. I arranged for her to come and stay with me so she and Ingrid could be in the delivery room with me and be around to help out with Tre'.

I went to the hospital for my appointment and Nate showed up. I was so disappointed ... *why had he come?* I couldn't deny his rights as the father, so he came into the delivery room with me and Ingrid and my mom waited outside. The delivery room is still a blur to me, but when it was all over I had a healthy baby boy weighing in at 10 pounds, 2 ½ ounces. The same feelings of awe, wonder, and unconditional love washed over me just as it had when Tre' was born. When I held my little boy everything else receded. Nothing else was as important as taking care of this little one and loving him with all my heart. I still didn't have a name for him, and I had promised Tre' that he could name the baby since he had prayed for one with such unwavering faith.

When Tre' saw his brother in the hospital nursery he said without even thinking, "I know what we can name him."

"What?" I asked, chuckling at his enthusiasm.

"We can name him King 'cause he looks like he's the king of the nursery!"

"King it is!" I said, laughing. I had no qualms with the name King because the greatest king I knew was the King of Kings, Jesus Christ, son of the living God. Tre's excitement could not be contained, he was overjoyed to have a brother of his very own. He was so proud that his brother was bigger than all the other babies. He couldn't wait to hold him and wanted to know when we could take him home. Tre' named King, but Nate also wanted the baby to have his name too, so we settled on Nate King Newton for this special baby boy. I celebrated his arrival with true joy. Baby King was a gift from God—this was undeniable.

I was released from the hospital and went home. Nate went off to training camp, so there was peace while I recovered from delivering King. When he was just six weeks old, Nate came home from training camp for a court appearance regarding the woman's accusation of sexual assault. I received a subpoena to appear in court as a witness. Because I had received so many calls from this woman, giving me details about their trips together and how he took care of her and her child, my testimony was needed to prove that they were in a consensual relationship. The woman had been harassing me with phone calls from the time I was three months pregnant with King. I was humiliated to do this and upset that I had to leave King and go down to the courthouse to testify on Nate's behalf.

I arrived at the scheduled time and stood outside the court room, waiting for my turn to go in. Nate stood outside with his attorney, but neither of them engaged me in any conversation. Never once had I been given any details about the trial or Nate's part in the relationship with the woman. I never asked about anything and

Nate never volunteered anything. I felt hollow inside, no emotion, just numb. I didn't really care what happened to Nate. I didn't believe he had raped the woman, but I honestly could not manage to find any warm or concerned feelings for him. I was filled with disgust for him. I was just so happy he was away at training camp—I wanted nothing to do with him.

I was called into a room with the jury. It was not the courtroom, but a private room. I was told to tell exactly what it was that I had been experiencing with the plaintiff and I gave all the information as it had happened. I also told the people in the room that Nate and I were experiencing serious marital problems, but I believed God would fight that battle for me. I told them that it was important for me to be able to separate those things and focus on the facts at hand. I asked them to concentrate on the facts relevant to the case and not on his status as a cheating husband. I told them that I did not believe this was a case of rape, but that it had been consensual. I told them I was upset—very upset—but the truth is what it is, I did not believe Nate had raped this woman.

When I came out of the room, I was completely convinced that Nate would not be convicted. I just knew it.

"What happened in there?" Nate asked.

"Don't worry," I said, "you'll be free as usual."

Nate and his attorney finally had a conversation with me, a detailed conversation that made me sick to my stomach. I was shocked. I shouldn't have been shocked after everything I had been through with Nate, but I was shocked nevertheless. I was speechless. I stared at Nate like he was a total stranger. I wanted him to stay away from me forever. I wanted to leave that courthouse and have it all be over. I walked away from them and went to the restroom. I kept my distance from them until I was free to go.

I left the courthouse and drove to Ingrid's house to pick up six-week old King. She asked me to come inside and I sat down in a chair, wanting to cry, but I couldn't. My tears had dried up. I had no feeling whatsoever. Inside I was crumbling, but on the outside my tears were damned up, no longer able to flow. I was drowning in sorrow, but unable to cry anymore.

Ingrid and her mother were in the room with me, but I was unable to speak. I couldn't tell them anything. They didn't know what to say to me and I couldn't find any words to say to them. I just kept thinking to myself, *I can't believe my baby is six week's old—Nate's baby—and I am in the courthouse to defend him over sleeping with another woman. I can't believe it …*

Nate was not convicted. We had been through so much in the last six months I thought to myself, *surely nothing else will happen.* Things were calm, Nate kept his distance from me, I suppose giving me time to get over having to testify on his behalf against his lover. I used the calm to approach Nate.

"I think it is best if we just go our separate ways. I need to be free of this marriage—it isn't really much of a marriage anyway. I will take care of the boys. If you will just help me out with three months rent, I will be able to get a job by then and won't need anything else from you. You owe me that much, Nate," I said.

"Dot … just wait awhile. Just a little while. Can you just wait a little while? Everything is going to be better," he replied.

I let out a deep, heavy sigh. I knew he wasn't going to give me a divorce. I knew he wasn't going to give me rent or money for childcare. How was I going to find a job and move away from him without some help? I felt totally trapped. Powerless to change my situation.

No one knew what I was experiencing. Even Ingrid and T. Hayes didn't know everything. People assumed I had a lot of money. I knew it wouldn't make sense to any of my friends if I went to them to ask for financial help. I thought of going to Ingrid, and I know she would gladly have helped—but how could she give me money without telling Monte what it was for. I didn't want him to know. *You're on your own,* I said to myself. *Just you and God.*

From that day on, I prayed more than ever before. I asked God to help me change things in my life. I trusted no one. I had lived my entire life being afraid. I had lived in fear, placing Nate's needs, Nate's career, Nate's wants ahead of everything else. Something inside of me was twisted and broken so much so that I thought more of Nate than of my own safety. I felt like I had done something to deserve the abuse—like I had to pay for my past sins. I was too afraid to go to the police. I knew if I did, Nate would worm his way out of any trouble, he always did. The rules were different for him. He was a celebrity. I thought about all the trouble he had caused, yet he managed to escape from suffering any real consequences from his actions. Every time ... not guilty, not convicted ... I felt like every effort on my part was completely futile.

No one really knew what life was like for me behind those closed doors. Ingrid and T. Hayes had some idea, but even what they knew was limited and filtered. To my friends and the world around me, I lived a dream life. I was married to a celebrity, professional athlete. We had money. We had a nice home. We had nice cars. Nate was the life of the party, showering everyone with gifts, giving them what they wanted and treating them well—it was all they cared about, what they could *get* from Nate.

Nate was the star. I was the trusty side-kick, part of the package. I can't remember anyone asking how I was doing, if I was happy, was I alright? The attention was always on Nate. I lived a lie—a double life. I played my role as devoted, faithful wife well in public, so no one ever suspected a thing—never knew I was miserable, broken and bruised, crying out for deliverance and desperate to escape.

Why didn't I tell my family? Surely if I had made my situation known they would have stepped in and intervened. I was too frightened to take the chance. Nate had threatened to kill me if I told anyone his business, and the image of him pointing that gun at my head was as fresh in my memory as the day it happened.

Growing up I promised myself to never get in the same situation my mother was in—trapped by economics, unable to escape because she was financially dependent on my abusive stepfather. Here I was, repeating history. I took the good with the bad and prayed for a way out.

Twenty-Three

MY SHIELD

God is my defender. He loves me and goes in front of me.
—PSALM 59:9b-10a NCV

$\mathscr{I}$lived my life going through the motions. The cycle of abuse—verbal, physical, sexual, rotated with cycles of calm—Nate keeping his distance, Nate promising to change, Nate going through some trauma. I found a way to separate myself into two people. I was one way with Nate. I did what I had to do. Whatever he asked of me or demanded from me, I found some way to comply. Sometimes I yelled back and said horrible things, sometimes I struggled against him, and sometimes I just gave in like a wounded dog, but I did what I had to do to survive.

The other me lived a totally different life. When I left the house, I tucked away that abused, weary, broken Dorothy and put on the strong, tender, kindhearted Dorothy that cared deeply about other people's pain and reached out in any way I could. When I spent time with Ingrid I was a different person. When I spent time with people I was a different person. When I spent time alone with God, He strengthened me and filled me and taught me things about my own character and my own faults. He spoke to me about my hatred and the bondage I was in.

I prayed, "Lord, please keep me safe from all danger and harm. Help me to have a better attitude and plenty of gratitude. Lord, please make the best of each and every day to clear my mind so I can truly hear from you. Broaden my mind so I can accept what you are saying to me. Lord, help me not to whine and whimper over the things I have no control over. Renew my mind so I won't feel guilty about all the bad choices I have made that led me here. God, help me with the right response when I am pushed beyond my limits, help me in those moments just to trust You. Lord, I know that even when I cannot pray, you listen to my heart … so remove the hatred that is lurking there. Cleanse me from it. Cleanse me with Your goodness, Your kindness, Your fruit of the spirit."

I kept praying, "Lord, please continue to bless me even though times are hard for me right now—really hard. My struggles, trials, and tribulations are beyond belief right now and only You really know what they are. God, help me through them so I can be a blessing to others some day. Keep me strong so that I will not give up, Lord. Keep me uplifted that I may have words of encouragement for others, even during this time. Let your Word be in my heart and in my mouth."

And in earnest, passionately I continued, "God, I pray for those who are lost and cannot find their way to you. I feel like I am lost right now. I am in the wilderness and I haven't been able to find my way in a long, long time. I need Your guidance. Lead me in the path that brings me closest to You. Lord, I believe in You. I believe You can change people and You can change things. Bring a change in my life ... bring it quickly, please hasten. I pray now, today, for peace, love, joy, and I pray that you will bring a change quickly. I will not give up. I will not give in. I am Your child. I do not have the strength to take any more, to carry this burden one moment longer. I need you. I need you *now*."

I repeated this prayer over and over and it gave me peace. I meditated on the Book of Acts, where Paul and Silas were in prison, their backs beaten badly, their feet shackled, and yet at midnight, they sang praises to God and worshipped Him—even in the middle of their horrible, hopeless situation. They sang praises to God even when they were powerless to set themselves free. This was me! I could sing praises to God in the midst of my situation and His peace came upon me and surpassed all my understanding. I felt just like Paul and Silas, it didn't matter, I would be okay.

I began to spend more time asking for forgiveness and less time pleading for mercy. I started listening more and talking less. I learned how to be still. Tentatively, I began trusting God. Ingrid and I continued studying the Bible together and attended Bible studies during the day while the kids were in school. We spent time together, feeding our spirits in the Word. This kept me encouraged—it kept me alive.

God spoke to my heart. He had been speaking all along, but I was finally still enough to hear His voice. God's goodness penetrated my heart, penetrated my spirit, and change took root inside of me. Nate's antics no longer had the same effect. It was like I lived inside a bubble of God's peace. I controlled every word that came out of my mouth, every move that I made, I concentrated on God's Word. I thought about God giving His only Son so I could have eternal life and this comforted me.

When I thought about not being able to make it on my own supporting two kids, when I was filled with regret over giving up my career to support Nate, I quoted Philippians 4:19, "But my God shall supply all your need according to his riches in glory by Christ Jesus." When I felt too weary to go on, I called up Matthew 11:28-30, "Come unto me, all ye that labour and are heavy laden, and I will give you rest. Take my yoke upon you, and learn of me; for I am meek and lowly in heart: and ye shall find rest unto your souls. For my yoke is easy, and my burden is light." I committed Scripture to memory and inscribed it on the tablets of my heart. It was my weapon. It was my shield.

I prayed diligently for Tre', concern growing about how our home life was affecting him. He was, for the most part, a happy-go-lucky child. He was very smart and very protective of me and King. Still, there was too much heaviness on a boy so young. He had seen too much. He had heard things no little boy should ever have to hear, and I was worried about what kind of man he would grow up to be. Would he solve his problems by lashing out in selfish anger? Was history doomed to repeat itself? I prayed that it would not. I spoke words of life over him. I prayed over him and declared good things over his future. I declared that he and King would grow up to love God with all their heart, soul, mind, and strength and not repeat my mistakes, not repeat Nate's mistakes. I loved these little boys with a fierce, protective love that words could not describe. They filled my life with purpose and gave me a mission greater than mere survival.

Twenty-Four

DIVORCE

If the numbers we see in domestic violence were applied to terrorism or gang violence, the entire country would be up in arms, and it would be the lead story on the news every night.

—REP. MARK GREEN

The 1997 season began and Nate was calm with me. It was almost as if we were living separately under the same roof. I never asked him about the details of anything going on with his life outside our home. He was getting into trouble more frequently—DUI's, car accidents, he even faced a misdemeanor for disorderly conduct after a loud argument in a Fort Worth restaurant with a fan seeking out his autograph. I kept my distance from these things and did my best not to get too involved.

During this season of calm, I approached Nate, "I think it is best if we go our separate ways. I think I need to be free from the marriage. We can each just go our own path. I'll take care of the boys. You can keep all the money ... just help me out with three months rent while I get a job."

"Dot ... just wait a while. Just wait a little while. Everything is going to be better," was Nate's answer. I knew he didn't want me to leave. I knew he wouldn't give me a divorce. I knew in his own twisted way he loved me, but I wanted out. I didn't want to live a double life anymore.

The Cowboys had a "White House" scandal sometime during all this. There was a house located near the team's Valley Ranch practice facility where some of the players brought women for sex and had frequent parties. When questioned about this by the Star-Telegram, Nate removed all doubt about his involvement, "We got a little place over here where we're running whores in and out, trying to be responsible, and we're criticized for that too." I was disgusted.

My humiliation seemed to know no end. I was constantly embarrassed by Nate's public behavior, but I stood by him no matter what. It seemed like every time I approached him about leaving, he got into some crisis again and needed me. I would feel guilty and stay to see him through.

His temper was unpredictable. We had seasons of relative calm, and seasons of violence where he would curse and be verbally abusive, push me, shove me, grab me by the throat ... I just never knew exactly what to expect. I drew closer and closer to God for my strength. It seemed like the worse things were for me physically and emotionally, the more my spirit soared. I was filled with the Holy Spirit and He was indeed, my Comforter. No matter how bad things were with Nate, my soul was at peace with God. Nate had no control there. He couldn't spoil it. He couldn't interrupt it. He couldn't harm it. I lived on the Word of God. It sustained me. The worse things got, the deeper I dug my well of living water, the further down I put my roots in Christ. *I shall not be moved. I shall not be shaken. Jesus is my rock, my shelter, my fortress, my strong tower. In Him will I trust. I will not be afraid, neither shall I fear. He is my refuge. He is my all in all* ... I felt closer and closer to God.

Nate knew I was close to God. When it came to this area of my life, he still had me on a pedestal. There was almost a reverence coming from him over my relationship with God—he never wanted to mess with that. He counted on the fact that I prayed, and on rare occasions still asked me to pray for him, though he wasn't willing to pray on his own. God was reserved for "good" people who already had their act together.

Nate was involved in another affair. Once he was careful to protect me from knowing about them, but he had grown careless with the evidence. Not only was he coming home in the wee hours of the morning, I found condoms, notes, receipts ... I began collecting these items, wanting to have physical proof of his indiscretions so I would at last be able to leave, even if he wasn't willing to consent to a divorce.

A few times I asked him about other women, but Nate always denied that anything was going on between him and another woman. Any time I mentioned it, he got very angry. He would shout profanities, shove me around, and threaten worse things—it would last for hours. I don't even know why I asked him about it. I knew what he was doing, even if I didn't know who it was with. I knew he was unfaithful and had probably been so our entire life together. When he wanted sex, I was frightened. *What if he gives me a disease?* I thought. I didn't want to be with him that way. He was demanding and controlling. It hurt me. I didn't trust him. I was deeply wounded.

In the summer of 1998 just before Nate went off to training camp I found evidence of yet another relationship. I became enraged. Nate came in and I lost all my fear of him. I screamed at him. Accused him. I was crying and shouting and storming around the room. It took Nate completely off guard—he wasn't used to this behavior from me. It was completely foreign. He grabbed me by my arms to bring me under control.

"F_____ you!" I screamed.

It was like I had thrown ice water on him, he was so startled. I *never* used that kind of language and it shocked him.

"Dot," he said, his face contorted, "Dot … what's wrong with you? That's not like you. Calm down, now. Calm down …"

"That's right," I said through clenched teeth, "I said it … f_____ you!"

Nate was mortified. He shook me, "Get hold of yourself, Dot! Settle down!" He let me go and I crumpled into a heap on the floor.

"Who am I?" I said, almost in a whisper. I was genuinely frightened at my own anger. This wasn't me.

Could I hurt him? I wondered. I shuddered. *Yes. I could.* In fact, I wanted to.

I shuddered again, trying to shake myself out of whatever it was that had taken hold of me. I went to my room, got on my face and began praying. I knew I could never give in to that anger again. I rolled over looking up to heaven, "God, You've got to do something spectacular to get me out of this situation. I don't ever want to feel this way again. I never want to lose control like that again. Help me, Jesus. Help me now …"

I never did act like that again, but the memory of my own anger in that moment stayed with me. It shook me up. It was proof that I could allow Nate to change who I was and that was power I didn't want him to have.

Once again I found refuge in God. I poured out all that anger at His feet, asking Him to bear burdens that were too heavy for me to carry. I sought His mercy and found it. I felt Him lift the load and promise to always be with me. He poured out His grace and comforted my weary heart.

1999 came and Nate was cut from the Cowboys. It was a crushing blow to him and he worked to get a contract with the Carolina Panthers. Tre' was having frequent stomach pains. He was troubled by things at home, and I took him to the doctor regularly, concerned about the stress he was managing. It seemed wrong for a boy his age to bear so much. I wanted him and King to have normal lives, not live under dark, stormy clouds of anger and dysfunction.

Nate got the contract and announced that we were moving to North Carolina. This was my way out! I told Nate, "No. I can't take the boys to Carolina. Tre' is involved in sports and has good teachers, taking him out of school is not good for him. Think of Tre'. We need to stay here."

Miraculously, I convinced Nate that I should stay behind in Texas with the boys while he moved to Carolina. My heart lifted. It felt as if God had stepped in and offered me a way of escape. I was rescued! I could use this time to find a job and get established. I knew this was the beginning of my breakthrough.

Tre' attended school Monday through Friday and he played football on Saturdays, so we only went to North Carolina on holidays. We couldn't go watch Nate play all the games. I didn't want to go. I was happy on my own with the boys. Another American Express bill came to the house and I saw charges for airline tickets back and forth to Carolina ... another woman. I didn't care. At least I was safe. I was spending time with Ingrid and other friends. I was involved in Bible study and enjoying "normal" life. I felt lighthearted. If Nate needed another woman in Carolina so I could stay at home, so be it.

At Christmas Nate demanded I come see him and bring the boys. I couldn't think of any good reason why we couldn't go, so I packed them up and flew out to meet him. When I arrived and began unpacking, I found female jewelry at his place. Right there in plain sight was proof that Nate was seeing someone. I spent one day and flew back home.

A member of Nate's team was under suspicion that he had murdered his girlfriend who was carrying his baby. I was horrified. I remembered all Nate's threats that he would kill me if I told his business to anyone or tried to leave. This news reinforced my fear that Nate was capable of the same thing. I was somehow prepared for the worst.

I knew if he killed me, Monte and Ingrid would take care of the boys. Then there was the letter … still locked up in Ingrid's safe. If Nate ever did go that far, surely he would find himself in prison, with my own handwriting telling the police that he had killed me. He wouldn't get the boys. They would be safe.

I was glad to be away from him. I was happy he was living in North Carolina. He could stay there as long as he liked.

In January the season came to an end. I was dreading it, knowing that meant Nate would move back home with us. He had injured his shoulder and it required surgery to repair the damage. It had not been a good season for Nate, and with the injury, his football career was in serious jeopardy. I had physical evidence of a long-term affair and I was ready to go to an attorney. Nate asked me to stay with him during the surgery and his recovery. He promised that if I stayed and if I agreed to use his attorney and if I agreed to accept his terms, then he would give me the divorce.

I consented to everything. All I wanted was out.

"Fine," I said. "I'll stay until you are recovered. I'll use your attorney and I don't care what the terms are as long as I get to leave," and I meant every word.

Nate knew there was something different about me. In the past, I took care of everything for Nate—I mean everything. He never had to wash clothes or pack, never had to prepare for any appearance, never had to cook or wash a dish ... and anytime he had ever been hurt or sick, I stayed by his side every moment and made sure all his needs were met. He didn't want me out of his sight.

"Dot, you can put King in a playpen and stay with me," he said.

"You'll be fine," I said. "I promised I would stay and take care of you, Nathaniel, and I'm doing just that. I have to take care of King too, though. I can't just sit in here with you. I still have to take care of King. I'll be back."

February came and we scheduled an appointment with Nate's attorney. The attorney told me that we could split everything down the middle and Nate would pay $2,000/ month in child support. "Down the middle?" I asked, shocked, "Down the middle ... what does that look like?"

I didn't need to be shocked, there wasn't anything left to split. Nate was out of money. He had managed to spend everything he earned. All that remained was the house. We had paid cash for the house and owned it outright.

The arrangement was for me to stay in the house with the boys until it sold, then we would split whatever it sold for and that would be the end of that. March was coming and we already had an all expense paid trip to Jamaica booked. Tre' had learned about Jamaica in school and had wanted to go for a long time. The Martin's son Drew was flying in from Jacksonville to join us. I didn't know how to back out of the trip without letting Tre' down and I wasn't ready to tell the Martins about the divorce. They had been so good to Tre' and treated him like one of their own, I just didn't feel like I could cancel. I told Nate I would go on the trip, but we would not sleep together. This would not change anything—I still wanted a divorce.

On the trip Nate was very relaxed and attentive to the boys. It was a wonderful time. It was actually the best trip we ever took together. I felt as if a giant weight had been lifted from my shoulders and I was totally relaxed also. I didn't want Nate out of the boys' life completely. He was their father. He had never been abusive to them, so this arrangement was like an experiment for me.

When we returned from Jamaica, Nate disappeared. I have no idea where he went. I didn't hear from him again until June. It was time for us to appear in court and the attorney told me only one of us had to be present, so I didn't worry about trying to find Nate. I didn't have to worry though, he called. "Dot, are sure you want to do this? I mean really sure? I'm out of football now. I promise you. I always promised you if you would wait until after my career was over I would be the best husband ever. You don't need to do this. There won't be anymore football. It will be different now. Things are gonna be totally different now."

"No," I answered, feeling genuinely sad that things never worked out. "I'm sorry ... I'll be before the judge tomorrow."

Morning came and I went to the courthouse. I had not cried in a very long time. I couldn't even remember the last time I cried, I just didn't allow myself the luxury of tears. I didn't have time to cry and feel sorry for myself, but standing there before the judge the tears flowed unchecked. He asked me to state my name ... no words came out of my mouth. I couldn't talk because I was crying.

"Mrs. Newton," the judge said sternly, not an ounce of sympathy in his voice.

"Mrs. Newton, you do need to speak up," he addressed me, frowning.

It sounded like Nate's voice, stern and cross. The firmness affected me mentally. I shook myself, snapped out of it, and went through the proceeding without another tear.

I made arrangements to have dinner with Ingrid that night. I had not told anyone I was getting a divorce. I left my kids with Miss Amy, the babysitter, and pulled into Ingrid's driveway to pick her up. She slid into the passenger side, smiling, ready for an outing.

"Ingrid," I said, "We're not going anywhere, okay? I need to be by myself right now ... " I paused and Ingrid studied me, sensing something was wrong. "I'm divorced," I finished.

"What?" she said, then repeated, "You're what?"

She was shocked. I confided many things to Ingrid, but I didn't tell her everything. I suppose I wasn't sure if it was actually going to happen—until I had actually signed the papers and knew it was for real, I didn't want to tell her. I wanted to be sure it went through.

"Divorced," I said again, letting out a long, slow sigh. "I'm divorced, Ingrid. I need to make some calls to my family. Do you mind if we skip dinner?"

I called my mom, my biological dad, my aunt and uncle in Virginia, Lynn and K-Mart, T. Hayes … In days and weeks to come, I slowly began telling people. Shock was the common response. No one but my closest friends knew anything at all about the abuse. To the public, I lived the perfect life of a celebrity wife, so my divorce seemed sudden. The media reports of Nate's trouble with women and fighting and drinking were an ugly thread through our public life, but I had stayed with him through all of that. Every time Nate got into trouble, I stood by him. No one knew how rough things had been for me, and I guess the news seemed sudden or even rash without understanding the journey that brought me there.

As agreed, I stayed in the house. In July I held a birthday party for King and Nate showed up. He was pleasant and amiable and friendly … then he disappeared again. One night he called and wanted to know where we were, telling me he was in town and wanted to see the kids.

I wouldn't tell him where I was, but reassured him that I would make sure he could see the boys. We drove up to the house and saw Nate's truck parked at the back where the guest house was. The boys were excited, bouncing up and down, "Daddy! Daddy!" they shouted. I drove around to the back so the boys could run and find him and there he was … with a woman. I was furious. I got out of the car and picked up a rock throwing it in his direction. "Get off the property!" I shouted. "Just go! Get off the property!"

Nate rushed toward me and held me, "Calm down, Dot. Calm down. Don't worry, I'm gonna get her off the property."

"Don't you touch me, Nathaniel Newton! You will not hurt me again!" I pulled out my cell phone and called the police, then T. Hayes.

The officer came and was jovial with Nate. With me he was firm and authoritative. "Mrs. Newton, I've been told that his name is on the deed same as yours. He has every right to be here. You need to calm down." I stared at him in shock, it was just as I imagined it would be if I ever found the nerve to call the police. T. Hayes arrived and I ran over to him. I was in total disbelief.

"Do you see how the officer is treating me? Look at him with Nate! He's over there laughing and talking about football. It is always like this when I need help!" Bad memories flooded my mind and I fought to regain control.

Being divorced was supposed to keep this from happening again. Nate was supposed to be out of my life, unable to harrass or threaten me any longer. Even my divorce was a disappointment.

Twenty-Five

WORKING
THINGS OUT

"Disappointment to a noble soul is what cold water is to burning metal; it strengthens, tempers, intensifies, but never destroys it."

—ELIZA TABOR

I moved out of the house. I rented an apartment closer to Tre's school in North Richland Hills and we lived there for the next year. It was like Nate was a demonic force oppressing me, always oppressing. He bothered us constantly, as if he took pleasure in making me miserable. He told me he wanted to see the kids more. I had begun graduate school two nights a week and so I told him he could be with the boys on those two nights while I was in school. This lasted for one semester before he grew tired of the responsibility. When the spring semester began, he was no longer interested in this arrangement. He decided to move to East Ellijay, Georgia. I was glad to see him go.

He called from Georgia occasionally. "I can't believe you divorced me!" he would say. "You're gonna pay for this ... and I can't afford no $2,000 child support so you're gonna have to figure something else out."

The house had not sold. It was a large, beautiful, expensive home but few people expressed any interest in purchasing it. Nate was out of money and growing desperate to find some cash. He lowered the price of the house to $650,000 and called to tell me I better agree to the offer.

I did agree. Whatever the house sold for, I would be fine. Things would work out. I would also receive a portion of Nate's retirement. This included a small settlement now, and would eventually include a portion of his 401(k) when he reached retirement age. So, I decided to stop renting and build a home. I knew I needed to be close to Ingrid so she could help me with the kids while I went back to work. We looked for the least expensive spot we could find in Southlake. I wanted to build my house close to her. I had to take Tre' out of Fort Worth Christian, no longer able to afford the tuition. He loved the school and taking him out and putting him into public school was an extremely difficult decision for me. It felt as though

Tre' was being penalized because of the divorce. It didn't seem fair. It was very hard for me to do this.

In May, Nate served me with papers. He took me to court to get joint custody of the children and didn't want to pay the $2,000 monthly child support. I would not agree to joint custody. I wanted full custody of the children and I didn't care what he paid me, he could pay whatever … so he stopped paying support.

I was lost. As a single mom looking at legal battles and legal bills—I felt totally outclassed. Nate Newton was still a celebrity and everybody loved him. I was overwhelmed by the responsibility to find an attorney—who could I trust? What should I look for? How was I going to afford it? I didn't know what to expect or where to turn for help. The bills were staggering, unbelievable. I was on my own. I felt as equipped for this as a rowboat stranded alone in the middle of a stormy ocean.

By July 2001, our house was ready. We had been members at Southlake Blvd. Church for about a year. Tre' was getting baptized, King was having a birthday, and we were moving into our very own home. We had a huge celebration—at last we seemed to be finding our own way.

A court appearance was scheduled, and when I arrived I was escorted into a mediation room. I was asked to explain why I didn't want to let my boys go to Georgia with Nate. I explained that they would be in danger. I told them that something was wrong with Nate, that he had a violent temper. I told them about the dogs he kept in Georgia—pit bulls. "They won't be safe," I said in earnest, "Nate is not stable. It will not be good for the boys to go to Georgia."

"Can you prove he's not fit?" I was asked.

I told them some of the things that happened in our marriage, about the violence and abuse.

"Did he ever hurt the children?" I was asked.

"No," I sighed. "He never hurt the children ... but he is violent ..." I pleaded.

"That has nothing to do with him not being able to take care of the kids," came the reply.

A second appearance was scheduled. I sat there stunned, listening as they told me I had to allow Nate visitation rights. I needed to think about which holidays the children would spend with him. Then the subject of child support came up, and because Nate no longer had any income, he was no longer obligated to pay the amount agreed upon for child support. Once again ... everything seemed to be coming out in Nate Newton's favor. I felt a hard knot forming in the pit of my stomach. *Will I ever be free of this man? Even now, he gets to call all the shots.*

I left the courthouse dejected. I thought about my friends, who I could call, but what could they do? How could they help? I wasn't used to sharing my problems with people. I didn't really know how to ask for help. I was used to trying to figure things out on my own. God was the only one I really trusted, I had trouble with trust even in my closest relationships. All I knew to do was pray.

December was approaching and I had one last court appointment. I had paid out more than $40,000 to the attorney, and I was at the end of my rope. I was fasting and praying. I emptied myself completely. I wanted every breath I took to be filled with the Holy Spirit. "Please God," I prayed, "intervene."

I called my best friend from college, Sheila, and asked if she would come to court to stand with me. She agreed right away. The mediator asked me which holiday Nate could have the boys and I said, "New Year's Day."

I looked across the courtroom. There was Nate and his girlfriend. He was smiling and hugging her. He caught my eye and my heart sank. It seemed as if he was proud to hurt me. I thought about all the things I had been through with him. I had never done anything to tarnish his reputation. I stood by him whenever he was in trouble. I took care of him and lived with his abuse in silence. I watched him lavish gifts on others while all I got were angry words and curses. *Why did he have to take the boys too?*

One more court appearance was scheduled where everything would be finalized. I left with Sheila, broken hearted. I prayed and submitted it all to God. "It's up to you, now ..." I whispered.

Nate was arrested on November 4, 2001 in St. Martin Parish, Louisiana. The police discovered 213 pounds of marijuana in his van, but there was no conviction. I continued to pray. I was desperate that the boys not be allowed to go to Georgia with Nate.

The Church of Christ located near Fort Worth Christian called one day, asking me to speak at a women's event. I was surprised. *Why would they ask me?* I wondered. I immediately felt like I was supposed to do it, so without hesitation, and without understanding why, I agreed.

I poured energy into preparing for the message. I focused on Galatians 2:20, "I am crucified with Christ: nevertheless I live; yet not I, but Christ liveth in me: and the life which I now live in the flesh I live by the faith of the Son of God, who loved me, and gave Himself for me." This verse had sustained me throughout my life and I was passionate to share Christ with others. God filled me with insight on courage and He ministered to me as I prepared to minister to others.

A week before I was supposed to speak, just a few days before my fortieth birthday, five weeks after Nate's arrest, it happened. Nate once again made national headline news. He was caught with 175 pounds of marijuana on Interstate 45. This time, however, he was not released, but convicted and sentenced to thirty months in a federal prison.

Tre' was devastated. He was so embarrassed. He had just started public school, so he was away from the friends he knew and the support structure he had come to depend on. I was embarrassed too, and angry. It was a nightmare.

My speaking engagement came and I was too dependable to bow out. God used it to keep my focus on others and not get lost in my own circumstances. No matter what happened in my life, God constantly put people in my path for me to minister to. I couldn't wallow in my own sorrow. I couldn't retreat into depression. Others needed me. I thought I was helping them—it turns out they were keeping me from giving in to self pity. The more I poured out, the more God poured in. When I saw someone else in pain, I gladly reached out. I was happy to pray with them and offer them encouragement. In return, I was strengthened. God protected me from too much introspection and filled my life with purpose greater than myself.

Twenty-Six

STANDING STRONG

Vitality shows in not only the ability to persist,
but also in the ability to start over.

—F. SCOTT FITZGERALD

If my kids are going to survive this, I am the one who is going to have to show them how to do it. I looked at myself in the mirror, measuring the reflection that I saw. Instead of sadness, I saw determination. I saw hope—even confidence. "We're going to make it," I said out loud, lifting my chin. I twisted the tube of lipstick and applied the color. I nodded to myself and squared my shoulders. "Better."

The boys and I grew even closer in the days that followed. I didn't ask for help. I had a fierce independent streak in me and I believed we could deal with things on our own. I didn't allow the boys to watch television during the week, and we had Bible study every day. We were active in church and we spent lots of quality time together—healing, coping, finding our way. I got involved in women's ministry and began looking for a job. I had not been employed professionally for some time and knew I needed something more than an entry level position to take care of our needs.

I really needed the child support, but with Nate in prison, there was none. The attorney's fees, renting an apartment, and building a house required all my resources, even with careful management. I felt like I needed to stay home with the boys during the transition, but I began to accrue credit card debt just to make ends meet. That was something I was not willing to continue. It was time to take a job—any job, even if it wasn't enough to sustain us, it would be income.

My friend, who is an internist, knew I needed a job. He spoke with the office manager at the clinic where he worked and got me an interview. I was hired to work in medical billing. It was an entry level position and the salary was not enough to meet expenses. The job responsibilities were not challenging for me, and did not seem the best match for my knowledge, education, and experience. It was a job though. It was local and allowed me to remain accessible to my kids. I took it, praying and asking God to make things stretch and grant me favor.

There were still occasional stories on the news about Nate's arrest and prison sentence, and my picture would show up in connection with him. I was humiliated. Three months after I began working, a position opened in management. I went to speak with the lead physician at the clinic about it, telling him I was interested and qualified. I was concerned about all the publicity and afraid that because of it, I might not be given a fair chance as a candidate for the job.

This compassionate man asked me to tell him about the kind of person I was. Then he asked about my experience and how I would be an asset to the company. I answered his questions openly and honestly.

"You are the person I am interested in," he told me. "I'm not interested in who you've been married to, not what the media has to say about you. I will not judge you, nor will I penalize you for someone else's actions. All I ask is that you remain focused while you are here and not let that life interfere."

From that time on, my career blossomed and I was given the opportunity to work with the best boss anyone could ever have. She had lots of wisdom to offer along with a vast knowledge of the industry and years of experience. She never once made me feel like any question I asked her was dumb or a waste of her time. I had not physically been part of the work force for twelve years—her patience was limitless. She taught me everything I needed to know to bring me up to speed and set me up for success.

While Nate was serving out his sentence, he called often and sent letters asking repeatedly to see the kids. I wasn't sure what to do. *Should I keep the boys away from their father? Should I take them to visit Nate and expose them to prison? What's best for them? What's best for me?* I honestly didn't know what to do. Tre' missed his father and was old enough to understand that he had been caught breaking the law and was serving time as punishment. He knew right from wrong. King was so young. He didn't understand anything about it, but he also missed his daddy and kept asking to see him. I had reservations about exposing the boys to prison, but I felt so sorry for Nate and was heartbroken for the boys.

I decided that keeping the boys away was selfish. I made a decision to take them to Texarkana once a month to visit Nate in prison. I had no idea what to expect. As the date for our first visit drew near, I longed for someone I could talk to that could prepare me for the experience. I could think of no one, so once again, I prayed about it. I was scared to death as I made the long drive, but I knew God was with me—watching, guiding, protecting. I hoped that seeing Nate in jail would not disturb the boys.

Visitation was on Sunday and it was too far to drive there and back in one day, so we drove over on Saturday and found a hotel to spend the night. On Sunday I took the boys to visit Nate. It was awkward and strange, but Tre' seemed relieved that he had seen with his own eyes that his dad was okay. King was more interested in the playground out front, but Nate seemed glad to see him. We made the long drive back home and I put the boys to bed. I went to my room and fell on top of my bed, completely drained. My bed had never felt so comfortable. I fell asleep in my clothes. I woke up the next morning with my comforter wrapped around me. Sometime during the night I must have kicked off my shoes, but I didn't remember waking up to do it.

This became our routine every month until the last year of Nate's sentence when he was transferred to a prison in Louisiana. Monday mornings after our trip were difficult. We were all so tired. Mornings were already hard. Tre' had to be on the field for football practice at 6:30 AM. Every day I had to wake up five year old King, put him in the car and drive Tre' to practice. Then I drove back home, got King fed and ready for school, and then I went off to work.

For all the years I was married, I never had to worry about money. Nate gave me enough money to pay the household bills each month—I didn't have any bills. If the kids needed clothes or shoes or fees for any of their activities, he gave me his credit card to take care of it. When I scheduled his appearances I received a small percentage for my work and that took care of my personal needs, and I had never needed much. Now I thought about money all the time. Now I had to be super frugal. I had to manage and balance and adjust and balance again. It was a fight to survive. It was a struggle not to surrender to anger or depression, but even this struggle was a light load in comparison to what I had lived through. I gladly dealt with financial issues in exchange for peace of mind and safety. My heart was filled with gratitude that God had brought me through.

We had wonderful friends around us who made our lives better. I thought about our friends, *the Fords, the Ervins, the Martins, the Freemans, the Grays, the Brainards, ... so many to be thankful for, Lord ... the Taylors, the Johnsons, the Dents, Sheila, Bug ... yes, thank you God ... the Swackers, the Marylands, the Parchues ... every one of them, Lord, I thank you for sending them to us ... for Coach Dodge and his wife, Elizabeth, for how good they have been to Tre'* ... my heart was filled with thanksgiving for them and I prayed blessings over them. Had I asked any of them for help, I know they would have gladly stepped in to meet our needs. I didn't want to ask. I couldn't ask.

Our friends didn't want to talk about Nate's situation, and we didn't volunteer any information. I believe part of us wanted to open up and share what we were going through—we just didn't know how. We didn't even know where to begin! Even with caring people all around us, it sometimes felt as though we stood alone in our past and in our pain. It was our burden to bear. It was our responsibility to deal with.

I knew God wanted to do great things through me and the boys. I wanted us to focus on others and not get bogged down in our troubles and what we were dealing with concerning Nate. We got involved in the Presbyterian Night Shelter and many other outreach and service opportunities. We supported food drives and clothing drives and were actively involved in touching others.

Tre' held a Bible study in our home. He was a phenomenal athlete and an outstanding student. He was friendly even though he was quiet, and open about his faith. Instead of turning bitter when things were hard or allowing the trauma experienced in his childhood to overwhelm him, he excelled in everything he did. I was immensely proud of him.

King was getting older, and he and Tre' were close to each other. Tre' was very protective of King, and became his hero. King loved watching Tre' play football. He followed him around and listened to him, discipline was never a problem for me when Tre' was around.

One night we were at the game, watching the Dragons play. The Southlake Carroll Dragons were a championship team. The games were always exciting to watch, and I was proud of Tre'. I sat in the stands, cheering him on and visiting with other football moms, keeping an eye on King when out of nowhere ... Nate! He had been released from prison and wanted to surprise us. I had not heard from him in months. Now here he was, looking like a wild man, and he brought the woman he was with the night I called the police to make him leave the property ... and after all this time away in prison! I was surprised all right. I knew it was close to time for his release, but I hadn't given it much thought. I was completely shocked!

After the game, Nate found Tre' and they talked for awhile. My friends just kept looking at me, perhaps for an explanation, but no one said anything. I never talked about Nate to any of them and I certainly didn't know what to say now. My thoughts were racing everywhere. *He's back. What does this mean? Is Nate going to leave us alone? Does he expect to come around the house now to visit the boys?*

It had been nearly three years since Nate left. While he was in prison, I felt completely safe, knowing that he couldn't show up to bother us. I wasn't sure how to handle it now that he was back in Texas. I found it very unsettling.

I didn't have to wait long to find out what it was going to mean having Nate nearby again. First he wanted to come retrieve all the belongings I had stored for him while he was gone and then he wanted to take me back to court over custody.

"What do you want?" I asked him, not wanting to go back to a courtroom.

"What is it that you really want?" I asked again. "Surely you don't want joint custody of the boys. They are settled in their life. They are active in school. Tre' is very involved in sports. Why would you want to interrupt their stability?"

There had been no child support the entire time Nate was in prison. He didn't want to pay back child support, and he wanted the monthly amount reduced. I knew he didn't have any income, didn't even have a job. We had gone all this time without any help from him and I didn't care about that, all I wanted was custody.

Our attorneys argued back and forth and we finally agreed that Nate would pay $850 a month to support the boys and would pay 20% of the back child support over a period of time. I wondered if he had any idea how hard it had been on us financially while he was away. It didn't matter. He was giving me full custody and we would stay out of court. That was what mattered. The boys would stay with me.

Twenty-Seven

FAMILIAR TUNE

Difficult things take a long time, impossible things a little longer.
—ANDRÉ A. JACKSON

*N*ate was back.

While in prison, he was as active in the boys' life as prison allowed him to be. Whenever he called he was nice to us. He was interested about the details of their life and expressed concern for the boys in his letters, so I was hopeful that things might be amenable between us now that he was back. But that wasn't to be. It seemed like every encounter with Nate was difficult and disagreeable. He was angry whenever he got around me. I didn't want his anger spilling out around the boys. I avoided him as much as possible.

Family time was very important to me. Now that I was working and a single mom, it was important to me that when I spent time with the boys I focused on them. I didn't talk on my cell phone or answer email. When I was spending time with them, I gave them my full attention. My friends knew this and respected our family time.

One Sunday afternoon I took King to his little league baseball game. He was so cute in his uniform! I loved watching him play ball. Nate came to watch also. I kept my distance and sat near some other parents. Another little boy on the team was hitting home runs every time he got a turn at bat. He was having quite a streak! All the boys wanted to use his bat—after all, it *must* be the bat responsible for all those home runs. When it was King's turn to hit, he picked up the boy's trophy bat to give it a try. I was smiling from ear to ear as he took his turn at home plate.

Then I heard, "Dot!"

"Dot, what bat is that?" Nate shouted at me across the stands.

I didn't answer. *What difference does it make? King is up. Watch.* I thought to myself.

"Dot!" Nate shouted again. "I said who's bat is he using?"

People around me got restless. I was embarrassed. Why did Nate have to shout and make a scene? This was just little league. *Stop it!* I thought to myself.

"I spent my m_____ f_____ money on a bat for King and he's using someone else's bat? Why?" Nate ranted.

He continued shouting at me in front of everyone. I was mortified. The parents in the stands were uncomfortable. I couldn't bring myself even to look at Nate. I took my cell phone out and called Ingrid. "Hi Ingrid," I said, "can you come and sit with me at King's game?"

I never called Ingrid during their family time, so when I called her on a Sunday afternoon, she immediately knew something was wrong. "On my way," she said and hung up. She arrived within a few minutes and came to sit by me. Nate would not let it go. He was stirred up and kept demanding to know who's bat King was using and why wasn't he using the bat he had bought for him. It was awful.

King knew something was wrong. All during the game he kept looking into the stands and saw Nate yelling at me. We had made plans for after the game to have dinner with some friends from a Bible study group that Ingrid facilitated. When the game ended, I gave Ingrid a quick hug and she looked me in the eyes, knowingly. I gathered King's things and hurried him to the car.

"I WILL be talkin' to King!" Nate shouted as I drove away.

I called Tre'. "Your dad's in a rage," I began. "I don't know what is going to happen, but as soon as I get home I want you to take your brother upstairs. He's following me home. I'm not going to let him in. I don't know what's going to happen ..."

I pulled into the driveway and Nate was no longer behind me. I hurried inside and sent King up to shower. Maybe Nate decided not to come after all. I hoped not. I let out a sigh of relief.

Bang. Bang. Bang. Nate pounded on the door. I jumped.

"Let me in, Dot!" Nate shouted, still banging on the door.

"Don't let him in Mama! Don't let him in!" Tre' called to me from upstairs.

I went to the door, double checking to make sure it was locked.

Bang. Bang. Bang. Bang. Bang. Bang. Nate was pounding on the door so hard I feared he would break the hinges and knock it down.

"If you do it again, I am going to call the police. Do you hear me?" I shouted, "I will call the police. Go away. I'm not letting you in here like that,"

"Dot, I just want to see the kids," Nate said much more calmly. "I want to apologize. Please ... just let me in. I want to talk to King."

I stood there, my hand on the bolt. I hesitated.

"Mama, don't," Tre' said.

"I just want to apologize, Dot," Nate repeated.

King was on the stairs, crying, "Let him in, Ma, let him in .... please ... "

"King, baby ... " I began

"Ma, please, he just wants to talk to me," King pleaded, tears streaming down his cheeks.

Tre' was shaking his head no. "Don't," he mouthed. King was crying and Nate was still pleading to enter. Slowly, I turned the deadbolt and cracked the door. "You are going to be calm or I am going to call the police. Do

you understand?" I knew that if I called the police it would mean a return to jail for Nate. He didn't have any room for a parole violation, so it gave me confidence that he would behave.

Nate pushed past me, "Tre', King," he called. "Come down here boys."

Reluctantly, the boys came down the stairs, their faces betraying their apprehension.

"Nate," I warned, "you said you were coming in to apologize, remember?"

"I bought that bat. Why were you using someone else's bat?" Nate asked, his voice growing very loud and thick with anger.

"This isn't working out," I said. "You're too mad to talk right now, and that doesn't sound like an apology. I think you better leave."

"Why were you using someone else's bat?" Nate shouted and slammed his fist down on my marble table. The table broke.

Fear gripped me. "Get out!" I shrieked. "Get out, NOW!"

I opened the door and gestured for him to leave. "Get out right now! You leave right now, do you hear me? NOW!" I said. I was shaking. Nate left.

I shut the door and King ran and hugged me. Tre' was angry. Furious.

"Why?" he asked me, "Why are we still having to deal with this?" he shouted and punched the wall.

I had never seen him do anything like that and it scared me. For the first time I was scared for Tre'. I saw the potential for anger to grab him like it grabbed Nate and I was terrified for him.

"Tre' ... baby ..." I said, crying. "Oh God, why can't this be over?"

I was too upset to go to dinner. I called Ingrid and told her we couldn't come. I asked Monte if he would come over. Tre' needed him.

Monte came and took Tre' out. He spent time talking to him, like he always did. Monte was really good to the boys. He was a wonderful mentor and friend. He cared deeply about them and made as much time as he could for them. I was grateful. Monte was a good family man. Monte and Ingrid treated Tre' like one of their own and gave him the opportunity to travel extensively with their family. It was good for the boys to be around functional families loving each other—families with a mom and dad who respected each other, treated each other kindly, and poured out their love freely. I was very blessed to have these amazing people in my life. He spent lots of time with his boys and I was grateful that he made time for mine too.

We also had Lynn and K-Mart. They had moved away in 1993, but returned in 2002 shortly after the divorce. They found a house nearby in Keller and were wonderful friends to us, like family. Their son and Tre' were just five days apart, and all I ever had to do was pick up the phone and they were quick to help out with my boys.

Any time I called, one of them would ask, "You bringing the kids over?" I never had to ask them—it was like they knew I had a hard time asking for help, so they made it easy on me and just offered. They never took no for an answer. There were many times I was involved with work or ministry that one of them drove to wherever I was to pick up the boys and take them back to their house.

There were more angry episodes with Nate. Even in public he was quick to verbalize his anger and speak to me disrespectfully. He showed up often for the kid's sporting events—that was when they saw him. It was never nice between us, though. It seemed like just being around me stirred up the worst inside of Nate. Whatever he felt towards me, he didn't know how to express it in any other way except anger.

Twenty-Eight

GIVE AND RECIEVE

There is nothing on this earth more to be prized than true friendship.

—THOMAS AQUINAS

It was August 2005. We were members of Southlake Boulevard Church and had made many wonderful friends there. Tre' was involved in youth group, I led Bible studies, and things in our family had settled into a comfortable routine. Nate was still the wild card, and we never knew exactly what to expect, but we had learned how to deal with things and we were strong and stable.

My family still lived in Buras, Louisiana where I grew up. It is located just sixty miles south of New Orleans. Hurricane Katrina hit with violent force. My mother, siblings, aunts and uncles lost everything. It was total devastation. There was nothing left.

They took refuge at my house. For the next three weeks Tre', King, and I shared our home with seventeen people. It was total chaos. They sat up all night, glued to news reports, trying to learn about the damage. Then as dawn approached, one by one they fell into restless, exhausted, fitful sleep. Their days and nights were completely backwards. They were in shock, trying to cope with the loss of their property and personal belongings. Time stood still for them.

The boys were in school, and I was working every day. Every square inch of our home was occupied. The bathroom was never empty. There were pillows and blankets and clothes and shoes strewn everywhere. Just making sure there was enough food to feed everyone was a full time effort. I had tremendous support from my church and from friends. They contributed groceries and finances, even the organization I worked for helped out by providing them with free health care.

The whole family was trying to figure out what to do next. The news was on all the time. Every moment of any broadcast about the storm damage found them watching in horrified attention. I felt their sadness and anxiety and wanted to help in any way I could. My home was their home.

Friends offered them transportation to go to agencies to work things out like birth certificates, social security numbers, bank records—all destroyed in the storm. It was a nightmare. People helped out as much as they could. They donated money for food and clothing and the church helped us get them all into temporary apartments or houses over time. They bought groceries for them and tried to help them get established in a living situation.

There were lots of tears and laughter too. Having my family around was wonderful. The circumstance was horrible—total, sudden, irreplaceable loss. The damage was massive. There had been no opportunity to salvage anything, to put anything into storage, or adequately prepare. They had only enough time to flee for their safety.

I took them down to Reunion Arena in Dallas, hoping to help them connect to people they had lost track of. Everyone was so spread out and cell phones and postal connections were not available to find out if people were dead or alive. It was very traumatic. I was grateful for the kindness and support we received throughout the ordeal.

My family is resourceful. They researched where to find help and were able to access available supplies. I was proud of them. They didn't give up. They didn't quit. I saw their strength and admired their tenacity. Eventually everyone in the family moved back to Louisiana to rebuild and start again. Only my mom decided to remain in Texas. She moved nearby and I was glad she stayed.

Once again I was reminded that no matter what we have to endure, we can live a blessed life. God surrounds us with a blanket of love. He touches every area of our lives and makes sure we have exactly what we need. Even when things are bad—in the valley of the shadow—He is with us. He is always with us.

I am cautious with relationships. Trusting people is difficult for me and I prefer seclusion. While attending Southlake Boulevard Church, a woman named Freda began calling me. She didn't just call occasionally, she called me every day! I thought this woman had lost her mind. She would not stop calling. She just called to check on me, to say hello and see how I was doing. She had no idea about my past and at first I was annoyed that she kept calling me. I wanted her to stop, but was too polite to say so.

I didn't realize that God brought her into my life. It was His plan for her to put herself in my path—knowing I wouldn't reach out for this kind of friendship. We began sharing Scriptures with each other over the phone and praying together. Without realizing it, I now had a prayer partner. I had someone to be accountable to. I had someone to pray with and pray for—and someone to pray for me. It was amazing.

During Tre's junior year of high school he started looking at colleges, and colleges started looking at him. He was an amazing athlete, and this opened up opportunities to provide for his education. Several schools expressed their interest and he received offers from many of them. He wasn't interested. Tre' would not settle. He would not compromise. He wanted to go either to the University of Texas or Notre Dame. Three weeks before we were scheduled to attend "Junior Day" at U.T., Coach Mac Brown called Tre' to come to his office. He offered him a scholarship and we were totally blown away. There hadn't even been a letter from them, so we had no idea they were even interested in him, and here they were offering him a full scholarship while he was just a junior in high school!

Tre' wanted Nate to be part of his decision and he asked Coach Brown if he could call his dad and talk to him about it. "Of course," Coach said. Tre' called Nate and asked him if he would drive to Austin and he did. When he arrived, he and Tre' talked about it, going over the pros and cons. I didn't get involved. Football was definitely Nate's area of expertise. I felt it was best to defer to him in this decision. I would have been happy with any choice Tre' made.

Tre' decided to accept the scholarship and so he did that same day. When we returned home we cancelled a planned trip to visit Notre Dame. In his heart, University of Texas had been his first choice. There wasn't a need to look any further.

Tre' graduated in December of 2007, a full semester early. He was anxious to begin college and didn't want to wait, so in January of 2008 he began his studies at the University of Texas.

This was a difficult time for King. He was in the sixth grade when Tre' left and everything changed for him. Tre' leaving was hard for both of us. We depended on him. We were an inseparable family unit. We cared deeply about each other. We loved each other. When Tre' left, an emptiness hung over the house. Nothing was quite the same.

One of King's teachers gave him an assignment to write about something that affected his life. King wrote about Tre' leaving home to go to college. He talked about Tre' being the person he looked up to for everything and how he was his best friend. King's world was shattered. It took him a long time to adjust to Tre' being in college. It didn't feel quite right being just the two of us. Something was missing.

During Tre's senior year of high school I had often visited Gateway Church. I loved hearing Pastor Robert Morris preach. I would attend services at Gateway on Saturday night, then attend Southlake Blvd. Church on Sunday mornings. I felt drawn to Gateway, but as long as Tre' was at home, I wasn't ready to move my membership. Tre'

was so involved at Southlake Boulevard Church, and I didn't want to disrupt things for him. Now that he was in college, I felt like I had a green light to begin attending Gateway regularly.

One day I had dinner with my friend, Rayne. She said to me, "Dorothy, I notice that you know a lot of people. I see you reach out to a lot of people. Rodney and I love you, Dorothy. You have helped me through a very difficult time in my life, but I don't feel like I know *anything* about you."

I froze. I didn't expect this.

"How do I get to know you?" she asked. "You never share anything with me about yourself. How can I find out more about you? Can you be open and honest with me? I want to have a transparent relationship so I'll know what you need as much as you know what I need."

I was shocked. We had been friends for a long time. I was surprised at her observation, and that she was offering this kind of close friendship to me. I looked at her, overwhelmed by her generosity of spirit.

"I feel stuck," I began, pausing, not sure if I should continue. "Right now things are very strange in my life.

There are things I believe I need to talk to someone about, but it is really hard for me to trust people. It isn't that I don't love you ..."

"You hurt me when you won't let me help you with the needs you have." She continued, "You are always giving, but you are not willing to receive. You won't let me in. Quite a few people have noticed that you have a wall built around you. As nice as you are ... as giving as you are ... you won't let anybody inside your space."

"It is hard for me to trust," I told her. "I have a difficult time trusting people. I want to. Will you be patient with me? I need time to figure things out."

After my time with Rayne, I thought about my cousin Scarlette. Until Hurricane Katrina, she was the only family that lived near me. She was a single mom raising two girls, Ariel and Whittney, on her own. I couldn't remember a single time that she had asked for my help. She was an incredibly strong woman. She went back to school and got her degree while raising her daughters by herself. I was proud of her. Though I felt close to her and it was my privilege and pleasure to help her out with the girls, and even though she was my flesh and blood family, she didn't seek assistance from me. Maybe this difficulty—this inability to ask for help—was something that was part of my family's culture. We were strong and independent. I thought about it some more. My desire to never be a burden to anyone had made me close myself off, unwilling to seek support even when I needed it most. I knew I needed to learn how to receive. I needed to learn that asking for help is not a sign of weakness, it is giving others the opportunity to be a blessing. For the first time, I considered that receiving from others was not less than giving to them.

Twenty-Nine

PERFECT LOVE

*Greater love has no one than this, than to
lay down one's life for his friends.*

—JOHN 15:13 NKJV

Robert Morris concluded his message. It went straight
to my heart. At the time, Gateway Church was much
smaller than it is now, so at the end of each service Pastor
Robert would come down the stairs and mingle with the
congregation. I was visiting that day with Arnita and
Mike Taylor, who were friends of Pastor Robert. He came
over to where we were standing and introduced himself
to me. Nate had just told me a few days before that he had
a conversation with Pastor Morris, so I said, "It is so good
to meet you. Just last week Nate mentioned that he had
seen you and had a chance to visit."

"Oh," he said, "So you're Dorothy, Nate Newton's ex-wife? My wife, Debbie would love to meet you."

"I'll give Dorothy's number to her," Arnita volunteered.

The next day, Debbie Morris called me and we set a lunch date. This began a series of lunch dates a few times a year. We didn't get to visit together very often, but when we did it was an extra special time for me. Debbie was amazing. Soft-spoken, tender, kind-hearted, gentle … a beautiful example of a godly woman. The church was growing rapidly and her schedule was very full, so I was careful to respect her time. We texted each other often and managed to stay in touch.

I always assumed the reason we were friends was because she needed a safe place. By now Pastor Robert was well known nationally and internationally, and I knew what it was like to be the wife of a famous husband. I figured Debbie had reached out to me for what I could do for her … since everyone else came to me, I thought she needed someone to be friends with who was interested in her for herself, not because of who she was married to. I knew all too well what it was like to be sought out because of who my husband was, not because of who I was. I wanted to be friends with

Debbie, whatever that looked like. I wanted to be there for her. I understood her position. I understood that she had to be careful about sharing her private life with others. Trusting people is very difficult when you've got a famous husband.

It was the end of February in 2008. Debbie and I were enjoying lunch together. We had visited for nearly two hours when she said to me, "Dorothy, I know you are involved in a lot of things. What are you doing now, what is your passion?"

I paused for a moment, wondering if I should share what was going on inside of me. "Well," I began, "as of January I decided to completely erase my calendar. I have been involved in so many things and I just didn't want to do them anymore."

I took a sip of tea. My stomach felt like it had butter-flies inside. "I feel stuck, Debbie … I don't know, maybe I just need to take time out to be still and not do anything for awhile. I need to hear God and know what the next steps are. The place I am in right now feels foreign to me. From the time I was a little girl I felt close to God—like I could always feel him hugging me, and I was hugging Him back. It was always personal and intimate.

"For the first time in my life, I can't feel Him," I said. I looked across the table at her and her attention was completely focused on my face. "I know He's there, Debbie, but I can't seem to *feel* Him anymore. I have never felt so stuck spiritually, like I can't grow. For the first time I don't want to lead a Bible study, I don't want to feed the homeless, I don't even want to go to lunch or spend time with friends. I have no desire even to meet their spiritual needs or pray for them.

"People have always been my passion, and now I no longer have a desire to reach out to them. I just feel numb … just numb."

Debbie sat there quietly, not interrupting, keeping her steady, loving gaze on my face. She smiled, encouraging me to continue without saying a word.

"I don't know, Debbie," I said. "I have always looked forward to opportunities to minister. I have ministered to so many people in the past. Many of them mentioned that they sought professional help. Maybe I need a counselor … I don't know. I'm not sure. I think right now I am just going to be still and wait. God will reveal it to me."

"Well, Dorothy, if you want to see somebody," she offered, "I have someone I trust that I think you would enjoy knowing and visiting with."

I looked at her, knowing she was in earnest. "I don't know, Debbie. If it's not you, I mean you yourself, then there is no way I would trust them. I'll be honest with you, I have some trust issues. The life I have lived … it is hard for me to know who I can trust."

I sat there for a moment and images of people I had trusted, but who betrayed me flashed across my mind. I had been disappointed so many times. Hurt by people I loved.

"To be honest, the worst is over in my life. It is in my past. I don't really think I need to talk to anybody. I was just thinking about it, that's all. I haven't really decided to do that. I'm fine," I told her.

"Let's pray about it," Debbie said. "I have someone in mind you would really enjoy talking to. I love her. I trust her. I believe she can help you, Dorothy."

She smiled again, the laugh lines around her eyes were inviting. Everything about her reflected the peace and love of God.

"So, I guess that explains what your passion is," she said.

"Right," I said. "Nothing. Nothing is my passion right now."

"Think about it," she sipped her tea and let a pregnant pause hover. "I believe the Lord has a lot planned for you. This would be something good for you."

"Are you gonna be there with me?" I asked.

"Yes. If that's what you want, then I'll be there with you. If you decide you want to see her, I will come with you," she offered.

"You know I come to Gateway regularly, but I still pay tithe at Southlake since that is where I am a member. I don't even give money to Gateway. Are you sure that's gonna be okay?" I asked.

"I'm sure," she said. "I believe this is what God wants. It doesn't matter."

Lunch was over. I always enjoyed lunch with Debbie, but we didn't get to spend very much time together. I knew it would be months before I saw her again. I knew we would send text messages and stay in touch, but I was thinking, *Yeah, right. Debbie does not have time to check into this. She has a million things to do. She travels with Pastor Robert. She's not going to check into this.*

Remember, I said to myself. *This is not about you. You are here for her, not so you can be needy.* In truth, I cared about her very much. I wanted her to have a friend in me that she could lean on, that she could trust. The last thing I wanted was to be someone else she needed to expend energy on. I felt a little remorse that I had shared my problem with her.

A half hour after I left the restaurant, my phone rang. I pulled it from my purse and looked at the screen to see who was calling. It was Debbie.

"Dorothy! I checked with Rebecca, and she has three dates open," she said, telling me the three openings. "Which one is good for you?" she asked.

"Debbie," I answered, "I'm surprised you called, but … wait …"

"I'll hold on while you decide," she said, not giving me a chance to back out. The excitement in her voice was unmistakable. Quiet, sweet Debbie was bubbling on the other end of the line.

"Okay, let me look," I said.

"If you still want me there, I'll be there," she reassured me. "What day is best for you?"

Pink Impact, Gateway's Women's Conference was just a few weeks away. I checked my calendar and picked a date after the conference.

I can't believe this, I thought to myself after I hung up. *I just can't believe it.* Debbie took the time to ask me what I was passionate about. She was genuinely interested in me. I wanted to be there for her, and here she asked about me, getting me to open up to her and share what was going on in my life.

I couldn't wrap my head around the fact that she had called and followed through the same day ... just thirty minutes after I left her. I thought about the excitement in her voice and how authentic and real her attention to me was.

The next time I saw Lynn Martin I told her, "I think I need to see a counselor, Lynn. I just feel stuck."

Lynn is a strong woman. She loves God. She doesn't like even the hint of gossip. Any time I went to her feeling down or dejected, she would look at me and say, "Snap out of it, Dot." Then she would remind me of how strong

I was. She would remind me of the person I was and who God made me to be. She would tell me that I was not a quitter—that I could get through this. Never once did she allow me to think of myself as a victim or enable me. This was often exactly what I needed. She was the "tough love" person in my life.

When I told her I was thinking about seeing a counselor she said, "You don't need a counselor. All you need is God, the One you have been depending on your whole life. Who brought you through everything you've been through? God, right? Why do you need a counselor now?"

"I don't know, Lynn," I answered. "I've just been thinking about it, that's all."

A few days later I saw Ingrid. I was wavering a little, not sure if I wanted to go through with the appointment, but not wanting to back out after Debbie had gone to so much trouble.

I told Ingrid I was thinking about perhaps seeing a counselor. Without hesitation she said, "That's a very good thing. I always believed you should be able to talk to somebody. You've been through an awful lot. It will help," she encouraged.

I was scared to death. I sat outside in my car, trying to talk myself into going inside to Rebecca's office. *Why did I agree to this?* I thought. *You know why,* I answered myself. I had prayed much about this since my lunch appointment with Debbie. I knew for sure I was supposed to do it, but I was nervous. I didn't know what to expect or what was expected of me. I had never seen a real counselor before— Nate and I saw one once for two sessions, but I hardly counted that. I wasn't sure how I was supposed to act or what I was supposed to say.

I got out of the car, locked the door and went inside. Debbie was already there, as if sensing that I would need to see her right away. I was grateful.

"Where would you like to sit?" Rebecca asked.

Simple question, right? But I froze.

"Dorothy?" Debbie reached out her hand, "Where would you like to sit down?"

At first I wanted to sit next to Debbie, like close enough to hold her hand because I was so afraid. I stood there and looked at the loveseat. I knew if I sat next to Debbie,

I would have dependency on her. I was independent. *If this is going to work,* I thought, *then I'm gonna have to be able to do it on my own. Debbie is <u>not</u> going to be able to come to every session with you.* I looked at the chair, standing there by itself—it was independent, strong, and represented courage. I sat down in the chair.

Rebecca suggested that we pray together first, and that really helped me. She encouraged me to talk about anything I wanted to talk about. I assumed this was how it worked, I would tell her everything, then she would tell me what I needed to do to fix it. I rushed through my whole life story as fast as I could, wanting to get it all out and be done with it. I talked fast, my nervousness causing me to speed up even more.

As I shared, tears welled up. *I cannot cry,* I told myself. *I cannot cry. If I start crying, I might not be able to stop.* That was the last thing I wanted. I swallowed hard and forced the tears back inside. I just wanted to get through this.

"Dorothy," Debbie said gently, "It's alright to cry."

"No," I said, shaking my head. "No, if I start, I won't be able to stop." I had not cried in a very long time. Even when tears had come in my past, I didn't allow myself to give in to them. I believed that I needed to be strong. I didn't believe I should take time crying over things I couldn't change.

I continued sharing my story, and so much pain came to the surface. More than I ever expected. I kept stopping myself to gain composure. It felt like the flood gates were trying to open and I was terrified that if I allowed myself to cry, I literally might not be able to stop.

For years I had suppressed everything. I never dealt with anything, I just pushed it down. I set the hard things aside and concentrated on moving forward. The more I talked, the more pain surfaced, but I refused to cry.

I wanted to finish my story. I wanted to tell the whole thing in one session so I would never have to do it again. I didn't ever want to think about these horrible things again. I figured if I could get all this out, then the next time I came, Rebecca could tell me what I needed to do to fix things and stop feeling stuck.

I finally finished. I looked at my watch—it had been almost three hours. I knew I had bounced around all over the place as memories long buried came rushing out, but I had done it. I felt relieved.

"So, are you going to be able to help me?" I asked Rebecca. "Is this going to be a quick fix?"

Rebecca smiled at me and said, "Let God decide how it's going to be. If you will commit, then I am willing to do whatever I can to be a vessel for God. I just need a commitment from you."

"What type of commitment?" I asked. I wasn't sure what she meant.

"Well, why don't we just schedule next week's visit," she said, offering me no clue about the length of time we would work together or how many sessions we would have.

I was exhausted. I had scheduled dinner at Brio with a friend. She was going through a difficult divorce and I had been ministering to her, encouraging her and praying with her to get through it. I sat outside in my car for thirty minutes, composing myself. I could not believe I had just told a complete stranger my whole, private, painful life story.

I flipped down the visor and touched up my makeup. I breathed deeply. I was an expert at separating myself from painful things and dealing with matters at hand.

I adjusted my focus to my friend and didn't give my experience with Debbie and Rebecca another thought.

After dinner I went home. I had prepared for that day by taking off work. King was staying with Lynn and K-Mart, so I was by myself. Exhausted, I went to bed and slept soundly. I didn't wake up until the next morning.

The next week I met with Rebecca again. We scheduled meetings once a week, but I wanted a quick fix. I wanted her to give me the steps to getting un-stuck so I could follow them like a diet or exercise plan.

I couldn't open up any more. Rebecca encouraged me to talk about whatever I wanted to, but I couldn't open up … so it took many, many sessions. I felt guilty about going and taking up this woman's time. *There must be other people she could help if I wasn't taking up the appointment,* I thought. She was so patient with me. She was a loving, caring, sensitive person. Session after session I came, but couldn't bring myself to open up again.

"I'm so sorry," I told Rebecca in one session, "I am wasting your time. It has been four weeks. You shouldn't be wasting your time on me because I'm going to be okay. I'm a strong person. I've been through terrible things, but that is all in my past. There are other people you can help, you must be impatient with me showing up and not able to talk about anything."

I was upset that I had dragged Debbie through my story. I was worried that I might have damaged her as she sat through my entire spill. I wondered what she thought. *Would she judge me? Would she see me differently?* I regretted that she knew my past. I wished I had not agreed.

I genuinely felt like I was wasting Rebecca's time. I had told her everything on the first day, there wasn't anything left to say. Taking up her time to spend with me when I knew she must have other people who really needed her made me feel selfish and guilty. Every appointment was a major struggle for me. I didn't want to go, but God gave me no release. I showed up, but I wasn't engaged. I was resistant to everything. The more difficult I became, the sweeter Rebecca was. There seemed to be no end to her patience.

One afternoon I came home from work, and had a session scheduled for later. I prayed, "God, this is just not working out. It was sweet of Debbie, but nothing is happening. I am wasting this woman's time. I feel guilty and that is certainly not helping me feel less stuck. Other people need her. She can actually minister to them. I am going to cancel. Okay?"

Nothing ... I didn't hear a yes or a no, just nothing. I decided to take a long, hot bath and stay home. I would call Rebecca and cancel. I ran my bathwater and put in a CD that Gateway had given out for Mother's Day. It was music, mixed in with voices reading Scripture. It relaxed me. I sunk down in the water, letting the Word wash over my soul. There it was ... I recognized that voice! Right there on the CD was Rebecca's voice, reading Scripture to me. I couldn't believe it ... I could not escape!

I sat up, got out of the tub, got dressed as quickly as I could, and hurried to the office. "I know you want me to be there," I prayed. "I feel guilty, though. I don't understand the purpose for going. I don't want to go anymore. Help me know what to say to her tonight so I won't hurt her feelings when I tell her that this is my last session."

I got to Rebecca's office and told her what happened in the tub. She smiled. It was a turning point. I can't explain it, but it was true.

Continuing with the sessions was the hardest thing I had ever done, but Rebecca was persistent. She was easy to talk to, even when what we talked about seemed totally irrelevant. *How could I not want to be here?* I thought, *Oh well, I guess I'm not a quick fix after all.*

Session after session, Rebecca was consistent and patient. She never gave any indication that she was bored or tired of listening to me. It was incredible. It was a gift— for as long as I needed it, she was there. Other people would have given up on me long before now. If I had been paying a therapist, I would have spent thousands and thousands of dollars by now—and I knew I would have quit. God knew I needed Rebecca. I had been the giver my entire life. I had never received anything of this magnitude.

Anger began to surface. Anger that I had pushed down and pushed away and convinced myself I didn't have. As my sessions with Rebecca continued, I began having to deal with anger. I was shocked by it. I was a Christian. I loved the Lord. I wasn't supposed to feel like this. I had forgiven Nate, so where was all this anger coming from?

My anger began to consume me. Literally, every moment of my day—it was there with me—ugly, taunting, pushing me to explode. I was ashamed of it.

In order to remain focused on my job and taking care of King, I gave myself "containment time" during the day—

time when I would allow the anger to surface so I could deal with my issues, then dutifully I would put it away, push it to the back of my mind so I could function.

Little by little I allowed myself the joy of receiving comfort. I received attention with nothing asked in return. It cracked my shell. I can't even begin to describe how much anger there was inside of me. I couldn't comprehend how I had lived for so long with all of that buried so deep, not even realizing how much space it had occupied in my subconscious.

One evening I was in a session with Rebecca, but I was still holding things back. I didn't want to deal with one more ounce of anger. I believed that I had talked about so much already—surely God would do whatever needed to happen in my life with what I had already shared. Did I really need to bring up one more thing? Then finally, breakthrough came.

I started to cry. First a few tears, then it was like a dam broke and tears, so long kept under control, burst forth. It was a sweet release.

I felt dirty from the moment I agreed to have sex with Nate before we were married. I had never felt pure and whole again from that night. I had been through so much.

I had suffered so much. I had compromised. I had made bad decisions. My boys had suffered. I had lived with shame, never feeling pure.

As I cried, the tears cleansed me. God showed me that no matter what my life had been before, He could make it new again. The tears flowed. I felt completely poured out—emptied of all the guilt, sorrow, and shame. Everything of me was emptied and replaced by Him.

I cried so much that I thought I would never be able to stop. I didn't realize there were so many tears inside of me that needed to be shed. I was at last free to receive. It was as if the Holy Spirit took complete control over everything and I was finally free. I didn't have to think about anything. I didn't feel guilty any more. I was overwhelmed by God's love.

The tears finally ended. I was completely spent, exhausted, but completely at peace.

Rebecca prayed with me and God showed me a vision of a girl in a plain, white dress. It was raining. I was in the mud and my dress was getting dirty, filthy. The weather got worse and it turned into a storm with thunder and lightning. I cried out to God and the rain stopped. Soaking wet I looked up to the sky, the clouds began to break. I twirled around and around, holding my arms up to Him. I looked up into His face and began thanking Him, still twirling. As I twirled around, my dress got beautiful. I got beautiful. Suddenly, there was no dirt anywhere, just green grass and sunshine and the lover of my soul.

My entire body reverberated with gratitude. He loved me so much. I could feel Him with every breath. I could sense Him in every heart beat. He had collected every tear and they were precious to Him.

"Rebecca, can you see things pouring out of me?" I asked. "Can you see the joy? Can you see the love?"

It was then I realized that God did have great plans for me. I wasn't disqualified because of my past. I would never be the same. My past did not define me. I had a whole life stretched out before me—a lot of living to do. I was God's vessel, pure, sanctified. I was cleansed. I was holy—set apart for His perfect use.

I was free.

Thirty

NEW

And He that sat upon the throne said,
"Behold, I make all things new."

—REVELATION 21:5a

---

*T*hings were different now. Instead of being God's vessel struggling to survive, working hard not to walk in hypocrisy, now I was God's vessel, poured out and ready to be used by Him. I was ready to let Him put people in my path when He chose, how He chose, and why He chose. I no longer felt the need to protect myself or manipulate things.

I was totally free from my guilty past. I no longer felt ashamed about the choices I had made. I thought I had forgiven Nate—I thought I had forgiven a lot of people, but I had much to learn about forgiveness. Most importantly, I had to learn to forgive myself and accept God's forgiveness without any strings attached. It was much deeper than emptying myself. It was God filling me, equipping me. Because of the time I spent with Rebecca, I would never be the same.

I had always known God. I had never walked away from Him, even in the most difficult times of my life. My relationship with Him had been strong—yet incomplete because I closed off part of myself, not allowing His forgiveness to free me from shame. I had not received all He had to give. Now I freely surrendered every part of my heart, soul, and mind to Him—we were inseparable and I was filled to overflowing with joy.

For six months I had met with Rebecca weekly. After the breakthrough came, we met less often. We spread the sessions out to every other week, then monthly, and finally, quarterly check-ups. I was a completely different person. I had always had trouble receiving from others. I went to God for what I needed, on my own. Rebecca would not accept anything from me. She wouldn't allow me to give her anything. I wanted to show her how much I appreciated her, but she wouldn't accept anything from me. She wouldn't even allow me to take her out to lunch. I longed to shower her with my appreciation, but she wanted me to receive from her as a free gift—and give nothing in return. It was very, very hard for me to do. Rebecca had prayed about it, and God had told her that there should be no exchange. He told her to minister to me from her heart, not for pay.

April 1, 2010 I met with Rebecca for my quarterly check-up. It was God-ordained. It felt like a reunion. I had come so far from that first afternoon in her office. I had kept in touch with my biological dad and he had been sick. I traveled to Maryland every month to visit him. As our session ended, my cell phone rang and it was my brother. He called to tell me that my father had died. In the past, when something tragic happened to me, I pushed it down, dealing with it on my own, and never sharing my pain with anyone else. I just moved on. I got this terrible news while I was there with Rebecca. I talked with her about how I would handle it. I shared with her how close I had grown to him. I had been given the opportunity to get to know him much better and had bonded with my brother and his family. I knew he was sick, but I had not expected him to die. Rebecca was there for me. She encouraged me to connect with Lynn and Ingrid and let them know how this affected me. I promised her I would.

The following day I went to work and told no one. I didn't let anyone know how sad I was. As I promised Rebecca, I called Ingrid and Lynn and asked them to go to church with me. Both agreed. On the way to church, I told them that my father died. It was the strangest feeling—I was not used to telling someone when I was hurting or in need. Ingrid and Lynn were wonderful. Even this small act was a breakthrough for me.

Things with Nate were much better now. I could see evidence of change in him. He was no longer angry when he saw me. We could be civil to each other in public as well as in private. I knew he and his wife had gotten involved in church and I prayed that the changes in him were genuine—that at last he had truly found the Lord. I hoped he was also living a new life. I forgave Nate in my heart for everything—I was free—I wanted Nate to be free also. I wanted him to have a good relationship with Tre' and King. They had made their peace with him and I hoped, with their past. I truly wanted God's best for Nate Newton.

Tre' had experienced several concussions playing for the University of Texas. Nate and I flew to Austin and met with him and a team of doctors. Their advice was that Tre' should not play football any longer. We did our own research and found out as much information as we could. In the end, it was Tre's decision. He had information from his coaches, from the medical staff, and from us, but it was his decision to play or to give up football. Ultimately, he was the one who had to live with the choice, so we let the choice be his. In November 2010, he held a press conference and announced that he would no longer play football.

The news was hard on the whole family. Tre' had loved football since he was two years old. He was passionate about it. The only toys he ever wanted as a boy were footballs and little football men, he loved everything about the NFL. He loved watching Nate play and was proud that his daddy was a pro. He was also a scholar, and attending school on a football scholarship. Nate and I both expressed that we supported his decision 100%. He told me that he knew continuing to play would be selfish. Another serious injury could leave him an invalid for life—and that would have meant I had to take care of him. He didn't want that for me.

Remarkably, U.T. honored his football scholarship. They did not penalize him because he was injured and unable to play. He continued to support the team, working with them and being involved from the side lines. His passion for football now had to express itself in other ways.

In February 2011, I received an invitation to attend W.I.L.D. (Women in Leadership Development, a mentoring process through Gateway Church). The invitation indicated that all the meetings were held during the weekdays. I was working full time, so I knew I wouldn't be able to attend. I discarded the invitation without much thought.

A friend of mine asked me if I had received an invitation to W.I.L.D. I told her I had, but I didn't give it much thought because of work. "Dorothy!" she exclaimed. "Do you realize how many women would give anything for this opportunity? This is special. You should at least pray about it."

I had been a member of Gateway for some time by now. I hosted a Life Group in my home for a year, but I wasn't really the leader, just the host. Holly Smith had been the leader and had submitted my name for W.I.L.D.

"Did you have a chance to look at the invitation?" she asked one day.

"Yes, Holly, I did. I'm praying about it," I replied.

I forwarded the invitation to my boss. It was a leadership class, and we were encouraged to attend classes that developed our leadership and management skills. "This class will meet for two hours each week," I wrote in an email. "Do you mind if I attend?"

I had barely hit the Send button when the reply came back. "Absolutely!" it said. My last excuse was gone. I accepted the invitation.

Thirty-One

W.I.L.D.

For to be free is not merely to cast off one's chains, but to live in a way that respects and enhances the freedom of others.

—NELSON MANDELA

I showed up for the first class, feeling a little shy. I wasn't really sure why I was here. I had always considered myself a leader, but I was uncomfortable in small, intimate settings. They began by asking everyone to say their name and share something about themselves. *Oh, no,* I thought. *I do not want to do this!*

I knew I was supposed to be there, so I did my best. I enjoyed the class very much, in fact. The women were all really wonderful and Jan Greenwood, Lynda Grove, and Mallory Bassham were great teachers. I was learning a lot.

Early on, Jan announced that each member of the class would have to present a project at the end. This frightened me. What kind of project? I wondered. Jan put very few guidelines on the project and I preferred strict rules and expectations. This made me uncomfortable.

God had spoken to me on a Friday night two years earlier and told me that I was supposed to write my story. The next morning, Nate met me and a friend in a restaurant to drop something off for the boys. I told him, "Last night, God told me I was supposed to write a book." I even suggested that perhaps we should write it together.

I recalled the words of Ingrid, how she often encouraged me to become more involved in ministry—even to do it full time. I so loved ministering to people and Ingrid saw this gift in me. She had encouraged me to write a book ... but until that Friday night, I had never given it any serious thought.

Over the next few weeks I prayed about it in earnest. I asked a friend, Janet Gray, to pray about it with me, that I believed God was preparing me to be His vessel by writing a book someday.

About a month later I attended a function in Janet's new home and she gave me a tour. One very small room was designated as her prayer closet, and there I saw a picture of me with the boys and writing on the wall indicating that she had been praying for us. In that moment, I had confirmation that God was planning something great for me.

Some time later a friend of mine, Terri, gave me a luncheon for my birthday. She introduced me to her friend, Gracie. During the meal I mentioned that I was going to write a book. Gracie is an author and encouraged me to do it. She even graciously offered to help me when the time came and I was ready to advance.

I have always enjoyed reading books by Sheila Walsh. I had just read sample chapters of her book, *Beautiful Things Happen When a Woman Trusts God*, on her website. It had not even been released yet. There was an invitation extended to write your short story—about 120 words, and if selected, you would be interviewed by Sheila Walsh. *That's it!* I thought. Excited at the prospect of meeting this phenomenal woman, and motivated to exercise my trust in God, I called my friend Isabel to help me edit something I had already written. *This is my answer!* I told myself.

Faithfully I submitted my story, but I was not selected. At first I was very disappointed. *Maybe I'm crazy,* I thought.

But the weight of the assignment did not lift. I knew that God wanted me to write a book, to share my story. As soon as Jan mentioned the project, writing this book came to mind. "This can't be the project," I told God. "I cannot be that transparent with these people."

"You will write a book," God said …. over and over again.

The next class Jan Greenwood asked if everyone was comfortable with their project and told us that if we weren't we could ask her, Lynda or Mallory about it. After class I went over to her and said, "Excuse me. I don't want miss the last class just because I don't want to do this project. I really appreciate the class. I will complete the assignment, and I don't mind sharing it with you, but I really don't want to share this with everyone."

"What is it?" Jan asked.

"It's a book overview," I said.

"Does God want you to write the book?" she continued.

"Yes," I said, "I know for sure that I am supposed to write the book."

"Then why won't you be obedient?"

I stood there looking at her thinking, *You don't even know me. Why are you talking to me this way?*

My feelings were hurt. Jan was really friendly and when she spoke her words were powerful and full of anointing. I always looked forward to hearing her speak.

"Listen," she said. "God just wants you to be obedient, that's all. He's not asking you to write a best seller, He just wants you to be obedient."

This was not the same friendly, gentle person who went around the room and hugged everyone before class started. She was calling me out. She was so serious.

"I just think you need to be obedient. I don't know why I am being this strong with you, but I need to tell you that God wants to use you and that you need to be obedient." She didn't say another word after that. I left a little mad with her. *You don't have to be so mean,* I said to myself.

The day drew near for the class to present their projects. I had completed the overview, but I was feeling nervous about presenting it to the class. I called Christi, one of my classmates, and told her I was uncomfortable about being so open and transparent.

She replied, "Dorothy, you have to trust God. You've always been a woman of God, ever since I've known you. Be obedient. God will control it all. Every time you speak people want to hear what you have to say. They listen to you. They tune in. Don't miss out on this opportunity."

The next day I was to present my overview in class. I arrived 45 minutes early and sat in my car praying. God clearly said, "Do not fear. I'll be with you. Not just today either, but every day for the rest of your life. You are a vessel. I have purposed and planned your life and this book is by My design."

Total peace flooded me. I was at ease. I could do this. When my turn came I stood up and gave the overview. Everyone was affirming and applauded as I finished. "Thank you," I said. "I was happy to be obedient." I caught Jan's eye and she was smiling and nodding her approval.

I had done it. It was over … I thought.

The last class was a wrap up session. It was just me and my classmate, Mika. I sat down and she immediately said, "Oh my goodness, you were amazing! You're going to be a woman of faith speaker some day. I couldn't wait to tell my family about you!" I was SO uncomfortable.

There was more positive feedback after that. I was grateful for my experience at W.I.L.D.—to have developed some good relationships. I had been given the opportunity to get to know the leadership more personally and I felt even more connected as part of the Gateway family.

Jan mentioned that God was telling her to have a book club. A group of women felt led to write a book and she asked if I might be interested if she was able to pull something together. "Sure," I said, not expecting anything to materialize.

I had been obedient and completed the project. I stood in front of a room full of people and shared parts of my story. This was a big step. I was ready to let it go.

Not long after, I received an email inviting me to attend the writing club. Meetings were scheduled once a month on Monday evenings and would last for six months. Jan was taking time out of her busy schedule to provide structure and accountability for the women who felt God had called them to write. It was summer time, so King was out of school and there was really no reason not to accept. It was easy.

Jan provided great information and it was a good class. I got to know her even better through this opportunity and the more I got to know her, the more I appreciated her. She invested herself in us. Instead of working on her own project and advancing her ministry, she poured her time into us, encouraging us to complete the assignments that God had entrusted to us. She provided valuable resources and some accountability with the process. Her grace and generosity effortlessly combined with her wisdom, humor, and practicality. She is an activator and strategist and now, a treasured friend.

There was lots of encouragement during the class, and I began making progress on the actual writing process. Still, I felt like I didn't really know what I was doing. I went to lunch with two new friends that I was just getting to know, Kim and Kiasi. They asked about what I was doing, where I worked and I just boldly said, "I'm writing a book."

"What's the title?" Kiasi asked.

"I don't know. Something like *Unheard Cries* or *Cries Unheard* or something like that, I'm not sure," I said.

"What about *Silent Tears*?" Kim asked.

"Oh! ... that's what the book should be about!" I said, excited.

"What does publishing a book entail?" Kiasi asked.

"Well, it sounds like it is going to be an expensive thing to do. I'm not a writer. I just write it raw and by the time it gets edited, it is going to cost a fortune!" I said.

"We have a sister named Karissa who has a Master's Degree in writing, would you trust her with it?"

She lived in Chicago, so I wasn't sure if that would work. After a few months I had not made very much progress so I decided to give it a try. It didn't work out very well, the story was so personal, I felt like I needed someone face to face that I could get to know and spend time with. I prayed and asked God to direct me to the right person.

Some time later, Jan had scheduled a guest to appear in class. Her name was Wendy Walters. She came to speak to our group. She gave us really practical information about different kinds of publishing and what things cost and how the process worked. Before long she was asking each person in the room about their project. She was full of energy and found ways to motivate and encourage each person there that what they had to share was important and their unique perspective made it special. She didn't say anything about her business, or promote herself in any way. All I saw was a true vessel of God who had a heart for helping people reach their potential and succeed in whatever their endeavor was.

She gave simple, straightforward action steps and each one of us could feel her excitement and passion to ignite what was inside of us. The room was bursting with creativity and "I can do this!" She had a few of her books, *Marketing Your Mind*, with her. I bought a copy because I wanted to learn more about what she had to say.

When she spoke to our group that day, I knew instantly I was supposed to call her. She made the process seem simple and she was easy to talk to. Then I thought, *if Jan trusted her enough to bring her into the group that's good enough for me.* God spoke to my heart and I couldn't wait to read her book. I took it with me on a trip to New York. I read it from cover to cover. It was the final stamp of approval—complete confirmation that this was who I was supposed to work with.

A week later, I called to set up an appointment to meet with her. From that very first meeting, it never felt like business. It was like we were old friends talking about next steps to push my project along. I asked about how she could help, what all was involved—I was in charge of the conversation for all those details. I was blown away that I didn't have to pay for her time. She was just willing to share with me what she knew about writing and the publishing process. She was even willing to recommend other people to me if they were a better fit for the project.

I didn't want anybody else. I knew she was the one I wanted to work with. We set up another appointment and I started from the beginning. She asked me questions and listened attentively, taking notes as I shared my story. This book you are reading right now is the result of our collaboration. God brought me everything I needed to accomplish the task He assigned to me. He's like that. When we obey and take steps of faith in obedience, He provides all the resources—people, time, finances, opportunities, strategy—every single thing needed to complete the task comes from His hand. All we have to do is obey.

Now you know my story. The way I did things was not always the way God intended. He wants us to have relationships. He loves people and He gives us people to love and be loved by. I believed I was supposed to be strong and independent. I thought asking for help was a sign of weakness, or meant that I wasn't relying on God. I didn't open up to anyone and that was a mistake.

I should have sought help long before I did. I should have gone to the authorities. I should have told my family about the danger I was in. I should have trusted Ingrid and Monte, Lynn and K-Mart ... somebody. I didn't have to suffer as long as I did. It was not punishment for my sins or for my choices, it was abuse.

Looking back, I enabled Nate. By staying with him and not forcing him to be accountable for his actions, I enabled his destructive behavior. I put my children in a terrible situation. I was afraid. I was afraid for my life, and afraid of being alone. I was afraid I wouldn't be able to provide for the boys without Nate's help.

The abuse began as verbal. Horrible arguments that lasted for hours. Cursing, intimidation, demeaning language ... I should have reached out then and not allowed it to go any further.

But it did go further. The verbal abuse turned physical and got worse by degrees over time. Physical abuse turned to sexual abuse that was demanding and I was controlled completely. He was bigger than me. Stronger than me. I was overpowered. I felt completely helpless to escape. I believed that there was no one that could stop the abuse. I believed that the authorities would give Nate a pass for his celebrity status. I didn't think anyone was capable of helping me escape, but I was wrong.

More than ten years have passed since the divorce at the time I write this book. By no means can I say that I walk in that perfect freedom every day. There are times when the shadow of my past still tries to bring darkness to my soul. The difference now is that I recognize it and cast it off. I know how important it is to have people in your life to be accountable to—people you can be open with and trust not to betray you. Trust still doesn't come easily. I wish I could say it did, but God is still at work and I know He will bring me into His perfect design.

I celebrate my story, every part of it. If I were given the opportunity to go back and change things, of course I would. But none of us has that ability. I am the person I am today as a result of the journey I have walked. My strength and grace are a result of life lived and lessons learned.

I am stepping into a new chapter of my life. A chapter that I hope will offer freedom to other women who are in abusive situations. I pray that when they read my words or hear my voice they will understand that abuse is wrong—never deserved and should not be tolerated.

I pray that abusers will recognize they are hurting the people they love the most and need help. They need God. They need accountability. They need someone to guard them and help them through their anger and bitterness and not resort to violence.

God offers hope to us all. He has a way of escape when we are ensnared in a trap that is outside His design. We each have a purpose. We each have a reason to live. I pray that my story will offer hope for a new day. I pray my experience will touch others and cause them to reach out for help and not remain one day longer in the prison of abuse.

Mostly, I pray my story will honor God. He is my everything. His love and His light have guided and protected me, even when I walked a path He did not choose for me. He has restored my soul, delivered me from the pit, and set my feet upon a solid rock. I pray you will come to know Him as I do. I pray you will allow yourself to feel His love and accept His complete, total forgiveness and restoration.

He sees your tears. He hears your cry. He knows every detail of your life—even the things you think no one else sees or hears. He captures your every tear. There is hope. He will save you. Only believe.

Interview

MEET
NATE NEWTON

Success isn't permanent and failure isn't fatal.

—MIKE DITKA

*I*n preparation for the release of *Silent Tears*, it seemed important to give you not only a look into Nate Newton's past, but also his present. The purpose of this book is not to expose juicy details about a famous athlete, but to shine a light on domestic violence and help others escape the damaging downward spiral and find a victorious life on the other side. To that end, Dorothy arranged for me to interview Nate and learn more about the man he has become.

401

It was a chilly October evening. A mist of rain blanketed the atmosphere and allowed the chill to penetrate your clothing and target your bones. The weather was miserable the night I met Nate at a Starbucks in Southlake, Texas. He was dressed to watch his son, King, play football for the Carroll Dragons later that evening.

We had never met before and Nate entered the Starbucks scanning the room for who it was he was supposed to meet. I caught his eye and stood to meet him. "Nate?" I questioned, not positive it was him. He looked very different from the photos I had seen when researching him on the internet. "Yes, ma'am," he said, shaking my outstretched hand and sizing me up. This was definitely not his first interview.

I gestured to a corner where I had positioned some chairs to face each other in an attempt at privacy. I was grateful Nate had granted the interview and knew he was fully aware of the content of Dorothy's book. I could only imagine how he felt about the information soon to come to light. As a high profile alumni of the Dallas Cowboys, a well known member of the Dallas/Ft. Worth community, and a current radio personality (The Coop & Nate Show, 103.3 ESPN Radio), Nate is no stranger to public scrutiny of his personal life. Years of fame and infamy stretch behind him like yard lines on a familiar field.

As I prepared for our meeting, I came across his words in another interview where he was quoted as saying, "I don't care what you write about me. What I did, I did. That's on me." Other reporters have found him bluntly honest without any attempt to gloss over his missteps along the way. I was curious to know how he would respond to my questions and wanted desperately to communicate that the focus of the interview was on who he had become, not on who he had been. I began by telling him the purpose of my interview was not to dredge up his past, but rather to offer a perspective on his future. I wanted others who had been abusers to understand that the cycle of abuse does not have to continue indefinitely. There is hope.

"Let me first tell you something about my past," Nate began.

"I always lived life to what I thought was the fullest for me. I'm an emotional person. I'm excitable. If I believe I'm right, I don't care what nobody say—how dumb it is or how dumb it may seem to somebody else—if I believe I'm right, that's the end of the story. My highs are very high. My lows are very low. That's what drove me, and sometimes I took things to extremes."

He took a sip of his coffee and settled in, he was ready to talk.

"My Uncle Charles died when I was in high school or college, I can't exactly remember," he said. "When I would visit him he always told me, 'Son, live life to the fullest. Live it how you want to live it.' Well, I took that beyond what he meant. He meant for me to live a good life and cherish every day how it comes. Me, being a young buck, I took that to mean for me to be the wildest dude in the world. I took his advice to mean do what you want to do, how you want to do it—and I did. I lived like that, whatever I did. Whether it was drinking … everything … I took everything wrong. Like the drinking, women, living on the edge, mistreating people, I just took everything too far. By the time I realized what Uncle Charles really meant, I had spent a good part of my life living on the edge, having fun … and believe me, I had fun. I ain't one of these people that look back and say, 'Oh man, golly, what have I done?' I had fun. The good, the bad, and the ugly, I had fun. But by the time I realized what life is all about—and thank God … thank God He saved me before

I got too far that I can't recover—by the time I realized who God was and what He really meant to me, I had done lived a whole life of pursuing the wrong things. So now this is where we are at now.

"I realize now that if you are a parent or a husband, your life ain't yours. I was married, but everything had to revolve around me. I had kids, but everything had to revolve around me. Now, since I've changed my life and God is a part of my life, now I know I have to make sacrifices for my kids—for my wife now (Michelle). It's kind of amazing the transformation because you just do things differently. That's basically all I can say."

"When did you find God?" I asked.

"It was once I got out of prison, you'll have to do the research, seven or eight years ago maybe. I got out of prison and I had to find a job. I went to Deion Sanders, I went to David Wells—he was a bail bondsman—and he said, 'Man I got just the guy. His name is Omar Jahwar. He's a preacher out of South Dallas.'

"I had to get a job, you see, because I was on parole in Louisiana and I was on probation here in Dallas, so I had to get a job or I would be in violation. They were giving me time to get a job, and I had a big fine I had to pay back, so I went to David Wells and Deion and they were trying to help me find a good job, not just any job. At the time I was just like ... I just need to get a job and start paying these people back their money.

"David Wells told me one night, 'Meet me at Hooters, I got this pastor I want you to meet' and I was like, 'Whoa, meet you at Hooters? Okay.' He told me he had the perfect guy for me to meet and he introduced me to Omar. I was like, 'I'm meeting a pastor at Hooters!' So Omar tells me that he has a job for me mentoring kids in South Dallas. I said, 'What do you want in return?' He told me, 'Nothing really, but I'll think of something.' As the evening went on, Omar asked me to introduce him to Deion Sanders and ask him to come to a function to raise money for Vision Regeneration. I said, 'Well, cool, that's easy.' We spent several more hours talking in that Hooters and it was like I had known Omar all my life. It seemed like I grew up with this dude.

"You asked me when I found God. Well, I don't know what day it was. I know most people can remember this epic day of when they recall finding God. I'm different than most people. How do you find God? God has always been there. When I decided I was going to be a part of God's plan, I was just in my truck—I think I had little diesel deal—something small because I had just gotten out of prison. I was driving around and I said, 'You know God, You've always covered me through everything—multiple car wrecks, bad marriage, how I was, drug-related deals, me selling drugs, and You've always covered me. I've never really had to work a day in my life and I've always known You. I've always known that You're about right and good ... but I chose the other route.'"

Nate stopped his remembrance here and looked at me right in the eyes, "I was never ignorant, you see. I always knew there was a God, but I also knew that ... and here is where Dorothy and I may disagree: when I met her, I never played like I ever wanted to be a Christian. I didn't ever even say I was gonna try to be a Christian. She'll say that through the bad times we went through I would say, 'I'm going to try to be better,' and I would ask her to pray for me, but I was trying to be a better husband, I never said I was trying to be better with God.

"So when I decided that I was going to better my life and get right with Christ, I knew that I was going into it whole-heartedly and if I saw it wasn't working, then

I wasn't going to stick with it. One thing about it, you're either with God 100% or you're going to hell.

"When I decided to change and get my life right I was well aware of what it took because of the people around me—I knew Dorothy was a Christian, I knew my son Tre' was a Christian, I knew my father, my mother, Deion Sanders, Tony Hayes, Charlie Biggers—these people were Christians. They never told me it was thunder and lightning and all of a sudden your life just miraculously changes. I knew it wasn't like that because I knew the struggles they went through.

"So, when I became I Christian I already knew what it was going to be like for me. I saw Dorothy, Deion, Charlie, Tony, Tre', my mother and father—I saw that they couldn't be shaken. I knew I would be like that. I told you if I believe something is right, I don't care what anybody else says or thinks. I did feel like they would probably be closer in their faith and in their walk with Christ than I could ever be—not because I started late, that isn't what determines it. Because I lived in the flesh for so long … I think if you could start earlier, you wouldn't have the habits, you see? The habits from my past … " his voice trailed off.

Nate chuckled and reengaged, "You see," he continued, "One thing I like about the Bible, and about God and Jesus Christ is common sense. It allows for a whole lot of common sense. Take Paul. Nobody was worse than Paul, you see? But nobody was greater than Paul. Once God said, 'Now I'm gonna use you,' nobody was greater. When Paul had to tell his own people, the Jews, that they could not deny the Gentiles—and nobody had been better at persecuting and murdering the Gentiles than Paul—but he told the Jews, 'Now that Jesus has died for these people and grafted them into the vine, they have been given the same rights that you have. As long as they stay in the belief of Jesus Christ, they have to be given every opportunity.' Do you understand what I mean?

"What I mean by that is, I think with Dorothy, or Tre', or Deion, they started earlier with habits of love, and the earlier you start with those habits, the easier it is if you fall off the wagon—to get back on. I'm not saying they love God more than me, but they're already at the meat of the Word and I'm just still getting past the milk and the mash. I don't have the same habits they have.

"I still have a lot of flesh to fight. The things that Dorothy went through with me … there is no way I could ever look good to someone. I would never look good to women, and I don't expect to look good. I'll deal with that. I don't need acceptance from you or anybody. All I need for you to understand is that even though I can't change what has happened, you can't stop it that now I live in peace. Who I am now, what I've been through, what Dorothy has been through, how we have come through it, how our kids have prospered … you have to let your kids know that you can change your mind. You can be different."

Nate talked for a few minutes about his parents and the differences about how he was brought up and how Dorothy was brought up. He spoke very fondly of his mom and dad and of his sons. He expressed that he believed he and Dorothy shared the same basic core values all along, just that his path caused him to make very different choices.

"When I did stupid things, there were only three entities that I apologized to for the wrong that I did. One was Dorothy and the boys—that's one because they are my family. Two was my mother and father. I had to apologize to them separately, you see? My mom was a school teacher and I put her through a lot. My father was self employed. He owned a store, a gas station, and several properties and he talked and bragged about his kids. I hurt them and I had to apologize to my parents separately. Finally, the third was that I had to apologize to the Dallas Cowboys' organization and fans. I mean, the Cowboys knew my antics ... they knew ... but I lived a dual life. I presented one thing and did another.

"I told some of my friends that Dorothy was going to write this book and they told me, 'Oh man, that's gonna make you look bad.'

"You know what? I prayed about it and I said to myself, 'I'll deal with that when it comes.'"

We both took another sip of our coffee. I shared with Nate that the purpose of this interview was not only to lend credibility to Dorothy's story and to keep the press from doing, "He said, she said," but my main purpose in interviewing him was to reach out to those who had been abusers—men who found themselves trapped in a cycle of violence, hurting those they care about the most. I was curious to gain his perspective not only on what caused him to be abusive, but even more what caused him to stop. I wanted to know what he would say to men who abused women.

Nate didn't even have to pause to think about what he would say, he just dived in, "Whether you hit a woman once, or you hit her 50,000 times, there is no place in our make-up as a man that allows for us to ever do that. It's unacceptable, that's the bottom line. Any man that knows God understands that as a man, hitting a woman is never ever acceptable.

"Will men do that? Yes. Men will fly off the handle and do that, but I am telling you that it is never okay. For a woman to think that she has to accept that (abuse) … she needs to seek help now—and much faster than that man does. For a man to beat a woman, and this is what I had to come to grips with, for a man to beat a woman, he's a coward.

"You're a coward! That's all there is to it!"

Nate took a moment to regroup. He was visibly stirred up.

"I went to God," he resumed talking, "and started seeing a change in my life and a lot of things started to fall into place. There were things I had to do right away. I went to Dorothy right after I got out of prison and apologized to her, but I had to go back again after I found

God and apologize again. When I made my apologies as a Christian, only then could I even begin to understand forgiveness. Only then could I start to feel good about it. Yes, I apologized when I got out of prison, and I was grateful for the way she stuck by me and showed love, but it wasn't until I was a Christian and then I made my apologies to Dorothy, to my mother and father, to the Cowboys and fans that I began to feel good.

"Do you feel free now?" I asked.

"I do feel free, but I never want to forget and fall back into that. I have a wife now (Michelle). I still get mad. I still have real, real bad days and real, real bad nights, but I don't ever want to get so angry that I would put my hands on her. It takes God to keep me from that. Only God can.

"For athletes I think it is worse. We're conditioned for aggression. We're conditioned to respond physically. Larry Allen asked me one time, 'Nate do you sometimes just get so wound up? So full of anxiety?' I told him, 'Yeah, I do. Let me tell you how to fix it—you gotta start praying. Don't go get a drink, don't go talk to your wife. When the anxiety attacks come you gotta start praying. That's the only thing that's gonna fix it.'

"I tried drinkin'. I tried going away and being by myself, but that didn't work. Nothing I tried worked. It takes God's intervention. Now I surround myself with Christians, even my doctor is a good Christian. Michelle and I have been married now for a long time. We attend North Dallas Community Bible Fellowship ... "

Nate looks down at his watch and reminds me that he doesn't want to miss the start of King's game. There is much more I want to ask him, but I know our interview has come to an end.

I am left with the impression that this man's journey has led him to a very different place than where he was many years ago, and that he has a journey ahead of him still. I am convinced that he deeply regrets his behavior and the pain he has caused—not only to Dorothy, but to his sons, his family, and his fans. I lift a prayer for Nate as he walks out into the cold mist. I ask God to fully reveal the power of His forgiveness and acceptance to Nate. I thank God that He is faithful to complete the work that is started. As I watch him drive off toward Dragon Stadium, I believe that God has much, much more in store for Nate Newton.

Interview

MEET
TRE' & KING
NEWTON

Train up a child in the way he should go: and
when he is old, he will not depart from it.

—PROVERBS 22:6

---

*T*his story would be incomplete without gaining the perspective of Nate and Dorothy's two sons, Tre' and King. I spoke with each of them separately, wanting to give them the opportunity to share their thoughts with you.

I spoke with Tre' over the telephone on November 11, 2011. He was an excellent communicator, a very articulate young man. He was reserved at first, unsure exactly what was expected from him during our interview. He knew this was important to his mom and wanted to get it right.

I told him that I wanted him to relax and be completely free to share anything he liked.

"What was it like for you growing up?" I asked. "Were you aware of the abuse? How did it make you feel?"

"I remember lots of arguing in my house," he began. "I would go to my room, but I still could hear what was going on. Sometimes I would pop out and see what was taking place.

"There were times I felt very helpless. This was all I knew. I didn't know other families were different. It felt like it was wrong at the time, even though I was little, and I knew it was bad. I just didn't know any other way of life.

"When dad started drinking, I expected something bad to happen. Like, I knew it would be bad for my mom. It hurt me, it made me feel bad. I was used to it. It was what I expected. I knew I couldn't do anything about it.

"When it was happening, I would hide out and wait for it to be over. I knew my mom would be sad, and the next day I knew we would act like nothing ever happened.

"I knew not to say anything. I tried to avoid my dad as much as I could. I only enjoyed going with him to the

Cowboys locker room because I loved football so much. At home, I never knew when he was going to go off, like he was bipolar or something.

"I have always felt real protective of my mom. I would tell her, 'Let's leave, we should go away.' I had a hard time understanding why we stayed so long. It was really bad sometimes and I wanted her to leave. I was excited when they got a divorce."

"How has it affected you as adult?" I asked.

"I don't want to be like that when I get older, get married, and have kids. I want to be careful to treat girls I talk to with respect. When I slip up I think to myself, *I don't want to be anything like my dad.* I'm aware of the statistics. But I don't plan to be one of them. I have always fallen back on my faith. My mom kept us in the Word and we always prayed together at night.

"When mom was abused or I would be in my room praying for her that she wouldn't be hurt or that he wouldn't do anything, I used to pray for my dad to be a happy drunk. There were times when he was a happy drunk and then he was actually a lot of fun to be around.

When he came home drunk I just hoped he would go to sleep. You just didn't know what to expect.

"When I spoke with your dad, he talked about how playing football had conditioned him to be aggressive. Sometimes it was difficult for him to turn that off at home. You have played a great deal of football how did that affect you?" I asked.

"When I step onto the football field I'm a different person. When I step off the field that part of me shuts down. When I'm on the field I'm really aggressive and violent and competitive. This switches off when I leave the football field."

"Tre', you saw your mom suffer for a long time. What would you tell women trapped in abusive situations?" I asked.

"I know there would be better ways, but in our situation my mom kept me away and protected me from the worst of it. She would send me off to my Uncle T. Hayes' house or to stay with friends and try to keep me from seeing it. She would always talk to me, 'Open Book Time' she called it, mostly on our way back and forth to school. She wanted me to be able to tell her anything that was bothering me. I guess I would tell women to keep an open relationship with their kids and make sure they can say anything. I knew I could tell my mom anything. I talked to my mom a lot. If nothing was bothering her, nothing bothered me. If I saw her happy, then I was happy. When she was upset, I was upset.

"I want people to know that if they can get help, they should. There is help out there. You don't have to go through what my mom went through.

Tre' changed directions a bit. "Growing up I thought this (abuse at home) was normal. I know now that how I grew up isn't normal at all, (he chuckles) but then I didn't know there was any alternative. I didn't know anything to compare it to. I guess normal to you is what you know.

"When I was a kid I never talked to anybody about what was going on at home, not teachers or anybody. I knew who my dad was and what he did. Family business was family business. I somehow knew I wasn't supposed to say anything to anybody else. I talked only to my mom but nobody else. Once in awhile my dad would act out with people around, but mostly that was only around close friends and they turned their backs and acted like it never happened. Maybe they didn't want to make him angry or rub him the wrong way. Because of who he was, they would ignore it. They wouldn't confront him.

"Have you talked to your dad about it since you grew up?" I asked.

"I have talked to my dad about the past. He'll ask me if I'm treating girls respectfully and he really wishes that his friends would have stepped in and stopped him. I wish they would have too. Everyone was afraid because he gave them money and bought them things and took them places. I guess they thought if they confronted him, that stuff would all stop.

"I wished someone had stepped in and stopped it. Uncle T. Hayes was best friends with my dad and good friends with my mom. I think he felt that if my dad knew that he knew about the abuse, that it would make things worse for my mom. I think fear of what might happen kept him from stepping in.

"You know what your mom's book is about," I said. "You lived through her story and gave her a reason to survive. She is concerned sometimes about how painful your childhood was and what you remember."

"The worst memory was one terrible day. My mom drove in the driveway and told me to stay in the car. She put some music on for me to listen to.

"So, I was in the car outside and I heard my mom and dad yelling. Stuff like, "I can't believe you told such-and-such ..." It was really loud and really angry. I didn't stay in the car though. I went up to where I could see through the window, I was peeking behind the grill.

"There was my dad, holding a gun and there were two bullets on the counter. He was yelling. I remember him flipping the table over and I thought it hit my mom in the stomach, I was really scared. Next thing I remember was seeing the window break and I ran and got back in the car. My dad stormed out, got in his car and left. I had always prayed for a little brother. I was scared that the baby (King) had gotten hurt.

"You know, I used to ask my mom, "Why can't you have another baby?" Now I understand why she was so hesitant.

Tre' paused, but I didn't want to interrupt his thoughts.

"In December," he said, "I graduate with a degree in Corporate Communications. I start graduate school in the spring and hope to get into Sports Management. I want to get into sports operations, player development or marketing. I want to do something within sports, but I don't want to get into coaching. Any sport is okay with me, but I'm drawn to football. I have always loved football. Basketball would be my second choice, and then baseball.

"Will you continue at U.T.?" I asked.

"Yes, I'll do graduate school at U.T. My scholarship for football doesn't run out until May 2013, so I can get a lot of my graduate school done. I was placed on medical scholarship and I am really grateful to be able to continue my education."

I asked, "How did you feel when you had to give up football?"

"That was a rough time. It still is. I've been around football my whole life. It was really hard to give up. I knew I had to stop because I couldn't recover from concussions. You can't play football worried or scared. I thought there was no way I could stop. Then I started second guessing myself, maybe I can avoid hits ... once I started doing that, I realized I couldn't play football if I was worried about getting hurt. When you play you have to be all in.

If you're worried about getting hit, you're going to blow it for the whole team. I was starting to feel selfish. I thought about what would happen if I ended up with permanent brain damage and how it would affect my mom.

"I'm still involved with the team and sometimes I still think about playing. I miss it more than I ever realized I would. I was really happy when I played football. I student coach now. For the games I'm in the press box and linked up with the running backs' coach. I still enjoy this. I still really love football."

"Tre', you know your mother is extremely proud of you. Is there anything you would like to say in this book to her?"

"I want her to know I love her and would do anything for her," he said without even a moment's hesitation. "I think its amazing that she was able to raise me how she did while going through all that. I think she's the best person in the world. She came out strong. She is always looking to help others and I hope that I will always have her same servant attitude. She puts others in front of herself. She doesn't even know how to be selfish. She is always worried about others. I want to take that from her."

"Anything you would like to say to your dad?" I ask.

"To my dad ... I want to say that I am proud of him and happy. He's done a lot of wrong things in his life, but all his sins are forgiven. Stuff he did in the past, I know it still affects my mom, it still affects me, but what is done is done. At the end of the day he's my dad and I respect him. I am happy that he has changed and trying to go in the right direction. I can see a big change in him. He's not the same person I grew up with at all.

"Uncle Monte and Uncle K-Mart really looked after me too. While my dad was in prison they treated me like I was their son. I know if anything every happened I know I could go to them and they would be there for me. While my dad was messing up, they stepped in and were role models for me. They were who I looked up to how a man should treat a woman, how a man should act. My Uncle K-Mart moved back to Keller when I was in 7th grade. I watched how he treated my Auntie Lynn. My Uncle Monte taught me more about the Bible and the business side of things. He shared his experiences with me. Uncle K-Mart taught me by example—I watched him and learned. Uncle Monte taught me by sharing experiences and talking to me about them. I am really grateful to them."

"Talk to me about King," I urged. "Your mom tells me that he really looks up to you and admires you, that when you went away to school it was hard for him for a long time."

"King is the person I care about most in life. I want to make sure he's alright. I would always tell King that he should be thankful how things have turned out (with the divorce). He is mad that my dad is not around now. He has a great mom. I don't know if he really realizes how great she is. He was really little during the worst part, so I don't think he remembers much. I try to talk to him when I see him ... we don't talk too much on the phone, he prefers to text. I mainly talk to him when I see him. I want him to do well in school and be close to God.

"King looks at other families and it bothers him. Most of the kids in Southlake have a mom and a dad. Dad only comes around for sports ... maybe King doesn't feel like he cares about other parts of life, I don't know. He is longing for a father figure in his life. When I left it bothered him. He isn't as close to Uncle Monte and Uncle K-Mart as I was. He'll be alright though. He's got my mom and she never gives up.

"Is there anything else you want to say? About the book release maybe?" I ask.

"Honestly, I'm not 100% excited about this, bringing up the past, but I trust my mom completely. She feels like God has told her to write the book. I trust her motive to help others—she is always about helping others, and she feels a calling on her heart to do this for a long time. I trust it will work out for the better. I'm proud of her and support her."

With that, Tre' needed to return to his studies. I hung up the phone feeling very much like I would like the opportunity to get to know this young man better. I felt like I already knew him through Dorothy's eyes, and my live encounter did not disappoint. He is a remarkable individual.

I met with King on a Sunday afternoon in Dorothy's office. I liked him from the moment I saw him. He was my kind of kid. Even though he totally didn't want to be talking to me, he was polite and willing to do it because his mom told him he had to. He was handsome, with a smile that makes you melt. He had a good sense of humor and I would much rather have spent the afternoon challenging him to play ping pong than have forced him to give me an interview. I just couldn't help it … I liked him.

King was a bit less open with me than Tre' had been. He sat in the chair, slouching down, eyeing the door. "Sit up straight, King," Dorothy told him.

"What?" he answered her, smiling and chuckling.

I was chuckling too. "Okay, King, let's get this over with shall we? What would you like for people reading your mom's book to know?"

"Not to listen to what other people say because some people just try to bring you down, but you have to keep looking forward and not worry about the past," he said, faster than I could type.

"Have you been practicing that?" I laughed. "Very good. Really, that is great advice, but lets slow down just a little and you tell me what it was like for you growing up. I know you were really small when your parents divorced and your dad went to prison. What was it like for you?"

With the rehearsed portion of the interview behind us, King took a moment to think. "Well, I didn't like how other kids would bring up my dad or how he was arrested for drugs just to get at me. You know, everyone thought we were rich because my dad played for the Cowboys and we really didn't have much. People always thought we had it made. I also didn't like that they expected me to be great at football because my dad was so good, that isn't true. You don't inherit sports.

"I remember going to jail to see my dad. I remember eating chicken wings from the vending machine, and that I would just go play on the see-saw while they talked.

"Some kids teased me because my dad was in jail. They would say stuff like, 'My parents told me he sold drugs and that he was a bad person.' It used to make me really mad. Some parents wouldn't let their kids play with me because of it. It didn't seem fair, I didn't sell the drugs!" King laughed.

Dorothy chimed in, "Nate would always tell the boys stories about him and his dad. He told them all the time that his dad was such a wise man. Well, one time during a visit, King was sitting on Nate's lap and he said to Nate, 'You always tell stories about your dad. Why you didn't never listen to him?" Dorothy and King both started laughing.

"That made Nate really, really mad," she said, still laughing over the memory.

"King knew something wasn't right, he was just too young to really understand what was going on," she continued.

"I'm kind of close to my dad now though," King said. "I go to his house sometimes. He comes to watch me play football. All he talks about with me though is football and my grades. Just football and grades.

"Well, my mom talks about my grades all the time too. Mostly when they're bad," he gives her an impish look.

"King!" she says, and I don't possess the words to describe the look she gave him back, but it was priceless.

"What about Tre' being gone?" I prompt.

"It's a lot different with Tre' being gone. It was a lot more fun when Tre' was around. My mom is too serious now. I text him sometimes, but we only talk when I see him. I miss having him around.

"I wish I would have been there when my dad hurt my mom," he changed the subject, "because I would have stopped it. I would have done something. I would have told him to stop or I would have pushed him or something. I would rather him hit me than her. I would have told the police ... I don't know, something."

Dorothy's face is very soft. King is looking down at the floor, but I can see her looking at him with so much love. I don't think they have talked about this in a very long time.

"I want my mom to start dating people. I wish she would relax a little more and have more fun. I mean she goes out with friends, but mostly she does stuff for other people, like charities and stuff. Every month we do SASO (Scholars and Athletes Serving Others), we also do Jack-n-Jill, and different activities for parents, lock-ins and team building and things like that. My mom works really hard. She always has to take care of stuff and she has too much stress. I want her to have more fun. I want her to date.

"He's always telling me he wants me to start dating," Dorothy rolls her eyes.

"What do you want to be when you grow up, King?" I ask, sensing the need to redirect before this got out of hand.

"I would like to go to the NFL and make some money. I would invest it in an international shipping business, you know, ship cargo and different things. I always wanted to own my own business.

"Tre' was my role model," he shifted topic. "He's a really, really good person. I'm like the opposite of Tre'. I'm talkative and happy, Tre' is more secluded. He was a really good football player, though.

"I used to worry that Tre' would grow up and be abusive like my dad. It would scare me when he got mad because he would yell. Like I watch to make sure how he talks to his girlfriend. I want him to be okay and not have anger issues.

"Me, I'm more verbal when I'm angry. I never get physical. People compare me to Tre' a lot, like teachers and coaches. He was a football champion and a super student, so they expect me to be just like him and I'm not. I'm my own person. I'm different than he is.

"King handles this really well," Dorothy interjected. "He is developing and becoming his own person, separate from Tre'. Tre's expectations of King are that he should be more like him, study harder, etc. He thinks I let King get away with things, but King is very, very different than Tre'. Every child has to be parented differently, in ways that suit their personality and gifts.

"King is the most affectionate, caring young man," she continued. "He is honest. He'll tell it all like it is without a filter," she laughs. "He is very wise for his age. He came home a few years ago and said to me, 'You know what mom? I'm glad you work. I'm glad you share the Bible with people. If you stayed at home all the time with just me, you wouldn't reach all those people.'"

"King loves to be around people. He likes crowds and is very extroverted. He wants me to remarry. He asks me about it all the time. I think he just wants a man around on a more regular basis. He notices things going on in other people's lives, he'll come home and tell me who we need to pray for. I just really, really want the best for him," she finishes.

King shoots her another look, admiration mixed with, *You're really embarrassing me.*

"Am I done?" he asks me, hopefully.

"Can I go now ... please?" he asks his mother.

"Alright, alright. You can go." she says.

King is out the door quick as lighting.

"Young man," Dorothy says with that *"Oh-no-you-didn't"* tone of voice. "You come back here. You shake Mrs. Wendy's hand. Tell her thank you. Where are your manners?"

"Sorry, Ma!" he calls, coming back to shake my hand. "Thanks!" and he's gone.

I told you I liked this kid.

Epilogue

FINDING HELP

*The most common way people give up their
power is by thinking they don't have any.*

—ALICE WALKER

$\mathscr{D}$orothy and I worked together for many months
bringing this project to press. As we struggled through
the painful memories necessary to tell her story, it was
important to both of us that we focus on the victory. We
wanted to offer practical steps to help women escape
abuse, to equip others with tools to assist the abused,
and even to encourage abusers that they do not have to
remain trapped inside their abusive patterns. There is
hope. There is healing.

When I began this project, my knowledge of domestic
violence was limited to what I knew from the experiences
of friends and family. My parents were pastors, and my
mother worked with troubled youth for the Georgia
Department of Juvenile Justice, so helping people through

435

the pain of domestic violence was part of life. It wasn't hard to find statistics on domestic violence, or see the impact on society from this darkness. A Google search gave me more websites with more information than I could possibly take in. A visit to the Bureau of Justice Statistics (www.ojp.usdoj.gov) opened my eyes, frightening me with the scope of reported violence in the United States. I searched website after website, finding corroborating statistics and soon realized that domestic violence is a far greater problem than I ever imagined.

The cold facts are that one out of four women in America will experience some type of domestic violence in their lifetime. Most of this abuse will go unreported, not just to law enforcement, but it will also be kept secret, hidden even from family and friends. Many women feel shame, as though they did something to cause the abuse. Other women convince themselves that it won't ever happen again, so there is no need to seek help. They treat each incident as an isolated event that had a plausible trigger, and will go away. Often, they genuinely love their abuser, and don't want to leave. Fear of reprisal keeps them from reaching out for help. Not only is there fear of suffering increased abuse, but there is fear associated with economics, logistics, and even just of being alone.

When abuse is present in a long-term relationship, it is hard to comprehend the steps leading to a permanent solution. As humans, our instinct is to survive in a present crisis. Cycles of abuse often repeat after time, sometimes significant periods of time where things are calm, even pleasant. The danger seems less imminent with every day that passes after a violent episode, so the urgency to leave subsides.

Abuse rarely begins with physical assault. Most starts out verbally—arguments that escalate and become increasingly irrational. Abuse is often expressed through control and intimidation. From there it can lead to pushing and shoving, perhaps even to hitting or throwing objects. Over time, the violent energy is directed to the physical and even sexual abuse of the victim.

From the Bureau of Justice Statistics, I learned that men are also victims of domestic violence, although women and children are the usual targets. I was surprised to learn that women of all races share equally in violence by an intimate partner. Vulnerability to abuse is apparently without prejudice, it can happen to anyone regardless of race, ethnicity, religion, culture, or even socio-economic status. The root of abuse is sin. We all begin with a sinful nature, so only by God's grace do we embrace the redemptive work of the cross and have the power to live free from the law of sin and death.

Sadly, like the divorce rate, abuse seems to be as prevalent inside the church as outside of it. Why is this? It should not be! If believers truly submit themselves to Christ, His love should abound and the fruit of the Spirit should be evident. Domestic violence should not exist where God's people dwell … but it does.

The question then is what can an abused person do? If you are trapped in an abusive relationship, where can you go for help? What steps can you take to protect yourself and your children?

Long before I ever met Dorothy, I had a dear friend living in an abusive relationship. On more than one occasion, she fled with her children to our home to find safety. Of course, we were happy to help. We always opened our doors and though she rarely shared details, her fear—and that of her children was evident. Her abuse was cyclical. It was not always physically violent, although control and intimidation were unceasing. Most of the abuse was verbal—cursing, demeaning, accusing, discouraging, labeling … horrible words and threats that no one should endure. Her abuser was magnanimous in public, generous, outgoing, and friendly—a real nice guy. His hold was largely financial. She had no control of assets, and little income of her own. His job took him away for long periods of time and though they were quite well off, I can remember having to loan her money for bread or gas sometimes when he was gone because he didn't always leave enough behind, and she had no access to his resources. His children resented him, despised him even, but accepted his gifts and grew into the lifestyle afforded by his income. I asked his son about it once and he told me, "I figure I might as well get something out of it. He's horrible. I hate the way he treats my mother, but at least I get paid to live with horrible. That's better than nothing."

Finally, my friend had enough. Evidence of extra-marital affairs, constant attacks to her self esteem, and outright physical assault had pushed her over the edge. She was ready to leave. I was more than happy to help her.

Risking serious reprisal, we searched through bank records, credit reports, asset inventories, anything we could find trying to pull together information for a lawyer that could help her make a case for divorce that wouldn't leave her financially destitute. We worked long hours making a plan and gathering information. She was always frightened that he would discover what we were doing. At times, I was too, concerned about what might happen to her or to me if he ever found out. We didn't even communicate over the telephone, for fear that he might record her conversations.

I was sitting in my office one day, in fact, praying for her when the phone rang. She called to tell me she had decided not to go through with it. She wasn't going to pursue a divorce after all. I am sad to say that instead of being supportive or understanding all that she was facing, I became angry with her. I had no frame of reference to take in all of the dynamics she was confronted with. In my mind, leaving him was the only sane course of action. She had biblical grounds for divorce, not to mention all the pain and suffering she and her children were enduring on a regular basis. I just could not understand how she got all the way to the edge of freedom with a workable plan in place, promised support from us and others, only to choose to remain trapped. I didn't know how to deal with it. I was frustrated and to be perfectly honest, I felt betrayed. I had put a great deal on the line to bring her through and was committed to the process, however long or painful. I just could not understand it when she backed down.

As I worked with Dorothy, I gained fresh insight into my friend's plight. She too believed she was the avenue for her husband to receive salvation. She feared that if she left, then all hope was lost that he would come to know God. She truly did love him and desired God's best for his life. She believed in the power of prayer and the promise of redemption. She knew that just one touch from God in his life could mean a totally different future, and she didn't want to quit before God had a chance to work. Like Dorothy, she was a motivator and an encourager, a mentor and friend—a safe haven where troubled souls sought refuge. She had one of the sweetest relationships with Jesus I have ever witnessed, and her heart of worship was passionate and pure. She wanted to cover her husband's sins rather than expose them in a court, or for the community to judge. She didn't want to damage him or the people she ministered to. She was terrified about how she would survive without any income. His anger to her was utterly vile. He convinced her that if she pursued a divorce he would thoroughly discredit her, take full custody of the children, and leave her penniless and alone. She wasn't willing to risk the uncertainties. She had found a way to live with the cycle—his instability had become her stability. She knew what to expect with him. She knew she was strong enough to survive, and she had no idea what to expect if she left him. In the end she stayed, and to my knowledge is with him to this day.

WHY WON'T SHE LEAVE?

Obviously, the safest choice is always to leave a dangerous or threatening situation, but many victims do not feel they can make this choice.

Nurturer by Nature

Many women struggle at placing their own well being above the love they have for their partner. Women are programmed to nurture, to sacrifice. Leaving can seem selfish to the victim.

Economics

Most families require two incomes to survive in our current economy. For many women, the male is still the chief bread winner. Some women work only part time or not at all. Concerns over how to provide for housing, transportation, clothing, shelter, and education are among the top reasons for staying with an abuser.

Custody

Losing custody of children is one of the greatest, and most threatening reasons for staying. When economics is an issue, a mother faces a genuine fear that she will not be able to keep custody. Leaving the children to live with an abuser, unable to be there as a buffer or to protect them is a raw but rational concern. This causes many victims to stick it out and deal with whatever evil is necessary so they can remain close to their kids.

Shame

Shame and the fear of isolation are also powerful re-straints. Victims are often convinced they did something to cause the abuse. They also believe they can do something that will make it stop. Physical abuse often leads to sexual abuse, even within the confines of marriage. This is a very difficult thing for a woman to talk about. At the bottom line, no matter how much support is offered, a woman will not leave an abusive relationship until she is ready.

Denial

Because abuse is cyclical, there are often seasons of calm or even "good times." In the "in between times" it can seem as if things have changed, maybe for good this time. Like Dorothy, many women believe each abusive episode will be the last. They convince themselves that the worst is over and will never happen again. The longer the time lapse between episodes, the harder it is to leave.

No Hope

For those trapped in abuse, the situation seems hopeless. To the victim it seems she has no choice but to suffer. She feels trapped, cornered, with no viable options. This is not the case, but in her mind she has no choice, no real alternatives that make sense. The emotional damage is severe. It cripples a victim's self-esteem and renders them powerless to make decisions, particularly as they affect her health, safety, and well-being.

HOW DO I HELP HER?

Build Her Up

When a woman shares her situation with you, even when she is unwilling to reveal all the details, it is important to acknowledge her feelings and underline that the abuse is not her fault. This is particularly difficult if you see things the victim might do to limit destructive behavior or ways to manage situations that are dangerous. Resist the temptation to say things like, "Listen, what you need to do is …" or "If anyone ever hit me, you know what I would do …" Such statements only damage her esteem more. It is easy to say what you would do or what she should do, but remember that you are not the one suffering the abuse. If you were, you might see things with less clarity.

You can let her know that what she is going through is terrible and that you are truly empathetic. You can give her the confidence to know that although she is walking through it, she is not alone. Remind her as often as needed that abuse is not her fault. She does not deserve to be punished by abuse. Give her strong encouragement. Help her understand the fact she is there, sharing with you means she is doing something right. Remind her that she has choices.

Pray

Pray for her. Pray with her. Pray for her safety, for her children and their safety. Even pray for her abuser. Let her know that you are a safe place she can come to talk and if necessary, to take action steps to intervene. Just knowing that someone is praying with her can bring enormous encouragement to her soul. I believe in the power of prayer. I know God can work miraculous intervention.

Create a Safety Plan

The National Domestic Violence Hotline is a resource you can use for practical planning. Their staff is available to assist victims and anyone calling on their behalf with crisis intervention, safety planning, and referrals to shelters and agencies in all 50 states. You can call anonymously and they answer the phones 24/7. The number is **1-800-799-SAFE (7233)**. Their website address is **www.thehotline.org**. They offer a great deal of valuable information for victims and victim support in addition to being able to talk with someone who can help.

Creating a safety plan is one of the most valuable and empowering things you can do. Visit **www.thehotline. org** to view and print their simple, two page plan. There is also a link to this website located on Dorothy's website, **www.DorothyJNewton.com**. This plan gives very practical advice for:

1. Personal safety while living with an abuser.

2. Guidelines for preparing to leave an abusive relationship—documents and evidence to gather, an action plan for economic survival, locating shelters and other agencies, important numbers, etc. Many women are not even aware that they can request a police escort to safely escape with belongings.

3. Guidelines for remaining safe after leaving an abusive relationship—information on restraining orders, opening a P.O. Box, instructions for your child care providers, etc.

4. Safety regarding the use of technology (how activity can be monitored or tracked).

Create a Financial Plan

An important part of creating an action plan is helping a victim assess where they are financially. Economics is one of the chief reasons women remain with their abusers. It is important to make an accurate assessment of what she has available, and put a plan in place to set money aside, improve job skills, access financial assistance through government or charitable organizations, and perhaps even speak with family members to lend a hand while she gets on her feet. Helping her develop a workable plan to function financially without her abuser's income will empower her and allow her to make better choices.

Remain Supportive

It may take some time before an abuse victim is ready to take action. It is difficult to remain patient and understanding when you know someone you love is living with abuse. You want to help her. You want to rescue her, to fix it! It can be very frustrating when the path seems clear to you, yet she is not convinced. Sometimes stepping in prematurely can cause her to be in great danger. You must be sensitive and aware. If you believe that her life is in danger, you should contact the authorities immediately. If you bring the authorities to bear, you should be prepared to stand by her through the process and make sure you are able to commit to her until she is secure that she is safe from harm. Victims of abuse have difficulty trusting other people. Betrayal is real to them and they have been hurt by someone they love. It is important that you be trustworthy. If she confided in you, rest assured, it was a big step for her. Take your cues from her and make sure she knows she can always trust you.

Self Defense

Learning self defense techniques is a valuable skill-set for everyone. It is even more so for victims of abuse. Depending on the situation, it may not be possible to take a self defense class, but if an avenue can be made to help her learn how to defend herself against physical attack, this should be done.

Self Awareness

It is very important for a victim of abuse to become self-aware. She can combat the emotional damage inflicted by her abuser by deflecting the ugly words and reminding herself of her value and worth. This is easier said than done, but the greater her self-awareness, the less power the abuser has over her. You can help by reminding her of her value and affirming her in her strengths. In Dorothy's case, she found refuge in God's Word. She filled her mind with His words to help deflect the damage of her abuser's words. This is powerful and should not be underestimated.

I AM BEING ABUSED, WHAT SHOULD I DO?

Reach Out

First, know that you are not alone. You have someone who can and will help you—a friend, a family member, a church, or an abuse shelter. Being abused is not your fault. You are the victim. One out of every four of your women friends has also experienced some type of domestic violence.

Don't isolate yourself by shutting people out. Isolation is dangerous. You need to reach out to someone and let them know you need help.

If you are uncomfortable speaking with a friend or family member, PLEASE call The National Domestic Violence Hotline. The number is **1-800-799-SAFE (7233)**. You can even call them anonymously. There are people available at any time day or night to answer questions, direct you to local assistance or just to talk. Their website address is **www.thehotline.org**. This can provide you with insight in protecting yourself. If and when you decide to leave, they can help you create a plan to break free.

Reach Up

Calling on the Lord is not a platitude or a last ditch effort. He does protect and defend, comfort, deliver and heal. Spending time seeking His face, meditating on His Word, and worshipping Him can bring hope and great inner strength. Giving way to bitterness hurts only you, not your abuser. Believing the lies you hear and all the negative things you have been told during a shouting match serves only to lower your self-esteem and give your abuser power over you. Shouting back is a natural response, but it only serves to escalate incidents and further lower your esteem.

Instead, learn what God says about you. See yourself through His eyes. Dare to believe His promises and that you have a destiny on your life that no one should ever be given the power to deny. You are beautiful. You are unique and special and one of a kind. You are precious in God's sight. He esteems you highly and has numbered the very hairs on your head. He is grieved when you suffer and he captures your tears in remembrance. Reach up to Him. Call on Him. He is always there.

Have you not known?

Have you not heard?

The everlasting God, the LORD,

The Creator of the ends of the earth,

Neither faints nor is weary.

His understanding is unsearchable.

He gives power to the weak,

And to those who have no might He increases strength.

Even the youths shall faint and be weary,

And the young men shall utterly fall,

But those who wait on the LORD

Shall renew their strength;

They shall mount up with wings like eagles,

They shall run and not be weary,

They shall walk and not faint.

—ISAIAH 40:28-31 NKJV

HELP FOR AN ABUSER

It is easy to sympathize with a victim and easier still to vilify an abuser. What makes someone abuse another human being? Why do some people turn to violence and cruelty, particularly with people they love?

Statistics clearly demonstrate that abuse patterns repeat for generations. If a child was abused, or witnessed a loved one being abused, they are much more likely to grow up and be abusive. No doubt watching cruelty go unpunished, or internalizing values that violence is normal and acceptable contributes to this generational curse. Likewise, victims of childhood abuse are more likely to seek out unhealthy or dysfunctional relationships where they again become victims.

People who deal with emotional discomfort through addictive behaviors such as alcohol, drug abuse, unrestrained shopping, or gambling are more likely to become abusive. Abuse itself becomes an addiction. It is a coping mechanism.

Abusers tend to deny their responsibility, even when they come back and apologize. Their oft repeated apologies ... "that wasn't really me" or "I lost control, I blew up" or some similar excuse do not repair the damage or guarantee a change. No matter how excessive the abusive behavior is, it is excused. A "trigger" event, not a lack of self control is blamed for the violent outburst. But, unless and until an abuser can accept personal responsibility for their actions—for choosing to harm another person, little can be done to help them.

Women I have talked with express that the day after an abusive episode, the abuser often seems to have little or no memory of what occurred. They act as if nothing ever happened. Stranger still, abusers often demonstrate outrage at the abusive behavior of others, without recognizing their own tendencies or any similarity in their own behavior. I don't know if this is a real phenomenon or just a convenient ploy. Perhaps they block it out because it reflects an ugliness they cannot or will not address within themselves.

Evidence supports the fact that abuse is cyclical. Abusers often express remorse after beating a loved one. Sometimes they will go to great measures to demonstrate their regret. They will desparately try to convince their partner that they didn't mean it and that it will never happen again. It is not uncommon for the abuser to seek pity from the abused, wanting to turn things around so the victim will feel sorry for them. "I need you ... you can't leave me ..." It is a sad and twisted thing, this cycle of abuse. It begins with a build up of tension, followed by a violent outburst, the denial of responsibility, an apology driven by guilt, followed by a period of calm. It can go on for years.

Of a certainty, abusers demonstrate behavior that is ego-centric and self absorbed. They see the world only as it impacts them, not as they impact their world. They excuse their violent behavior as a result of injustice or unfair treatment they have received. Their demands are self-centered and their need to control their victim is obsessive. Having to cover up their bad behavior leads to lies and deception, and that is a pattern that is difficult to reverse.

There is good news, however. Abusers have the potential to refocus and thus to reinvent themselves. But they cannot do it alone. If you are an abuser, or even show abusive tendencies, I strongly urge that changing this is a process best aided through the support of a qualified counselor. In addition to this, having an accountability structure in place is a must. You need to have a close friend (other than your spouse) with whom you will be honest, one who you know will be honest with you—who will hold you accountable for your actions and be willing to step in if you violate your partner with violence again.

Ultimately, the avenue for deliverance and restoration is God. God's love and forgiveness is available for you if you will receive it. It isn't partial. It is complete, total. It covers all your sins, not just select sins—allowing you both the room and the power to change. There is no need for you to live forever with guilt and shame for your past. You can be forgiven. God can rescue you. He can deliver you, heal you, redeem you and give you the opportunity to leave a whole, functional life.

Nate Newton found God. It was not until after the divorce and after his prison sentence that he came to the reality that he was never going to be "good enough" through his own efforts. He needed God to step in and cleanse him. But he chose to change, to let God change him—and you can too.

Maybe you are a Christian and wonder why you remain abusive. Have you admitted your sin? Acknowledged your guilt? Have you repented, taken it to the foot of the cross and laid it down there, asking for God's forgiveness through His atoning blood? Have you accepted His sacrifice, believing that it is sufficient for you? Do you understand that the same grace that covers lying and stealing and adultery and murder also covers cruelty and violence and abuse? Sin is sin in the eyes of God. Total forgiveness and amazing grace allows you the opportunity to live free again. Jesus paid the price for you. You have but to receive His sacrifice.

Breaking the Curse

I am blessed to have been raised in a family with loving parents. They argued over money and schedules and the usual things, but never once did I witness physical violence between them. Likewise, I have been married more than 22 years and I am extremely grateful that I have never lived in fear of physical violence from my spouse.

Knowing the statistics as I do, this is indeed remarkable. Boys who witness domestic violence are twice as likely to grow up and become abusers. In fact, the strongest risk factor for the continuation of violent behavior from one generation to the next is witnessing violence between parents or care-givers.

My husband came from an abusive home. His father was an alcoholic who physically abused not only his mother, but him as well, once breaking his ribs. He has painful memories of feeling helpless as he witnessed violent arguments and physical abuse. It impacted him deeply. He was twelve years old before his mother found the strength to walk away.

My husband is living proof that the cycle can be broken—it does not have to be repeated in subsequent generations. It requires much self-awareness and a commitment to break the generational curse and live free from the pattern. It requires having an accountability structure in place to keep anger under control and make sure it never turns to violence. It requires reliance on the grace of God and filling your heart and mind with His Word.

I shared my family's testimony with Dorothy's son, Tre', during our interview. He is keenly aware of the statistics and has already determined that he will not repeat the patterns he witnessed as a child. We talked together about the need for a close relationship with God, about the need for someone to be accountable to—other than your spouse—who will hold you to your word, encourage you through difficult times, and keep you from allowing anger or frustration to escalate into violence. I believe Tre' and King are well on their way to bringing honor to both their mother and their father by not repeating the damaging patterns of the past. There is hope. They can be the first generation that lives free.

I hope you come away from reading this book understanding that God can move in any situation. No situation is too far gone. Nothing escapes His knowledge or is too awful for Him to bear. Complete victory is possible. God wants you to experience His perfect healing, fully restored, and totally free.

ENDNOTES

Research for this chapter was taken from:

"Domestic Violence: Fast Facts on Domestic Violence." **Welcome to the Clark County Prosecuting Attorney's Office**. The Clark County Prosecuting Attorney. Web. 18 Dec. 2011. <http://www.clarkprosecutor.org/html/domviol/facts.htm>.

Van Der Zande, Irene. "Personal Safety to Help Stop Domestic Violence." **Kidpower Teenpower Fullpower: Personal Safety and Self-Defense**. KidPower Teenpower Fullpower International. Web. 21 Dec. 2011. <http://www.kidpower.org>.

"Domestic Violence: The Facts." **Safe Horizon: Moving Victims of Violence from Crisis to Confidence**. Safe Horizon. Web. 21 Dec. 2011. <http://www.safehorizon.org>.

Gundry, Patricia. "How to Tell If You Are an Abuser." **Abuseville**. Patricia Gundry. Web. 02 Jan. 2012. <http://www.abuseville.com>.

THE NATIONAL DOMESTIC
VIOLENCE HOTLINE

1-800-799-SAFE (7233)

www.thehotline.org